بسم الله الرحمن الرحيم

"The house of al-Arqam is the house of Islām"

Al-Ḥākim (d.405 h) in *al-Mustadrak ʿala al-Ṣaḥiḥayn* (6185)

IBN TAYMIYYAH SERIES
سلسلة الامام ابن تيمية

Ibn Taymiyyah on
Creation ex Materia

فَصْلانِ مِن النُّبُوَّاتِ وبَيَانِ تَلْبِيسِ الجَهْمِيَّةِ
لِشَيخِ الإِسلَامِ تَقِي الدِينِ ابنِ تَيمِيَّةَ

الخلق والإفناء

Taqī al-Dīn Aḥmad ibn ʿAbd al-Ḥalīm al-Ḥarrānī

DAR AL-ARQAM

ISBN: 978-1-7392940-1-4

British Library Cataloguing in Publishing Data
A catalogue record for this book is available from the British Library

Prepared and published by Dar al-Arqam Publishing,
Birmingham, United Kingdom

Translated by:

Mohammad Abu AbdurRahman

Translation and Arabic text edited by:

Dr. Nabeel Sheikh

He attained a BA in *Ḥadīth* and the Islamic Sciences from Dar ul Hadith, an MA in *Tafsīr* from Umm al-Qura University, and a PhD in *Tafsīr* from Umm al-Qura University. Whilst working for the publishing house Dār ʿĀlam al-Fawāʾid, he edited a number of volumes from large authorships of Ibn al-Qayyim and did the referencing (i.e. *takhrīj*) of volumes four and five of Ibn Taymiyyah's commentary on *ʿUmdat al-Fiqh.*

www.daral-arqam.co.uk
Email: daralarqam@hotmail.co.uk

If you would like to support our work, donations can be made via:

- www.daralarqam.bigcartel.com/product/donate
- www.patreon.com/daralarqam
- www.paypal.me/daralarqam

Printed by Mega Printing in Türkiye

IBN TAYMIYYAH ON

CREATION EX MATERIA

Taqī al-Dīn Aḥmad b. ʿAbd al-Ḥalīm
al-Ḥarrānī (d. 728/1328)

O My servants who have transgressed against themselves! Despair not of the mercy of Allah. Indeed, Allah forgives all sins. Indeed, it is He who is the Forgiving, the Merciful. [Quran 39:53]

الفهرس

Contents

Preface

In the Name of God. All praise is due to Him, and may He elevate the mention of Muhammad, His final messenger.

This book is the second in an envisioned series of translations from Ibn Taymiyyah's theological works that cover a wide range of topics from the evidences of God's perfection to the signs of Prophethood, and from the meaning of God's creative agency to the compatibility of divine predestination with human moral agency. The series aims to provide readers from the English-speaking world access to Ibn Taymiyyah's articulations of these important matters of the Faith in an effort to demonstrate the superior rationality embodied in Islamic Faith over the conflicting claims of rationality offered by other religions, philosophies and theological positions.

Such an English series is much needed nowadays, especially in response to current challenges posed by growing trends of atheism. Ibn Taymiyyah's exceptional insight and distinguished explanations of Qur'anic arguments have helped many Muslims remain intellectually satisfied in the face of doubts and challenges presented by competing world views. It is this observation that inspired me to embark on these translations, the second of which is a translation of selected passages on the topic of Creation from Ibn Taymiyyah's works *Nubuwwāt* and *Bayān Talbīs al-Jahmiyyah*.

In *Nubuwwāt*, Ibn Taymiyyah responds to the Ashʿari theologians' definition of miracles and their inability to make a rational distinction between the Prophetic miracles and the unusual feats of sorcerers and magicians who falsely claim to be Prophets. He writes at length to differentiate between the different kinds of miracles, clarifying that Prophetic miracles stand as clear signs and evidences of a true Prophet, for they are out of the reach of all the men and jinn to whom these Prophets were sent, with the sole exception of the Antichrist whom God will allow to perform many wonders as a test for mankind, having forewarned them of his appearance.

In one of the sections in the course of his explanation [Vol 1, pp. 245-328], Ibn Taymiyyah mentions that the Prophets of God must have clarified the sound rational evidences that lead to the fundamental theological matters of Faith, and he goes on to speak of how the Kalām theologians have strayed from these prescribed methods of attestation and verification. It is in this context that Ibn Taymiyyah writes the passage on creation ex materia that is fully translated in the first part of this book. There, he criticizes the counter-scriptural views of Kalām theologians and Philosophers regarding Creation and responds to an argument of Kalām theologians by which they attempt to demonstrate the Originator's existence. Ibn Taymiyyah then explains the alternative Qur'anic evidence for the Originator, an evidence which he maintains is characterized primarily by the origination of substances out of other substances, not merely by the rearrangement of matter.

In his other work *Bayān Talbīs al-Jahmiyyah*, which includes a detailed response to certain aspects of negative theology in the works of Fakhr al-Dīn al-Rāzī, Ibn Taymiyyah presents a rational argument for the creation of matter which demonstrates that matter is not an eternal substance [Vol 2, pp. 243-261]. He argues that matter in this world is fundamentally composed of a finite number of particles that have a physical existence, and he provides empirical evidence to support the claim that these fundamental constituents change totally and turn into other things. This is significant as it implies that natural bodies are originated in the context of prior creations.

Ibn Taymiyyah has written extensively on the topic of God's creative agency in many of his works. Here, I have chosen to translate the passage from *Nubuwwāt* due to its wonderful style and deep reflections. The passage from *Bayān Talbīs al-Jahmiyyah* is also included here for its clear and concise explanations.

Throughout this translation, I have included my own explanatory additions in brackets [like these]. I have also included many footnotes to define key Arabic and Islamic terms and to provide useful information to help acquaint the reader with the topic at hand.

The remainder of this preface presents a short introduction to the author and an overview of each of the two translations included in this book. In these two overviews, I draw the reader's attention to certain aspects on the topic of creation ex materia and the theory of the indivisible atom which are not explicitly mentioned in the translated text. My intention with this inclusion is to give the book an overall direction and emphasize the lesson to be taken from the translations. It is also designed to help the reader better understand why Ibn Taymiyyah chose to write on these topics in the first place.

About the Author

The Shaykh of Islam, Ibn Taymiyyah, was a famous Damascene scholar who lived in the Mamluk Empire in the seventh and eighth century of the Islamic calendar. His time was characterized by great political turmoil due to Mongol invasions from the east, as well as by intellectual dissent that existed among the different theological schools in the Muslim world. By the time Ibn Taymiyyah was born, many innovations attributed to Islam had slowly developed into branching sects of Kalām theology and various strands of philosophy. These innovations consumed the Muslim community and affected their fundamental beliefs in God, Prophethood, and the Last Day.

Troubled by the increasing confusion, Ibn Taymiyyah dedicated his work to reviving the original creed of Islam that is based on the understanding of the Pious Predecessors. With his deep understanding of authentic Islamic sources – the Qur'ān and the Sunnah – and his vast awareness of innovated opinions, Ibn Taymiyyah was able to defend the religion far better than any of his contemporaries. His student Ibn al-Qayyim states that "we were prisoners to the philosophers, our forelocks in their hands" but after Ibn Taymiyyah "their forelocks became in ours."

Perhaps one of the most noticeable features of Ibn Taymiyyah's argumentation is his genuine adherence to rational demonstrations in the Qur'ān and the Sunnah. Many of Ibn Taymiyyah's accounts are deeply intellectual explanations of intuitive theological statements and rational arguments. His writings can be very technical at times and are sometimes met with controversy, but they constantly bring the reader back to the instinctive beliefs held by the overwhelming majority of people. His works are extremely powerful and influential in this way.

Overview of the First Translation

The first translation from *Nubuwwāt* focuses on providing a definition of origination that is rational, intuitive and scripturally authentic. This definition involves the coming into existence of natural phenomena out of others that go out of existence. This is contrasted with the position of many *Kalām* theologians who claim that the substances of natural phenomena do not meaningfully come into existence unless they are originated ex nihilo or without prior materials.

By observing the created signs of God, a person with a sound *fiṭrah* (natural disposition) would realize immediately and without the need for an inference that they are a creation of God. If the *fiṭrah* however becomes corrupted by harmful influences, the person may no longer be able to recognize the existence of the Creator. In such a case, rational arguments are needed to infer the existence of a Creator.

A strong rational argument that demonstrates the dependency of the natural world on a Creator is the contingency argument. An even stronger argument that takes the same form as the contingency argument, and that is mentioned directly in the Qur'ān, is the argument from origination. God says in the Chapter al-Ṭur: {**Or were they created by nothing, or were they the creators?**}. By a method of reductio ad absurdum, the argument from origination demonstrates that an eternal Creator must exist for originated things to exist in the natural world. This argument can be presented in the following form:

Premise 1: **There exist originating substances that come into existence after nonexistence,** e.g. animals, trees and minerals.

Premise 2: If originating substances cannot exist without an originator, then either they must be the cause of their own origination, or they must be caused by an unoriginated Originator.

Premise 3: **Originating substances cannot exist without an originator.**

Conclusion 1: Therefore, either originating substances must be the cause of their own origination, or they must be caused by an unoriginated Originator *(from premises 2 and 3).*

Premise 4: **Originating substances cannot be the cause of their own origination.**

Conclusion 2: Therefore, originating substances must be caused by an unoriginated Originator (*from premise 4 and conclusion 1*).

Conclusion 3: Therefore, there exists an unoriginated Originator *(from premise 1 and conclusion 2).*

This book is solely concerned with presenting Ibn Taymiyyah's explanations and evidences in support of the first premise. Having a strong conviction in the first premise, and a proper understanding of what it means for things to originate, is critical to appreciating the Qur'anic argument from origination. The first part of the book presents this proper definition of origination as articulated by Ibn Taymiyyah in *Nubuwwāt*. Scepticism towards this definition is addressed in the second part of the book by presenting a sound rational argument of Ibn Taymiyyah to demonstrate that this understanding of origination is factually correct.

The third premise of the origination argument is self-evident for most and needs no demonstration, while the fourth premise has received some criticism from sceptics. Ibn Taymiyyah has written substantially to address objections against the fourth premise. Although these demonstrations are absent from this book, they will be the subject of a future translation on the existence of God – God willing.

The infinite regress

When refuting the claim that originated things can be the cause of their own origination, Ibn Taymiyyah argues that this claim leads to the impossible notion of circular dependency. Closely linked with circular dependency is the notion of an infinite regress of dependencies and originators. Both these notions, Ibn Taymiyyah maintains, are absurd and more irrational than things originating without an originator. By explaining how these two notions entail contradictions, Ibn Taymiyyah provides a solid justification of the fourth premise of the argument from origination.

Although Ibn Taymiyyah's demonstration of the fourth premise lies beyond the scope of this translation, it is nonetheless crucial to point out he did not believe that all types of the infinite regress are impossible. Instead, he makes a distinction between the regress of *dependencies*, *originators* and *efficient causes*, on the one hand, and the regress of God's *creative acts* and His *created effects*, on the other. For Ibn Taymiyyah, the latter type of regress is not impossible:

the regress of *created effects* is permissible, while the regress of God's *acts* is necessary as God's perfection entails that He has always been, since eternity, doing one thing after another.

Ibn Taymiyyah also believed that God has been creating materials out of other materials for an eternity such that the regress of materials continues indefinitely into the infinite past. For Ibn Taymiyyah, this view of Creation is not impossible as it does not entail a regress of originators. The regress in the material conditions only entails a regress in the created effects of God, which is a permissible type of regress. This is explained by the fact that God is a Primary Cause who independently originates the causal connections between material things. Even if the chain of natural causes is said to extend infinitely into the past, it must nevertheless owe its existence to an independent God who originates the effects by way of their necessary causes.

Definition of matter

We can now go on to explain Ibn Taymiyyah's definition of matter and the uniqueness of this definition within theological and philosophical discourse. Ibn Taymiyyah argued that his views on creation ex materia and the perpetual creative agency of God are both rational and in line with Scripture. However, his views were not always accepted without controversy. Many *Kalām* theologians and Philosophers did not understand how Ibn Taymiyyah could hold the view that God only creates things out of others while simultaneously claiming that matter is originated. This is because they gave matter an unnatural and counter-scriptural definition that Ibn Taymiyyah did not accept. Ibn Taymiyyah highlights the various definitions of matter in the translation from *Nubuwwāt*, which are summarized here accordingly.

One definition of matter, held by many Kalām theologians, is a general substance that is fundamentally composed of indivisible constituents (*jawāhir farda*, sing. *jawhar fard*) that continue to exist throughout the process of creation. These indivisible constituents do not originate during the processes of creation; they are only caused to rearrange into new forms. Kalām theologians who held this definition did not appreciate the origination of the very substance of natural bodies during creation, as these bodies are fundamentally constituted of unchanging components according to this definition. Nevertheless, these theologians believed that the fundamental constituents (or indivisible atoms) were originated in the past ex nihilo, which they attempted to demonstrate using an argument known as the Argument from the Origination of Bodies, also criticized by Ibn Taymiyyah in the translated passage.

In contrast, the Aristotelean philosophers defined matter as a universal substance that is shared ontologically by all the physical bodies. The primal matter (hyle, Arabic: *huyūlā*) is, in their opinion, unchanging and eternal, and only the forms of the physical bodies change in processes of generation and destruction in the natural world. However, unlike the Kalām theologians who described the forms in the materials as arrangements, the Philosophers believed that the forms are also substances. They claimed that the form is one of two substantial components that together comprise the physical body, the other being matter.

Ibn Taymiyyah rejected both these definitions of matter. For Ibn Taymiyyah, creation ex materia is not always a rearrangement of already existing matter, and physical bodies are not composed of an eternal matter substance. Instead, Ibn Taymiyyah promoted a more intuitive definition of matter, defining it as a prior substance out of which another is originated. In this view, the matter of one thing annihilates entirely and ceases to exist, whereupon the matter of a new thing is entirely created by God in its place and out of it as a substance. For example, the matter of a palm tree is the seed out of which that tree came into existence. Ibn Taymiyyah believed that this type of substantial origination is evident from direct empirical observations but can also be demonstrated using sound rational arguments.

The significance of Ibn Taymiyyah's definition of matter cannot be stressed enough. It has allowed him to reject the doctrine of creation ex nihilo while also maintaining a strict belief in Abrahamic monotheism. By the virtue of Ibn Taymiyyah's definition of matter, creation ex nihilo becomes unnecessary to prove that only God is eternal and that all substances besides God are originated and have a beginning. The observation that things come into existence in place of others becomes sufficient for that purpose. This view is articulated by Ibn Taymiyyah's statement that the *genus* of creations is eternal but none of the *individual* creations co-exists with God from eternity.

Ibn Taymiyyah's ontology

We now elaborate on the relationship between Ibn Taymiyyah's views on creation ex materia and his ontology in general. This helps deepen our appreciation of the originated nature of things and also expand our knowledge of the nature of the creative agency of God.

Ibn Taymiyyah's conception of Creation hinges on the understanding that all ontological existents fall into one of two categories: *substances (aʿyān)* and *accidents (aʿrāḍ).* These two categories are mentioned frequently in the translation.

Substances are self-subsisting entities like stars, trees and human beings, and also include unseen existents such as angels, jinn and souls. By contrast, *accidents* are attributes that subsist in substances. Accidents are inseparable from the substances they describe, meaning that each accident must exist in the very substance that is the subject of its attribution, not in other substances, nor on its own. Examples of accidents include life, colour, size, motion, temperature, and arrangement.

According to Ibn Taymiyyah, the origination of *substances* is a stronger and more direct evidence for God's existence than the origination of accidents, even though both the substances and accidents of natural bodies are equally created. Accepting the origination of both the substance and accidents of the natural world will lead to a stronger appreciation of the existence of the Originator. By contrast, accepting only the origination of accidents (such as arrangements) and not the substances will result in a weaker inference of the Originator's existence. People who hold the latter view are more likely to become confused by the atheistic position that this world is an eternal substance that is constantly rearranging into new forms, whereas the former view is immune to such claims as it entails that every part of the natural world is an originated substance.

Ibn Taymiyyah's view on Creation has many implications on his conception of the creative agency of God. In contrast to theologians who held that things change only through the rearrangement of atoms, Ibn Taymiyyah argued that there is more to God's creative agency than mere rearrangement. He argued that although creations rearrange at the macroscopic level, the creations are also subject to change totally as substances at the deeper and more fundamental levels. The fundamental constituents change substantially in many of the natural processes, whereupon they are destroyed and new things are originated by God in their place, such that nothing of the prior substance continues to exist in the new creation after these natural processes have been completed.

God's ability to create things as substances is also a defining feature of God's creative agency according to Ibn Taymiyyah. Only God can change the realities of existents by causing things to perish and originating completely different things, while other agents are limited in their creative power to rearranging the materials. For instance, human beings can build a house or knit a dress as this merely involves rearrangement of already existing materials, but they are unable to create as much as a fly.

In addition to believing that natural bodies originate substantially during their initial creation, Ibn Taymiyyah argued that natural bodies also undergo continuous processes during the span of their existence that involve varying degrees of substantial change. These processes can be placed on a spectrum ranging from total absence of substantial change on one end, such as in rotations of celestial bodies, to complete substantial change on the other, such as in wood that changes into fire and smoke. Ibn Taymiyyah places the biological development of living organisms on the higher end of this spectrum, indicating considerable levels of change in substance. This falls in line with his theological position that evidence for God in the origins of substances is found primarily in everyday observations, such as the creation of animals, trees, and minerals.

Relationship to modern science

Many people today may argue that Ibn Taymiyyah's views on Creation are incompatible with modern science. This is because they are convinced that natural processes are necessarily a rearrangement of already existing matter and therefore nothing really comes into existence during these processes. It therefore helps to point out that many scientific descriptions of change align perfectly with Ibn Taymiyyah's view of creation ex materia and provide a further empirical basis that supports the first premise of the origination argument.

In stark resemblance to claims of particle physicists, Ibn Taymiyyah argued that there fundamentally exist basic constituents that make up all composite structures in the natural world. These constituents are not eternally in existence but are subject to a total change in substance. This indicates, by extension, that the natural world in its entirety is originated as a substance in the context of a prior created world and that it is, therefore, dependent on the eternal Originator.

In agreement with Ibn Taymiyyah, scientists today believe that there exist natural processes through which matter is created and annihilated, referring to these as processes of 'Matter creation' and 'Annihilation'. The building blocks of matter at the subatomic level can be entirely annihilated in particle-antiparticle collisions, whereupon they change into photons of light, which in turn change totally into other types of energy in the surroundings such as kinetic and potential energy. The reverse is also possible; matter particles can be created out of photons, which in turn originate out of the heat and potential energy in their surroundings.

This change from energy to matter (or vice versa) constitutes origination or annihilation of substance, not a mere rearrangement. The process of rearrangement involves the relocation of basic ingredients that remain unchanged throughout the rearrangement process, such that the ingredients before and after the rearrangement process will be identical despite having a different configuration. However, in processes of 'Matter creation', the ingredients that are in existence before the process (namely the forms of energy) are not identical to the constituents that are in existence after the process has been completed (that is, the particles of matter). Therefore, 'Matter creation' is not accurately described as a process of rearrangement, but rather a case of complete substantial origination that is in full support of the first premise of the origination argument.

The ontological distinction between the prior forms of energy that subsist in the surroundings, and the consequent matter particles that come into existence therefrom, can be demonstrated in two ways. The first is that matter particles and energy forms belong to entirely different classes. Particles are self-subsisting *substances* while forms of energy (e.g. heat, potential, etc.) are *accidents* that subsist in a substrate, namely the surroundings. Secondly, it is impossible for accidents to detach from the systems that are the subject of their attribution and move on to exist elsewhere in isolation. This entails that particles cannot be identical to the heat and potential energy from which they emerged. Rather, particles will have been entirely originated out of energy that existed in the surrounding bodies.

That said, Ibn Taymiyyah probably would have criticized how scientists interpret natural processes at the larger scales, especially at the molecular level. Ibn Taymiyyah believed that substances are created out of other substances in what is today described as processes of chemical reaction, such as those present in biological development. This claim by Ibn Taymiyyah is more controversial. Scientists today believe that molecules are arrangements of smaller atomic constituents, which are in turn arrangements of even smaller subatomic particles such as quarks and leptons. The substances of molecules do not originate when the atoms combine, and the atoms do not come into existence when the subatomic particles come together. Instead, quarks continue to exist within the structure of the atom which in turn continues to exist within the molecular structures that are formed. Scientists therefore believe that the molecular compositions are divisible into smaller constituents.

When probing more deeply into Ibn Taymiyyah's notion of Creation, one can predict a way in which his view can be reconciled with the modern scientific conception. Ibn Taymiyyah seems to have believed that some arrangements and compositions in the natural world are necessary to the substance of their constituents. Any disassembly that is said to occur in these composite structures would be impossible, for the constituents do not continue to exist once the compositions have ceased. Perhaps the breaking down of a molecule would necessitate a substantial change in the components of the molecule such that these components must entirely change into a newly created substance. The components of the molecule before the reaction would not be identical to the components that arise afterwards within the product. This book does not attempt to argue for this reconciliation but leaves it as an open question for the readers to explore on their own.

I am personally inclined to believe that Ibn Taymiyyah's view of

Creation applies not only at the subatomic level (which seems to be supported by particle physics), but also at the molecular level. If this happens to be true, it would be of immense service to the cause of monotheism in general if one managed to revise the scientific descriptions of chemical change so as to introduce a robustly scientific understanding that is philosophically compatible with Ibn Taymiyyah's view of Creation. If the scientific community learns to embrace the idea that atoms change substantially in chemical reactions, the challenges of atheism would be immediately solved for most people. People will once again begin to appreciate the origination of substances in everyday observations such as a developing foetus and a growing fruit, and belief in the Originator will become more obvious and immediate. Moreover, theologians will no longer find it necessary to mention the changes at the deeper and more fundamental subatomic levels to demonstrate that matter is created as a substance. The evidence for God in the origins of substances would be right in front of all people in the creation of trees and human beings.

It is important to note that Ibn Taymiyyah did not believe that theological arguments based on rearrangement in matter are completely invalid. His writings imply that he believed that the continuous origination of accidents within the natural world (such as motions and arrangements) is a sound evidence for the Originator, particularly because these accidents are originated and effected from external causes. Whenever he criticizes this argument, it is to give credence and priority to the even stronger evidence in substantial origination.

The rearrangement in the matter also indicates the contingency of the materials, and therefore their dependency on a necessarily existing Maker via the contingency argument. More clearly, the materials in the natural world are *caused* into motion by external causes and are *made* into various arrangements, hence they are contingent and dependent on a Self-sufficient God whose agency is uncaused by another. According to Ibn Taymiyyah, this contingency of the materials can also be used as further evidence of their originated nature, and consequently of their dependency on the eternal Originator. This is because contingency and having an originated nature are mutually concomitant descriptions; all originated things are dependent, and all dependent things are originated. However, the origination of the materials is not ex nihilo or without prior material conditions according to Ibn Taymiyyah; it is strictly out of other materials.

Creation ex nihilo

Through my conversation with Muslim scholars and students of knowledge, I found that most are convinced that Ibn Taymiyyah held that creation ex nihilo is possible, even if the act is assumed to be in the context of a perpetual creative agency where God is always creating one thing after another. However, it can be shown from the explicit statements of Ibn Taymiyyah (presented at the end of the first translation) that he did not always hold this view. Ibn Taymiyyah explains in *Nubuwwāt* that creation ex nihilo is impossible because the materials serve as the substrate in which the possibility of the origination subsists. Without the substrate, there would not exist any potential for things to originate, and the origination would be impossible.

Nevertheless, it is important to stress that the impossibility of creation ex nihilo does not contradict the perfection of God's power for

Ibn Taymiyyah. This is because the omnipotence of God excludes impossibilities and self-contradictions by definition, such as the creation of things that are simultaneously motionless and moving or both alive and dead. Ibn Taymiyyah believed that creation ex nihilo belongs to this category of self-contradictions and incoherent estimations that do not possibly exist in reality. For Ibn Taymiyyah, it is meaningless to claim that God is able to create things without prior matter just as it is meaningless to claim that He is unable to do so, as such an act of creation entails a contradiction.

It also helps to add that Ibn Taymiyyah did not believe that the creative agency of God is *dependent* on the materials. For Ibn Taymiyyah, the materials do not act instead of God or assist Him in His acts of creation. Rather, God is entirely sufficient for Creation. The materials are equally created by God and are subservient to His will, and all is dependent on Him and is a consequence of His unconditional power. At the most, the materials serve as conditions for the next iteration of creatures without which their *origination* would be impossible.

Either way, whether the reader chooses to accept the position that creation ex nihilo is impossible or prefers to include it in the power of God, or perhaps is even undecided on the matter, it should at least be appreciated that creation ex nihilo is not necessary to determine the existence of the Creator. Sound rational arguments for God's existence are best predicated on the observation that things are brought into existence out of others. After all, nothing in the natural world is observed to originate ex nihilo.

Historical and theological significance

For Ibn Taymiyyah, the Kalām theologians who adopted incorrect methods in demonstrating theological matters were in many ways deficient in their *fiṭrah*. At the root of their argumentation lies an unhealthy scepticism towards the intuitive meaning of origination and a disregard for its adequacy in demonstrating the Originator's existence via the origination argument.

As Kalām theologians became prominent leaders within the Muslim world, they motivated a gradual departure from the sound and intuitive arguments of the Qur'ān (such as the origination argument) to more complicated arguments of Kalām theology. It is in this context that many Muslim theologians have attempted to prove that the world was originated ex nihilo and gave precedence to incorrect arguments like the Argument from the Origination of Bodies, an argument which attempts to demonstrate an initial act of ex nihilo creation by asserting that the regress of events is impossible and that an absolutely first event is necessary.

Ibn Taymiyyah observed that the arguments of Kalām theology had become a source of great confusion among Muslims in his time. They caused many people to think that the doctrine of creation ex nihilo is necessary to demonstrate the Creator's existence, leading them to doubt the existence of the Abrahamic God. The arguments also led to inadequate responses to the claims of the Philosophers who believed in the eternality of the universe, causing them to reject the models of Creation altogether and become more averse to the religion, associating the incoherence of the arguments to monotheism itself.

Similarly, when many theists speak of Creation today, they tend to refer to the origins of the universe and attempt to solve difficult questions that relate to the Big Bang theory, usually to demonstrate that the universe emerged from a singularity and that it is therefore originated by God ex nihilo. They may also deny the permissibility of acceptable forms of the infinite regress, such as the infinite regress of created effects, to prove that this world was originated ex nihilo and infer that God exists.

For Ibn Taymiyyah, it is self-evident that the Prophets of God never directed people to use the above mentioned theories and assertions as evidence. God's Prophets simply drew the attention of the people to the empirical fact that they begin to exist out of humble origins and that all things on the earth, both animate and inanimate, begin to exist out of one another. It is for this reason that Ibn Taymiyyah, in his unwavering support of this Prophetic call, defended through the use of rational argumentation that God is known to exist through His everyday acts of creation ex materia. In doing so, he paved the way for future intellectuals, those infected by Kalām and philosophy, to sincerely and rationally accept the existence of God in the same way laymen do.

Overview of the Second Translation

After explaining the proper meaning of origination in the first part of the book, the second part presents a translated selection from Ibn Taymiyyah's work *Bayān Talbīs al-Jahmiyyah* which seeks to answer the following question: "How can we know with certainty that the substances of natural phenomena do in fact originate after their nonexistence as opposed to being a rearrangement of already existing matter?" The translation presents a rational argument for the creation of matter which demonstrates that matter is not eternal, but that it originates and annihilates entirely. This argument is formulated by Ibn Taymiyyah as a solution to two extreme views on the nature of matter, both of which entail unavoidable contradictions.

The first one of the two extremes is adopted by Kalām theologians who claim that matter cannot be divided infinitely, but that the division must terminate at indivisible atoms that are extremely small to the point of not having any size or volume. In this view, physical bodies are constituted of a finite number of these unchangeable and incorporeal substances. This is known as the theory of the *indivisible atom* and is one of the key theories on which the theologians predicated much of their principal theological statements. By contrast, the second extreme is adopted by Aristotelian philosophers who claim that matter divides infinitely into smaller constituents. In this view, physical bodies potentially constitute an infinite number of components.

Because Ibn Taymiyyah rejected both views, it might seem that he is tangled in an absurdity. After all, to say that physical bodies divide neither infinitely nor finitely would entail a contradiction. To solve this seeming contradiction, Ibn Taymiyyah distinguished between two different types of divisibility: *actual* divisibility and *conceptual* divisibility. He rejected the existence of conceptually indivisible atoms or substances. He maintained that all particles must be conceptually divisible as it is possible to *conceive* of their different sides no matter how small and fundamental they are; all substances must have physical size and volume. Yet Ibn Taymiyyah rejected the existence of objects that can be divided indefinitely into smaller parts, whether actually or potentially. Such an infinite division would entail that the object is made up of an infinite number of particles, even though nothing can include an infinite number of parts no matter how large it is.

In this way, Ibn Taymiyyah concludes a third, middle position: that the fundamental parts that constitute the composite bodies of the natural world are conceptually divisible because they have size and volume, yet they are actually indivisible as they cannot be separated into smaller constituents. In other words, the composite structures of the natural world are divisible *conceptually* without an end, but are divisible *actually* only to a certain point of division.

At first glance, this third position seems to contradict a tempting intuition. Both the Kalām theologians and the Aristotelean philosophers agree over the notion that all physical bodies can be divided further in an actual sense, whereas Ibn Taymiyyah's position denies that the fundamental bodies can be separated further into smaller parts. What then does Ibn Taymiyyah make of the intuition (and well-established empirical fact) that natural bodies are not immutable but can be subjected to division by appropriate means without exception?

Ibn Taymiyyah answers that the fundamental matter particles within a composite body cannot endure divisions indefinitely. Rather, at some final point of actually dividing a body, the particles can no longer sustain and must change totally into other creations; they must cease to exist entirely, whereupon other things must begin to exist in their place. In other words, the matter must change substantially.

This solution by Ibn Taymiyyah allows him to maintain both sound propositions: (i) that every natural body can be subjected to division, and (ii) that no natural body can be divided ad infinitum in an actual sense. This is because there exists no meaningful sense in which natural bodies can be divided further once they have changed substantially into totally different bodies, as they no longer exist after the substantial change has taken place. This unique solution implies that matter is not eternal but ceases to exist, and thus forms the basis for Ibn Taymiyyah's argument for the creation of matter.

It helps to add that Ibn Taymiyyah believed that, unlike composite creations which consist of separate parts, God is actually and potentially indivisible. This entails that nothing can possibly detach from His essence and become separate from Himself, which is one of the arguments Ibn Taymiyyah uses to refute the claim that God begot a son. Moreover, for Ibn Taymiyyah, God is necessarily existing and therefore cannot be overpowered by any means or cease to exist, unlike the fundamental constituents in matter. Although everything in the world changes in substance, God is eternal and His essence does not perish.

However, it is important to understand that Ibn Taymiyyah did not believe that God is conceptually indivisible. Although he avoided the non-scriptural terminologies of 'body' and 'substance' when speaking of God, Ibn Taymiyyah believed that it is nonetheless possible to distinguish between different attributes of God. For example, it is possible to tell apart His exalted face from His two blessed hands and His right hand from His left hand. This is because God has various attributes and a tremendous measure that is greater than all things in existence. The Qur'ān mentions that: **{the whole earth will be in His fist on the Day of Resurrection, and the heavens will be folded in His right hand.}**

By the end of the second translation, the reader should be able to see how Ibn Taymiyyah located the empirical evidence for God's creative agency in the substantial origination of the different parts of the natural world. Everything in this world, from its biggest structures to its smallest components, is subject to total change and is therefore originated. The matter is created in the context of prior matter, which calls for the eternal Originator via the argument from origination.

Overview of the Third Translation

The final part of the book includes a supplementary translation of a selected passage from Ibn Taymiyyah's work *Ḥudūth al-ʿĀlam*, which argues for the origination of the world and responds to philosophical arguments for the eternality of the world and its celestial spheres. In *Ḥudūth al-ʿĀlam* [pp. 56-69], Ibn Taymiyyah identifies two lines of argumentation for the eternality of the world. The first is an Aristotelian line of argumentation that seeks to demonstrate the eternality of a matter substrate, and is usually reinforced by inductive arguments. The second is an Avicennian line of argumentation which states that God does not have any willful acts of creation, but that He is instead an eternally complete Cause for the world who emanates it by His essence, such that the celestial spheres must have co-existed with Him from eternity. The full translation of Ibn Taymiyyah's response to the first line of argumentation is presented in this book.

Ḥudūth al-ʿĀlam is a unique text because it provides a rare insight into Ibn Taymiyyah's early position on the question of whether the existence of materials is a necessary condition for the origination of created beings. Ibn Taymiyyah claims in *Ḥudūth al-ʿĀlam* that the materials are superfluous: God is able to create with or without prior materials. He objects to the soundness of Aristotle's argument for the eternality of the matter substrate, implying that further evidence must be provided in order to justify the position that creation without materials is impossible. Nevertheless, Ibn Taymiyyah suggests that Aristotle's argument does not lead to an eternal substrate even if it were true, explaining that the creations are known to originate entirely and substantially out of others, a position that is consistent with his definition of origination elsewhere.

However, in *Nubuwwāt*, Ibn Taymiyyah argues for a different position that the materials are necessary conditions for the origination of the next iteration of creatures: God may create things only out of prior materials which are in turn created only out of prior materials. The omnipotence of God cannot be said to include acts of ex nihilo creation, as such acts are incoherent and self-contradictory propositions that cannot be attributed to God in any meaningful sense. In this view, God's creative act is the sufficient cause that is needed to bring the created effect into actual existence from the prior material condition in which it is latent. God originates the created effect only after preparing its material conditions. Ibn Taymiyyah explains his rational argument for this theological position (presented at the end of the first translation), which has its roots in Aristotle's argument.

The conflicting positions in *Ḥudūth al-'Ālam* and *Nubuwwāt* is one example that supports the known development of Ibn Taymiyyah's position on aspects of philosophy that occurred later in his life. *Ḥudūth al-'Ālam* most likely predates *Nubuwwāt* with the latter being one of the last major works of Ibn Taymiyyah.

It should be noted that the transition in Ibn Taymiyyah's position regarding the material conditions does not affect his arguments for the origination of the world or his general understanding of the way God originates things after their nonexistence. These arguments remain consistent between his earlier and latter works. Ibn Taymiyyah argues in *Ḥudūth al-'Ālam,* as he does in his other books, that God has been perpetually acting from eternity by His will. Ibn Taymiyyah also suggests in *Ḥudūth al-ʿĀlam* as he does in *Nubuwwāt* that the evidence for God's creative agency lies in the contingency of the world and in everyday observations of the substantial origination of things ex materia. For Ibn Taymiyyah, the question on the plausibility of creation without prior materials is largely irrelevant when it comes to the rational demonstration of Abrahamic monotheism. However, as evidenced by *Ḥudūth al-ʿĀlam*, Ibn Taymiyyah did believe at some point in his life (perhaps mistakenly) that the impossibility of creating things without materials would contradict God's independence in His acts of creation, and that therefore such an impossibility is indemonstrable.

The evolution of Ibn Taymiyyah's position on the question of material conditions is an interesting observation with modern-day implications. The Shaykh of Islam Ibn Taymiyyah, one of the greatest exegetes of Islamic Scripture and a proponent of orthodox Islamic theology, was able to reconcile the impossibility of creation ex nihilo with an uncompromising belief in the absolute independence and maximal perfection of the God of Abraham. In the same way, it may also be possible to reconcile Abrahamic monotheism with modern-day sentiments in support of the necessity of the laws of physics, such as the laws of motion and energy conservation. Perhaps it is unnecessary for the naturalists of this age to sacrifice these philosophical commitments in order for their faith in God to find its proper expression. Perhaps they only need to see this world with sharper philosophical insight in the brighter light of God's Revelation.

كتاب النبوات

معنى الحدوث

On The Meaning of Creation

The Prophet Has Clarified the Foundations of the Faith

فَصْلٌ في أنَّ الرَسولَ لا بُدَّ أنْ يُبَيِّنَ أُصولَ الدِينِ، وهِيَ البَراهينُ الدالَّةُ علىٰ أنَّ ما يَقولُهُ حَقٌّ؛ مِنَ الخَبَرِ، والأَمْرِ؛ فَلا بُدَّ أنْ يَكونَ قَدْ بَيَّنَ الدَلائِلَ علىٰ صِدْقِهِ في كُلِّ ما أَخْبَرَ، ووُجوبِ طاعَتِه في كُلِّ ما أَوْجَبَ وأَمَرَ.

SECTION: On that the Prophet must have clarified the foundations of Faith, [which] are the [rational] evidences that show that [all of] what he stated is true, [both] the declarative statements and the imperative ones. [That is,] the [Prophet] must have clarified the evidences for his truthfulness in everything he **informs**, and [must have also clarified] the [moral] obligation of obeying him in everything he obligates and **commands**.

ومِنْ أَعْظَمِ أُصولِ الضَلالِ: الإعْراضُ عَنْ بَيانِ الرَسولِ لِلأَدِلَّةِ والآياتِ والبَراهينِ والحُجَجِ؛ فَإنَّ المُعْرِضينَ عَنْ هَذا إمَّا أنْ يُصَدِّقوهُ ويَقْبَلوا قَوْلَهُ ويُؤْمِنوا بِهِ بِلا دَليلٍ أَصْلاً ولا عِلْمٍ، وإمَّا أنْ يَسْتَدِلّوا علىٰ ذَلِكَ بِغَيْرِ أدِلَّتِهِ.

And among the greatest sources of misguidance is to turn away from the Prophet's explanation of the evidences, signs, and [rational] arguments. For indeed, those who turn away from this [explanation] either: (i) believe him and accept his claim without any evidence or knowledge at all, or (ii) [come to] infer the [truth of his claim] using evidences other than his [i.e. other than those which he cited].

فَإنْ لَمْ يَكونوا عالِمِينَ بصِدْقِهِ فَهُمْ مِمَّنْ يُقالُ لَهُ في قَبْرِهِ: ما قَوْلُكَ في هَذا الرَجُلِ الّذي بُعِثَ فيكُمْ؟ فَأمَّا المُؤْمِنُ أوِ المُوقِنُ، فَيَقولُ: هُوَ عَبْدُ اللهِ ورَسولُهُ جاءَنا بِالبَيِّناتِ والهُدىٰ، فآمَنّا بِهِ واتَّبَعْناهُ. وأمّا المُنافِقُ أوِ المُرْتابُ، فَيقولُ: هاه، هاه، لا أَدْرِي، سَمِعْتُ النّاسَ يَقولونَ شَيْئًا، فَقُلْتُهُ؛ فَيُضْرَبُ بمِرْزَبَّةٍ مِنْ حَديدٍ، فَيَصِيحُ صَيْحَةً يَسْمَعُها كُلُّ شَيْءٍ إلّا الثَقَلَيْنِ.

If they do not know the truthfulness of his [claim], then they will be among those who will be [tried and] asked in their graves [by the angels]: "What do you say of this man who was sent to you [i.e. Muḥammad]?" As for the believer who is certain [in his faith], he will reply: "He is the servant of God and His messenger; he came to us with clear evidences and guidance, and so we believed in him and followed him." [But] as for the hypocrite or the one who was doubtful [in his faith], he will reply: "Um, um, I don't know! I heard the people say something and so I said the same!" He will then be struck with an iron hammer, upon which he will let out a scream which is heard by everything, except mankind and the jinn.

وإنِ اسْتَدَلَّ عَلىٰ ذَلِكَ بِغَيْرِ الآياتِ والأدِلَّةِ الّتي دَعا بِها النّاسَ، فَهُوَ مَعَ كَوْنِهِ مُبْتَدِعًا، لا بُدَّ أن يُخطِئَ وَيَضِلَّ.

[But] if they infer the [truthfulness of his claim] through [means] other than the signs and evidences by which he called the people [to the Faith], then they will inevitably fall into error and misguidance, in addition to becoming innovators [in the religion].

فإِنَّ ظَنَّ الظانِّ أَنَّهُ بِأَدِلَّةٍ وبَرَاهِينَ خَارِجَةٍ عَمَّا جاءَ بِهِ يُدَلُّ[١] عَلَىٰ ما جاءَ بِهِ= مِنْ جِنْسٍ[٢] ظَنِّهِ أَنَّهُ يَأْتِي بِعِبادَاتٍ غَيْرِ ما شَرَعَهُ تُوصِلُ إِلَىٰ مَقْصُودِهِ.

Indeed, to assume that one may be guided to the [same Faith] which was taught by the Prophet through evidences and [rational] demonstrations that lie outside of what [he] brought [in Revelation], is analogous to assuming that one could attain the desired outcome [of worship] through innovated acts of worship which were not legislated by him.

وهَذا الظَنُّ وَقَعَ فيهِ طَوائِفُ مِنَ العُبّادِ الغالِطينَ: أَصْحابِ الإِرادَةِ والمَحَبَّةِ والزُهْدِ، كَما وَقَعَ في الظَنِّ الأَوَّلِ طَوائِفُ من النُظّارِ الغالِطينَ: أَصْحابِ الاسْتِدْلالِ والاعْتِبارِ والنَظَرِ.[٣]

And this [latter] assumption has befallen [many] groups from the erring worshippers, the people of *irādah*[4], love, and asceticism [i.e. the Ṣūfīs] – just as the former assumption has befallen [many]

---

١ في المطبوع: «تدلّ».

٢ في المطبوع: «فهو من جنس»، والمثبت من الأصل الخطي صواب.

٣ في المطبوع: «وهذا الظنّ وقع فيه طوائف من النظّار الغالطين، أصحاب الاستدلال والاعتبار والنظر؛ كما وقع في الظنّ الأوّل طوائف من العبّاد الغالطين، أصحاب الإرادة والمحبّة والزهد». والمثبت من الأصل الخطي هو الصواب.

4 *Irādah* translates as will or intention. *Aṣḥāb al-Irādah* is often used to denote those who tread the path of asceticism and taṣawwuf, usually because of their strong will power to forsake the pleasures of this life and engross themselves in worship.

groups from the erring *Nuẓẓār*[5], the people of [rational] demonstrations, contemplation, and *naẓar* [i.e. the Kalām[6] theologians].

وقَوْلُه ﷺ في خُطْبَتِهِ يَوْمَ الجُمُعَةِ: «خَيْرُ الكَلامِ كَلامُ اللهِ، وخَيْرُ الهَدْيِ هَدْيُ محمّدٍ، وشَرُّ الأُمورِ مُحْدَثاتُها، وكُلُّ بِدْعَةٍ ضَلالَةٌ» يَتَناوَلُ هَذا

5 The *Nuẓẓār* are people who engage in *naẓar*, a term that translates as the 'contemplation of rational arguments'. In this context, *naẓar* refers to specific arguments that were used by Kalām theologians to arrive at their theological conclusions, such as the Argument from the Origination of Bodies. The terms '*Nuẓẓār*' and 'Kalām theologians' can be used interchangeably in this book.

6 Kalām (literally 'discourse') is a science that was developed by the Kalām theologians, also known as the Mutakallimīn, for the purpose of demonstrating and defending the tenets of Islamic Faith in the face of doubt and irreligion. Kalām includes a variety of theological schools and arguments. Originally, it was represented by theological groups such as the Mu'tazilah who, based on their heavy reliance on Greek philosophy, ended up negating the attributes of God and deviating from the beliefs of the Pious Predecessors. For this reason, most of the leading scholars of that era like Aḥmad ibn Ḥanbal severely criticized the people of kalām and warned against it, clarifying that sound theology ought to be based on the word of the Qur'ān and the Sunnah of the Prophet and to avoid the irrational and counter-scriptural methods of demonstration that were used by the people of kalām. Other theological schools which were closer to the original beliefs of the Pious Predecessors, such schools like the Ash'ariyyah, were later developed as a reaction to the Mu'tazilah, but nonetheless drew from some of their key arguments and foundations. These latter schools became incorporated within the orthodox tradition of Islam over time, and so Ibn Taymiyyah wrote extensively to distinguish the truth from the falsehood in their theological demonstrations, insisting that the correct demonstrations are to be found in the prescribed arguments of the Qur'ān and the Sunnah, which also happen to be rationally sound since authentic Revelation does not contradict sound reason.

وهَذا.

And the Prophet's statement in Friday sermons "The best of speech is the speech of God. The best of guidance is the guidance of Muḥammad. The worst of matters are the newly invented. And every *innovation* is a misguidance" – includes both of these [kinds of innovations: in theological evidences and in religious practices].

وقَدْ أَرَىٰ اللهُ تَعالىٰ عِبادَهُ الآياتِ في الآفاقِ، وفي أَنْفُسِهِم، حَتَّىٰ يَتَبَيَّنَ[٧] لَهُمْ أنّ ما قالَهُ فَهُوَ حَقٌّ؛ فَإِنَّ أَرْبابَ العِبادَةِ والمَحَبَّةِ والإرادَةِ والزُهْدِ الّذينَ سَلَكُوا غَيْرَ ما أُمِرُوا بِهِ ضَلُّوا كَما ضَلَّتِ النَصارَىٰ. ومُبْتَدِعَةُ هَذِهِ الأُمَّةِ مِنَ العُبَّادِ، وأَرْبابِ النَظَرِ والاسْتِدْلالِ الّذينَ سَلَكوا غَيْرَ دَليلِهِ وبَيانِهِ أَيْضًا ضَلُّوا.

And God has [already] shown His servants the signs in the horizons and within themselves, such that it becomes clear to them that what He has said is the truth[8]. Indeed, the people of worship, love, *irādah*, and asceticism, [particularly] those who took [paths that are] other than the legislated one, were misled like the Christians. [Likewise,] the innovators within this [Muslim] nation, among the worshippers and people of *naẓar* and logical inference, who adopted evidences and [rational] demonstrations other than those of the Prophet, were also misguided.

قالَ تَعالىٰ: ﴿فَإِمَّا يَأْتِيَنَّكُم مِّنِّي هُدًى فَمَنِ ٱتَّبَعَ هُدَايَ فَلَا يَضِلُّ وَلَا يَشْقَىٰ

٧ في المطبوع: «تبيّن»، والمثبت من الأصل الخطي.

8 The author is alluding to Qur'ān, 41: 53.

﴿وَمَنْ أَعْرَضَ عَن ذِكْرِي فَإِنَّ لَهُۥ مَعِيشَةً ضَنكًا وَنَحْشُرُهُۥ يَوْمَ ٱلْقِيَـٰمَةِ أَعْمَىٰ ﴿١٢٤﴾ قَالَ رَبِّ لِمَ حَشَرْتَنِيٓ أَعْمَىٰ وَقَدْ كُنتُ بَصِيرًا ﴿١٢٥﴾ قَالَ كَذَٰلِكَ أَتَتْكَ ءَايَـٰتُنَا فَنَسِيتَهَا ۖ وَكَذَٰلِكَ ٱلْيَوْمَ تُنسَىٰ﴾ [طه: ١٢٣-١٢٦]

The Almighty God says: {**"And if there should come to you guidance from Me – then whoever follows My guidance will neither go astray [in the world] nor suffer [in the Hereafter]. And whoever turns away from My remembrance – indeed, he will have a depressed life, and We will gather him on the Day of Resurrection blind." He will say, "My Lord, why have you raised me blind while I was [once] seeing?" [Allah] will say, "Thus did Our signs come to you, and you forgot them; and thus will you this Day be forgotten."**}

وفي الكَلامِ المَأْثورِ عَنْ الإمامِ أَحْمَدَ: أُصولُ الإسْلامِ أَرْبَعَةٌ: دالٌّ، ودَليلٌ، ومُبَيِّنٌ، ومُسْتَدِلٌّ. فالدالُّ هُوَ اللهُ، والدَليلُ هُوَ القُرْآنُ، والمُبَيِّنُ هُوَ الرَسولُ؛ قالَ اللهُ تَعالىٰ: ﴿لِتُبَيِّنَ لِلنَّاسِ مَا نُزِّلَ إِلَيْهِمْ﴾ [النحل: ٤٤]، والمُسْتَدِلُّ هُمْ أُولوا العِلْمِ وأُولوا الألْبابِ الذين أَجْمَعَ المُسْلِمونَ عَلىٰ هِدايَتِهِمْ ودِرايَتِهِمْ.

And in the [famous] statement attributed to Aḥmad [ibn Hanbal[9]]:

9 Aḥmad ibn Ḥanbal al-Shaybāni (d. 241H) is the last of the four *imāms* of jurisprudence whose schools survive to this day. He was known for his piety and exceptional manners, powerful memory, and extensive knowledge. He compiled the *Musnad*, a collection of almost thirty thousand hadīths. During the Inquisition, he remained patient and refused to surrender to the doctrine of the created-ness of the Qur'ān, despite the torture and the immense pres-

"The foundations of Islam are four: (i) The one who **provides** the evidence, (ii) the **evidence** [itself], (iii) the one who **explains** [the evidence], and (iv) the one who **infers** [from the evidence]. The one who provides the evidence is God. The evidence is the Qur'ān. The one who explains [the evidence] is the Prophet, as God said: **{We have revealed unto you the *Dhikr* (i.e. the Qur'ān) that you may explain to mankind that which has been revealed for them.}** [Lastly,] the ones who infer [from the evidence] are the people of knowledge and understanding, those whom the Muslims unanimously agree to their righteousness and knowledge."

وقَدْ ذَكَرَهُ ابْنُ الْمَنِّيِّ عَنْ أَحْمَدَ، وهُوَ مَذْكورٌ في «العُدَّةِ» للقاضي أَبي يَعْلىٰ، وغَيْرِها. إمّا أنَّ أَحْمَدَ قالَهُ، أو قِيلَ لَهُ فاسْتَحْسَنَهُ.

This [statement] was reported from Aḥmad [ibn Hanbal] by Ibn al-Manni, and it was also mentioned in al-Qāḍi Abī Ya'la's *'al-'Uddah'*, as well as other books. [It is] either [the case] that Aḥmad said it, or that it was said to him and he approved of it.

ولِهَذا صارَ كَثيرٌ مِنَ النُّظّارِ يُوجِبونَ العِلْمَ والنَّظَرَ والاسْتِدْلالَ، ويَنْهَوْنَ عَنِ التَّقْليدِ، ويَقولُ كَثيرٌ مِنْهُمْ: إنَّ إيمانَ المُقَلِّدِ لا يَصِحُّ، أو أنَّهُ وإنْ صَحَّ لَكِنَّهُ عاصٍ بِتَرْكِ الاسْتِدْلالِ.

For this reason, many of the *Nuẓẓār* came to obligate knowledge, *naẓar*, and [rational] inference [as conditions for the validity of

---

sure from the authorities. When the Inquisition was over, he emerged victorious and was recognized by Muslims as an *imām* of the Sunnah by whom God preserved the religion.

one's theological claims], and they forbade blind following [in the theological matters]. Many of them say that the faith of the blind follower is invalid, or that he is [at the least] sinful in his forsaking of inference, even if his faith is valid.

The Argument from the Origination of Bodies

ثُمَّ النَظَرُ والاسْتِدْلالُ الذي يَدْعُونَ إِلَيْهِ، ويُوجِبونَهُ، ويَجْعَلونَهُ أَوَّلَ الواجِباتِ وأَصْلَ العِلْمِ: هُوَ نَظَرٌ واسْتِدْلالٌ ابْتَدَعُوهُ، لَيسَ هُوَ المَشْروعَ؛ لا خَبَرًا، ولا أَمْرًا. وهُوَ اسْتِدْلالٌ فاسِدٌ لا يُوصِلُ إلىٰ العِلْمِ.

[But] the *naẓar* and [rational] inference which these [*Nuẓẓār*] promote, obligate, and consider to be the first of [all religious] obligations and the basis of [all] knowledge, is a [method of] demonstration which they have invented, one that is not prescribed – neither in the declarative nor in the imperative [religious] texts. It is [also] a fallacious [method of] demonstration that does not lead to [sound] knowledge [of the Faith].

فَإِنَّهُمْ جَعَلوا أَصْلَ العِلْمِ بالخَالِقِ هُوَ الاسْتِدْلالَ علىٰ ذَلِكَ بِحُدوثِ الأَجْسامِ، والاسْتِدْلالَ علىٰ حُدوثِ الأَجْسامِ بِأَنَّها مُسْتَلْزِمَةٌ للأَعْراضِ لا تَخْلُو عَنْها ولا تَنْفَكُّ مِنْها[١٠]. ثُمَّ اسْتَدَلّوا عَلىٰ حُدوثِ الأَعْراضِ. قالوا: فَثَبَتَ أَنَّ الأَجْسامَ مُسْتَلْزِمَةٌ للحَوادِثِ، لا تَخْلو[١١] عَنْها، فَلا تَكونُ قَبْلَها[١٢].

---

١٠ في المطبوع: «لا يخلو عنها ولا ينفك منها».

١١ في المطبوع: «لا يخلو».

١٢ في الأصل الخطي والمطبوع: «فلا تكون مثلها»، والظاهر أنه تصحيف عن المثبت.

For they have predicated the knowledge of the Creator's existence on the argument that [all] **bodies**[13] are originated. And they predicated [the knowledge of this] origination of bodies on the notion that [bodies] are always accompanied by **accidents** and are never void of them nor detached from them. They then [sought to] demonstrate the origination of these [accompanying] accidents. Thus, they concluded that [all] bodies are accompanied by ***ḥawādith***[14] (i.e. ac-

13 In this context, bodies are things that have spatial extension and physical location. For Ibn Taymiyyah, the claim that all bodies are originated is problematic, as it implies an explicit negation of corporeality from God. Ibn Taymiyyah believed that every self-subsisting thing in existence, whether it is from the natural world or the world of the Unseen, must be spatially extended, physically located, and possible to see – if given adequate vision. However, although he believed that even God is spatially located and will be seen in the hereafter, he was careful to avoid the terms 'substance' and 'physical body' when describing God, and instead referred to Him as a concretely existing Creator *being* who resides above the creation and is described with various divine *attributes*, reserving the terms 'substance', 'body', 'corporeal', and 'accident' for created things.

14 *Ḥawādith* are things which originate. These may either be (i) concrete things, such as trees and human beings, or (ii) events and accidents that arise in concrete things, such as decisions, actions, motions and arrangements. In this context, *ḥawādith* is referring to events and accidents.

The first type of *ḥawādith* are always created by God. They are concrete *substances* that originate and are therefore dependent on a Creator who brings them into existence. As for the other type of *ḥawādith*, that of events and originating *accidents*, these may equally refer to created attributes and uncreated attributes. Those that are created by God are ones which arise in concrete creations. They include things like the arrangement of clouds, the motion of the wind, and the agency of a human being. By contrast, those that are uncreated are ones which arise in the essence of God. These are usually referred to as God's voluntary actions by Ibn Taymiyyah and not as *ḥawādith*, because

cidents that are *originating*), [and that] they can never be void of them or separate from them. Therefore, [bodies] cannot precede the [accidents].

ثُمّ كَثيرٌ مِنْهُمْ قالوا: وما لَمْ يَخْلُ مِنَ الحَوادِثِ، أو ما لَمْ يَسْبِقِ الحَوادِثَ، فَهُوَ حادِثٌ، وظَنَّ أنَّ هَذِهِ مُقَدِّمَةٌ بَدِيهِيَّةٌ مَعْلومَةٌ بالضَرورَةِ لا يُطْلَبُ عَلَيْها دَليلٌ، وكانَ ذَلِكَ بِسَبَبِ أنَّ لَفْظَ الحَوادِثِ يُشْعِرُ بِأَنَّهُ[١٥] لَها ابْتِداءٌ؛ كالحادِثِ المُعَيَّنِ، والحَوادِثِ المَحْدُودَةِ، ولَوْ قُدِّرَتْ أَلْفَ أَلْفِ أَلْفِ حادِثٍ. فَإِنَّ الحَوادِثَ إذا جُعِلَتْ مُقَدَّرَةً مَحْدودَةً، فَلا بُدَّ أن يَكُونَ لَها ابْتِداءٌ؛

Thereafter, many of the [*Nuẓẓār*] asserted [the following premise that is key to the argument]: "**Every substrate that was never void of *ḥawādith* (originating accidents) is originated**", or, [alternatively,] "**Everything that does not precede originating accidents is originated**", [therewith arguing that all bodies were originated ex nihilo in the past, which in turn calls for the existence of the eternal Originator.] They assumed that this premise [*"Every substrate of ḥawādith is originated"*] is known immediately and by necessity, without any need for [further] evidence. The reason for this [assumption of theirs] was that the term '*ḥawādith*' (i.e. originating accidents, events) gives the impression that they have a beginning [in time], just like a **particular** originating accident or a **limited** [set of] originating accidents [must have a beginning in time] – even if [the set were] assumed to include a billion originating

---

they are divine attributes.

١٥ في المطبوع: «بأنّ»، والمثبت من الأصل الخطي لا غُبار عليه.

accidents, for if the originating accidents are assumed to be definite and limited [in number], then they must have a beginning [in time].

فَإِنَّ ما لا ابْتِداءَ لَهُ لَيْسَ لَهُ حَدٌّ مُعَيَّنٌ ابْتَدَأَ مِنْهُ، إِذْ قَدْ قِيلَ لا ابْتِداءَ لَهُ، بَلْ هُوَ قَدِيمٌ أَزَلِيٌّ دائِمٌ. وَمَعْلُومٌ أَنَّ هَذِهِ الحَوادِثَ ما لَمْ يَسْبِقْها فَهُوَ حادِثٌ؛ فَإِنَّهُ يَكونُ إِمّا مَعَها، وإِمّا بَعْدَها.

Indeed, that which has no beginning [in time] does not have a definite limit from which it [may be said to] start, for it has already been assumed to be without beginning, eternal, and perpetual. And it is known that everything that does not precede this [kind of] originating accidents [that are limited in number] must [also] be **originated**, for it will either be with them [in time], or after them.

وكَثِيرٌ مِنْهُمْ تَفَطَّنَ¹⁶ لِلفَرْقِ بَيْنَ جِنْسِ الحَوادِثِ، وبَيْنَ الحَوادِثِ المَحْدُودَةِ؛ فالجِنْسُ مِثْلُ أَنْ يُقالَ: ما زالَتِ الحَوادِثُ تُوجَدُ شَيْئًا بَعْدَ شَيْءٍ، أَو ما زالَ جِنْسُها مَوْجودًا، أَو ما زالَ اللهُ مُتَكَلِّمًا إِذا شاءَ، أَو ما زالَ اللهُ فاعِلًا لِما يَشاءُ، أَو ما زالَ قادِرًا عَلى أَنْ يَفْعَلَ بِقُدْرَةٍ¹⁷ يُمْكِنُ مَعَها اقْتِرانُ المَقْدورِ بِالقُدْرَةِ، لا تَكونُ قُدْرَةٌ يَمْتَنِعُ مَعَها المَقْدورُ؛ فإِنَّ هَذِهِ في الحَقيقَةِ لَيْسَتْ قُدْرَةً.

Many [others] from the [*Nuẓẓār*] became aware of the distinction between the **genus of events** and the **limited [set of] events**[18]. As

---

١٦ في المطبوع: «يفطن».

١٧ في الأصل الخطي: «قدرة» بدون الباء، والمثبت هو مقتضى السياق.

18 And thus Kalām theologians added the further premise which states that

for the genus [of events], it is like saying: "There have always been events coming into existence, one after the other", "The genus [of events] has always been in existence", "God has always been speaking whenever He willed", "God has always been doing whatever He willed", and "God has always been able to act (and create) with a power whose conjunction with the empowered effect is possible" – i.e. there can never be any power whose acts under its potential are impossible, for this is not really a 'power' [in any meaningful sense][19].

ومِثْلُ أنْ يُقالَ في المُسْتَقْبَلِ: لا بُدَّ أنَّ اللهَ يَخْلُقُ شَيْئًا بَعْدَ شَيْءٍ، ونَعِيمُ أَهْلِ الجَنَّةِ دائِمٌ لا يَزولُ، ولا يَنْفَدُ. وقَدْ يُقالُ في النَوْعَيْنِ: كَلِماتُ اللهِ لا تَنْفَدُ، ولا نِهايَةَ لَها؛ لا في الماضي، ولا في المُسْتَقْبَلِ، ونَحْوُ ذَلِكَ.

Likewise, [the genus of events is] such as when it is said concerning the future: "God will continue to create things after others", and "The delights of the inhabitants of Paradise will continue forever and will never cease or end". Also, [the genus of events] may be affirmed in both types [of infinity, past and future], with statements such as: "The words of God cannot be exhausted and are endless

---

it is impossible for events to regress into the past. They specifically introduced this premise to rule out the possibility of an eternal genus of events. This is because it cannot be inferred that all bodies are originated if the accompanying set of originating accidents which they cannot precede is assumed to be eternal.

19 Ibn Taymiyyah is alluding to the Kalām theologians who on the one hand believed in Allah's eternal power, but on the other say that the genus of His acts of creation must have a start and cannot possibly be eternal. Their position entails that there must be a time when the act of creation was inaccessible to Allah's eternal power.

from the [infinite] past and into the [infinite] future".

فالكَلامُ في دَوامِ الجِنْسِ وبَقائِهِ، وأنَّهُ لا يَنْفَدُ، ولا يَنْقَضي، ولا يَزولُ، ولا ابْتِداءَ لَهُ= غيرُ الكَلامِ فيما يُقَدَّرُ مَحْدودًا لَهُ ابْتِداءٌ، أو لَهُ ابْتِداءٌ وانْتِهاءٌ؛

[Indeed,] what is said regarding the **continuation** of the **genus** [of events], its endurance, endlessness, and absence of a beginning [in time], is [very] different to what is said regarding [the set of originating events] that is assumed to be **definite** with a **beginning** [in time], or with [both] a beginning and an end.

فَإنَّ كَثيرًا مِنَ النُظّارِ مَنْ يَقولُ: جِنْسُ الحَوادِثِ إذا قُدِّرَ له ابْتِداءٌ، وَجَبَ أن يَكونَ لَهُ انْتِهاءٌ؛ لِأنَّهُ يُمْكِنُ فَرْضُ تقدُّمِهِ علىٰ ذَلِكَ الحَدِّ، فَيَكونُ أَكْثَرَ مِمّا وُجِدَ، وما لا يَتَناهىٰ لا يَدْخُلُهُ التَفاضُلُ؛ فَإنَّهُ لَيْسَ وَراءَ عَدَمِ النِهايَةِ شَيْءٌ أَكْثَرُ مِنْها، بِخِلافِ ما لا ابْتِداءَ له ولا انْتِهاءَ؛ فَإنَّ هَذا لا يَكونُ شَيْءٌ فَوْقَهُ، فَلا يُفْضي إلىٰ التَفاضُلِ فيما لا يَتَناهىٰ. وبَسْطُ هَذا لَهُ مَوْضِعٌ آخَرُ.

[This second nuance is noteworthy] as many of the *Nuẓẓār* have [indeed] claimed that the genus of events must have an end [in time] if it is assumed to have a beginning. For [every originating genus] could be assumed to begin earlier [than it did] such that it would include a greater number [of events]. However, [they claimed] that sets which are infinite [and endless] cannot be greater than others [that are infinite and endless], for there is nothing beyond an infinite that can be greater than it. [In this way, they argued that there can never exist an endless genus of events that has a beginning, arguing that this is] unlike [the other genus] that is [assumed to be eternal both ways] without beginning or end, for this [latter genus] is not surpassed [in magnitude when compared with any other set] and, thus, does not lead to [the impossible] disparity and inequality between infinites. The clarification of these [views of the *Nuẓẓār*] is mentioned elsewhere.[20]

والمَقْصودُ هُنا: أنَّ هَؤُلاءِ جَعلُوا هَذا أَصْلَ دِينِهِمْ وإيمانِهِمْ، وجَعَلوا النظَرَ في هَذا الدَليل هُوَ النظَرَ الواجِبَ عَلىٰ كُلِّ مُكَلَّفٍ، وأنَّهُ مَنْ لَمْ يَنْظُرْ في هَذا الدَليل فَإمّا أنَّهُ لا يَصِحُّ إيمانُهُ، فَيَكونُ كافِرًا عَلىٰ قَوْلِ طائِفَةٍ مِنْهُمْ، وإمّا أنْ يَكونَ عاصِيًا عَلىٰ قَوْلِ آخَرِينَ، وإمَّا أنْ يَكونَ مُقَلِّدًا لا عِلْمَ لَهُ بِدِينِهِ، لَكِنَّهُ يَنْفَعُهُ هَذا التَقْليدُ، ويَصيرُ بِهِ مُؤْمِنًا غَيْرَ عاصٍ.

The point here is that the [*Nuẓẓār*] have made this [Argument from the Origination of Bodies] into the very foundation of religion and faith, and have made the comprehension of this logical argument into a [religious] obligation upon every legally accountable person. As such [they claim] that the one who does not contemplate this argument will be either: (i) an **unbeliever** whose faith is invalid, according to some of them, (ii) **sinful** [in his forsaking of the contemplation], according to others, or (iii) a **blind follower** who has no knowledge of his Faith, but one whose blind faith [nevertheless] benefits him and makes him a believer who is not considered sinful [for not looking into the argument].

والأَقْوالُ الثَلاثَةُ باطِلَةٌ؛ لِأنَّها مُفَرَّعَةٌ عَلىٰ أَصْلٍ باطِلٍ، وهُوَ أنَّ النَظَرَ

20 Ibn Taymiyyah believed that infinite sets can vary in magnitude if they are infinite in one direction and finite from the other.

الذي هُوَ أَصْلُ الدِينِ والإيمانِ هُوَ هَذا النظَرُ في هَذا الدَليلِ؛ فَإنَّ عُلَماءَ المُسْلِمِينَ يَعْلَمونَ بالاضْطِرارِ أنَّ الرَسولَ لَمْ يَدْعُ الخَلْقَ بِهَذا النَظَرِ، ولا بِهَذا الدَليلِ؛ لا عامَّةَ الخَلْقِ ولا خاصَّتَهُمْ؛ فامْتَنَعَ أنْ يَكونَ هَذا شَرْطًا في الإيمانِ والعِلْمِ.

[But] all the three positions are false. For they stem from a false premise, namely that the *naẓar* which serves as the basis for religion and faith is to contemplate this [very] argument [from the Origination of Bodies]. For indeed, the Muslim scholars know by necessity that the Prophet never called the people [to the Faith] using this *naẓar* or this argument - neither the lay people nor the elect few. Thus, it is impossible for this to be a prerequisite for faith and [firm theological] knowledge.

وقَدْ شَهِدَ القُرْآنُ والرَسولُ لِمَنْ شَهِدَ لَهُ مِنَ الصَحابَةِ وغَيْرِهِمْ بالعِلْمِ، وأنَّهُمْ عالِمونَ بِصِدْقِ الرَسولِ، وبِما جاءَ بِهِ، وعالِمونَ باللهِ، وبِأنَّهُ لا إلَهَ إلا اللهُ، ولَمْ يَكُنِ المُوجِبَ لِعِلْمِهِمْ هَذا الدَليلُ المُعَيَّنُ؛ كَما قالَ تَعالىٰ: ﴿وَيَرَى ٱلَّذِينَ أُوتُوا۟ ٱلْعِلْمَ ٱلَّذِىٓ أُنزِلَ إِلَيْكَ مِن رَّبِّكَ هُوَ ٱلْحَقَّ وَيَهْدِىٓ إِلَىٰ صِرَٰطِ ٱلْعَزِيزِ ٱلْحَمِيدِ﴾ [سبأ: ٦]، وقالَ: ﴿شَهِدَ ٱللَّهُ أَنَّهُۥ لَآ إِلَٰهَ إِلَّا هُوَ وَٱلْمَلَٰٓئِكَةُ وَأُو۟لُوا۟ ٱلْعِلْمِ قَآئِمًۢا بِٱلْقِسْطِ﴾ [آل عمران: ١٨] وقالَ: ﴿أَفَمَن يَعْلَمُ أَنَّمَآ أُنزِلَ إِلَيْكَ مِن رَّبِّكَ ٱلْحَقُّ كَمَنْ هُوَ أَعْمَىٰٓ﴾ [الرعد: ١٩]

And the Qurʾān and the Prophet have attested to the [firm] knowledge of the Companions [of the Prophet] and others, and that they have sure knowledge of the truth of the Prophet and his message, as well as sure knowledge of God and (the fact) that "there is none worthy of worship but God"[21], even though the cause of their knowledge was not this particular argument [from the Origination of Bodies]. For example, God says: **{And those who have been given knowledge see that what is revealed unto you from your Lord is the truth and leads unto the path of the Exalted in Might, the Praiseworthy.}** And He says: **{Allah witnesses that there is no deity except Him, and [so do] the angels and those of knowledge – maintaining [creation] in justice.}** And He says: **{Is he who knows that what is revealed unto you from your Lord is the truth like him who is blind?}**

وقَدْ وُصِفوا٢٢ بِاليَقينِ والبَصيرَةِ في غَيْرِ مَوْضِعٍ؛ كَقَوْلِهِ: ﴿وَبِٱلْأَخِرَةِ هُمْ يُوقِنُونَ﴾ [البقرة: ٤]، وقَوْلِهِ: ﴿أُوْلَٰٓئِكَ عَلَىٰ هُدًى مِّن رَّبِّهِمْۖ﴾ [البقرة: ٥]، وقَوْلِهِ: ﴿قُلْ هَٰذِهِۦ سَبِيلِيٓ أَدْعُوٓاْ إِلَى ٱللَّهِۚ عَلَىٰ بَصِيرَةٍ أَنَا۠ وَمَنِ ٱتَّبَعَنِيۖ﴾ [يوسف: ١٠٨]، وأَمْثالِ ذَلِكَ.

[Furthermore,] God has described them with firm conviction and insight in more than one place, such as when He says, among other [verses]: **{Of the Hereafter they are certain}**, and: **{Those are upon guidance from their Lord}**, and says: **{Say: This is my way: I invite to Allah with insight; I and whosoever follows me.}**

فَتَبَيَّنَ أَنَّ هَذا النَظَرَ والاسْتِدْلالَ الذي أَوْجَبَهُ هَؤلاءِ، وجَعَلوهُ أَصْلَ الدينِ،

21 This is the first half of the testimony of faith. The other half is "Muḥammad is the Messenger of God".

٢٢ في الأصل الخطي: «وصف»، ولعلّ الصواب ما أثبت.

لَيسَ مِمّا أَوْجَبَهُ اللهُ ورَسولُهُ. ولَوْ قُدِّرَ أَنَّهُ صَحيحٌ في نَفْسِهِ، وأنَّ الرَسولَ أَخبرَ بِصِحَّتِهِ= لَمْ[٢٣] يَلْزَمْ مِن ذَلِكَ وُجوبُهُ؛ إذْ قَدْ يَكونُ لِلمَطْلوبِ أدِلَّةٌ كَثيرَةٌ.

Thus, it becomes clear that this [rational] inference which is obligated by those [*Nuẓẓār*] and considered to be the basis of the faith is not [something that was] obligated by God and His Prophet. Even if we assume that it is in itself a sound [argument] or that the Prophet did vouch for its soundness, that would not necessitate that it is obligated [in the religion]. For a single conclusion can have many evidences [that lead to it].

ولِهَذا طَعَنَ الرازِيُّ وأَمْثالُهُ عَلىٰ أَبي المَعالي في قَوْلِهِ أَنَّهُ لا يُعْلَمُ حُدوثُ العالَمِ إلَّا بِهَذا الطَرِيقِ، وقالوا: هَبْ أنَّهُ يَدُلُّ عَلىٰ حُدوثِ العالَمِ، فَمِنْ أَيْنَ يَجِبُ أنْ لا يَكونَ ثَمَّ طَريقٌ آخَرُ؟ وسَلَكوا هُمْ طُرُقًا أُخَرَ.

For this reason, [Abū ʿAbdillāh] al-Rāzī[24] and others have responded to Abu al-Maʿālī [al-Juwaynī][25] in his claim that the origination of the world can be known only from this argument [from the Origination of Bodies]. They said: "[Even if we] grant that this [argu-

---

٢٣ في المطبوع «ولم»، والتصحيح من الأصل الخطي.

24 Fakhr al-Dīn al-Rāzī (d. 606H) is a famous late Ashʿarī theologian who authored books in Kalām and Qurʾanic interpretation. He is known for bringing the Ashʿarī school closer to the views of the Philosophers, and his works are the target of many of Ibn Taymiyyah's theological criticisms.

25 Abu al-Maʿāli al-Juwaynī (d. 478H) was a scholar of the Shāfiʿī school and a leading Ashʿarī theologian. He was given the title *Imām al-Ḥaramayn* (Imām of the Two Mosques) for having spent time teaching in both Mecca and Medina.

ment] demonstrates the origination of the world, why can there be no other [sound] argument [for demonstrating the Maker's existence]?" And they took other routes [in demonstrating the Maker].

فَلَوْ كانَتْ هَذِهِ الطَّرِيقَةُ صَحِيحَةً عَقْلًا، وقَدْ شَهِدَ لَها الرَّسولُ والمُؤْمِنونَ الذين لا يَجْتَمِعونَ عَلىٰ ضَلالَةٍ بِأَنَّها طَريقٌ صَحيحَةٌ= لَمْ تَتَعَيَّنْ[٢٦] مَعَ إمْكانِ سُلوكِ طُرُقٍ أُخْرَىٰ.

[Indeed,] even if this argument [from the Origination of Bodies] is [assumed to be] rationally sound, and even if the Prophet [is assumed to have] testified that it is a sound argument, [along] with [the Community of] the believers who are never to [unanimously] agree on a misguided opinion, it doesn't necessitate exclusivity given the possibility of taking other routes [of demonstration].

كَما أَنَّهُ في القُرْآنِ سُوَرٌ وآياتٌ قَدْ ثَبَتَ بِالنَّصِّ والإجْماعِ أَنَّها مِنْ آياتِ اللهِ الدالَّةِ عَلىٰ الهُدَىٰ. ومَعَ هَذا، فإذا اهْتَدىٰ الرَّجُلُ بِغَيْرِها، وقامَ بالواجِبِ، وماتَ ولَمْ يَعْلَمْ بِها، ولَمْ يَتَمَكَّنْ مِنْ سَماعِها= لَمْ يَضُرَّهُ؛ كالآياتِ المَكِّيَّةِ التي اهْتَدىٰ بِها مَنْ آمَنَ وماتَ في حَياةِ النَّبِيِّ ﷺ قَبْلَ أنْ يَنْزِلَ سائِرُ القُرْآنِ. فالدَّليلُ يَجِبُ طَرْدُهُ، لا يَجِبُ عَكْسُهُ.

This is just like how the Qur'ān includes chapters and verses that are known [both] scripturally and by the consensus [of Muslims] to be among the signs of God that lead to guidance. Even so, if someone was guided by other means, performed his duties, and died without

---

٢٦ في المطبوع: «يتعيّن».

learning of them or having the ability to hear them, that would not harm him [in any way]. This is like the Meccan verses were a means of guidance for the [Companions] who believed and died in the lifetime of the Prophet (may God elevate his mention) before the rest of the Qur'ān was revealed. For the evidence necessarily leads to its conclusions, but the converse is not necessary [i.e. absence of a particular evidence does not mean that the conclusion cannot be reached].

ولِهَذا أَنْكَرَ كَثيرٌ مِنَ العُلَماءِ عَلىٰ هَؤُلاءِ إيْجابَ سُلوكِ هَذِهِ الطَرِيقِ، مَعَ تَسْليمِهِمْ أَنَّها صَحيحَةٌ؛ كالخَطّابِيِّ، والقاضي أَبي يَعْلىٰ، وابْنِ عَقيلٍ، وغَيْرِهِمْ.

For this reason, many of the scholars disapproved of those who obligate this method [in demonstrating the Maker's existence] while conceding to its soundness, [scholars] such as al-Khaṭṭābi[27], Qāḍī Abū Ya'lā[28], Ibn 'Aqīl[29], and others.

والأَشْعَرِيُّ نَفْسُهُ أَنْكَرَ عَلىٰ مَنْ أَوْجَبَ سُلوكَها أَيْضًا في رِسالَتِهِ إلىٰ أَهْلِ الثَغْرِ، مَعَ اعْتِقادِهِ صِحَّتَها، واخْتَصَرَ مِنْها طَرِيقَةً ذَكَرَها في أَوَّلِ كِتابِهِ المَشْهورِ المُسَمَّىٰ بـ«اللُّمَعِ في الردِّ عَلىٰ أَهْلِ البِدَعِ»، وقَدْ اعْتَنَىٰ بِهِ أَصْحابُهُ حَتّىٰ شَرَحوهُ شُروحًا كَثيرَةً. والقاضي أبو بَكْرٍ شَرَحَهُ، ونَقَضَ

27 Abu Sulaymān Ḥamad ibn Muḥammad al-Khaṭṭābī (d. 388H) was a Shāfi'ī scholar of ḥadīth and jurisprudence.

28 He is the jurist Muḥammad ibn al-Ḥusayn ibn al-Farrā' (d. 458H), one of the leading scholars of the Ḥanbalī school.

29 Abu al-Wafā 'Alī ibn 'Aqīl (d. 513H) was a Ḥanbalī scholar and a student of Abu Ya'lā.

كِتابَ عَبْدِ الجَبَّارِ الذي صَنَّفَهُ في نَقْضِهِ، وسَمَّاهُ «نَقْضَ النَقْضِ لِلُّمَعِ»٣٠.

Likewise, [Abu al-Ḥasan] al-Ashʿarī[31] himself disapproved of those who obligate the [argument] in his *Risālat ilā Ahl al-Thagr*, while at the same time believing it to be sound. And he provided an abridged version of it in his famous book that is entitled *al-Lumaʿ fi 'l-Radd 'ala Ahl al-Bidaʿ*. His students paid [exceptional] attention to this book and wrote many commentaries on it. Qaḍi Abū Bakr [al-Bāqillānī][32] also wrote a commentary on it and refuted the book of Abd al-Jabbar[33] which he had authored in refutation of *al-Lumaʿ*, and he called it *Naqdu Nadqi al-Lumaʿ* (*the Refutation of the Refutation of al-Lumaʿ*).

وأمّا أَكابِرُ أَهْلِ العِلْمِ مِنَ السَلَفِ والخَلَفِ، فَعَلِموا أَنَّها طَريقَةٌ باطِلَةٌ في نَفْسِها، مُخالِفَةٌ لِصَريحِ المَعْقولِ وصَحيحِ المَنْقولِ، وأَنَّهُ لا يَحْصُلُ بِها العِلْمُ بالصانِعِ، ولا بِغَيْرِ ذَلِكَ، بَلْ يُوجِبُ سُلوكُها اعْتِقاداتٍ باطِلَةً تُوجِبُ مُخالَفَةَ كَثيرٍ مِمَّا جاءَ بِهِ الرَسولُ، مَعَ مُخالَفَةِ صَريحِ المَعْقولِ؛ كَما أَصابَ مَنْ سَلَكَها مِنَ الجَهْمِيَّةِ، والمُعْتَزِلَةِ، والكُلّابِيَّةِ، والكَرّامِيَّةِ،

---

٣٠ في المطبوع: «نقض نقض اللمع». والمثبت من الأصل الخطي.

31 Abu al-Ḥasan ʿAlī ibn Ismāʿīl al-Ashʿarī (d. 324H) is the father of the Ashʿarī school of Kalām theology. He was once an adherent of the Muʿtazili school before changing his views and effectively preaching against the Muʿtazili.

32 The jurist Abu Bakr Muḥammad ibn al-Tayyib al-Bāqillānī (d. 403H) was a leading Ashʿarī scholar and an adherent of the Maliki school of jurisprudence. He is one of the closest theologians to the views of Ahl al-Sunnah. Elsewhere in *Nubuwwāt*, Ibn Taymiyyah responds extensively to his definition of Prophetic miracles.

33 He is the Muʿtazili jurist ʿAbd al-Jabbār ibn Aḥmad (d. 415H).

ومَنْ تَبِعَهُمْ مِنَ الطَوائِفِ، وإنْ لَمْ يَعْرِفوا غَوْرَها وحَقيقَتَها؛

As for the most eminent scholars, from the [Pious] Predecessors[34] and those who came after them, they knew that the argument [from the Origination of Bodies] is in itself false and contradicts sound reason and Revealed tradition. [They understood] that it does not lead to knowledge of the Maker or anything else. Rather, it leads to false [theological] convictions that contradict much of what the Prophet has brought, in addition to its contradiction to sound reason – as has befallen the proponents [of the argument] among the Jahmiyyah, the Muʿtazilah, the Kullābiyyah, the Karrāmiyyah, and the [theological] groups that followed in their footsteps, even though they were unaware of the depth and reality [of what the argument entails].

فإنَّ أئِمَّةَ هؤلاءِ الطَوائِفِ صارَ كُلٌّ مِنْهُمْ يَلْتَزِمُ ما يَراهُ لازِمًا لَهُ لِيَطْرُدَها، فَيَلْتَزِمُ لَوازِمَ[٣٥] مُخالِفَةً لِلشَرْعِ والعَقْلِ، فَيَجِيءُ الآخَرُ، فَيَرُدُّ عَلَيْهِ، ويُبَيِّنُ فَسادَ ما الْتَزَمَهُ، ويَلْتَزِمُ هُوَ لَوازِمَ أُخَرَ لِطَرْدِها، فَيَقَعُ أَيْضًا في مُخالَفَةِ الشَرْعِ والعَقْلِ.

For indeed, every one of the leading figures of these groups came to hold conclusions which he deemed necessary in order to stay true to the argument, thereby adopting conclusions that contradict Revelation and [sound] reason. Thereafter, another [figure] comes along and refutes him, explaining the fallacy of [the conclusions] which

34 The Pious Predecessors are the first three or four generations of Muslims. They were described by the Prophet (may God elevate his mention) as the best of generations.

٣٥ في الأصل الخطي: «لوازمًا»، خطأ.

he held, only to adopt other conclusions which also cause him to contradict Revelation and [sound] reason.

The Disunity Ensuing from the Argument from the Origination of Bodies

فالجَهْمِيَّةُ الْتَزَموا لِأَجْلِها نَفْيَ أَسْماءِ اللهِ وصِفاتِهِ، إذْ كانَتِ الصِفاتُ أَعْراضًا تَقومُ بالمَوْصوفِ، ولا يُعْقَلُ مَوْصوفٌ بِصِفَةٍ إلا الجِسْمُ[٣٦]، فإذا اعْتَقَدوا حُدوثَهُ، اعْتَقَدوا حُدوثَ كُلِّ مَوْصوفٍ بِصِفَةٍ. والرَبُّ تَعالىٰ قَديمٌ، فالْتَزَموا نَفْيَ صِفاتِهِ. وأَسْماؤُهُ مُسْتَلْزِمَةٌ لِصِفاتِهِ؛ فَنَفَوْا أَسْماءَهُ الحُسْنىٰ، وصِفاتِهِ العُلا.

Thus, [in staying true to this argument], the **Jahmiyyah**[37] committed to negating the names and attributes of God. For attributes are accidents that subsist [only] in a subject of attribution, and it is inconceivable [according to them] for a subject of attribution to be anything but a body. Therefore, if they believe that [all bodies] are originated [via this argument], they [must also] believe that every subject of attribution is originated. But [since] the exalted God is eternal [and not originated], they found it necessary to negate His attributes. Additionally, [since] His names entail His attributes,

٣٦ في الأصل الخطي: «إلا لجسم»، خطأ.

37 Jahmiyyah is a sect named after Jahm b. Ṣafwān (d. 128H), who denied all attributes of God. More generally, this appellation is used to describe all theological groups which, totally or partially, negate the attributes of God, especially the attribute of God's elevation above His throne, and His speech. Glorified is God above their claim.

thus they found it necessary to negate [both] His beautiful **names** and His majestic **attributes**.

والمُعْتَزِلَةُ اسْتَعْظَموا نَفْيَ الأَسْماءِ لِما فيهِ مَعَ[٣٨] تَكْذيبِ القُرْآنِ تَكْذيبًا ظَاهِرًا= الخُرُوجُ[٣٩] عَنِ العَقْلِ والتَناقُضِ؛ فإنَّهُ لا بُدَّ مِنَ التَمْييزِ بَيْنَ الرَبِّ وغَيْرِهِ بِالقَلْبِ واللِسانِ، فَما لا يُمَيِّزُ مِنْ غَيْرِهِ لا حَقيقَةَ لَهُ ولا إِثْباتَ. وهُوَ حَقيقَةُ قَوْلِ الجَهْمِيَّةِ؛ فإنَّهُمْ لَمْ يُثْبِتوا في نَفْسِ الأَمْرِ شَيْئًا قَديمًا البَتَّةَ.

And the **Muʿtazilah**[40] found [this] negation of the names of God [by the Jahmiyyah] to be unacceptable, for in addition to being a blatant rejection of the Qurʾān, it is in opposition to [sound] reason

---

٣٨ في المطبوع: «من». والمثبت من الأصل الخطي هو الصواب.

٣٩ سقطت الألف من لام التعريف في الأصل الخطي، فأثبت محقق المطبوع: «ظاهرَ الخروجِ» على الإضافة، والسياق على ما أثبتنا.

40 The Muʿtazilah is a name given to a wide range of theological groups that are characterized by five false principles: (i) the negation of God's attributes and that He will be seen in the hereafter (a doctrine which they refer to as *Monotheism*), (ii) a profession of the freedom of human acts, such that these acts must not be created or decreed by God, but that they occur in the world without God's will (a doctrine which they refer to as *Justice*), (iii) the claim that the Muslims who commit grave sins will remain in Hellfire forever and that (iv) they are neither believers nor unbelievers but in a third state between the two, and finally (v) the belief in the legitimacy of rebelling against Caliphs and their Muslim subjects in order to enforce these theological views. The Muʿtazilah gained great influence during the reign of the Abbasid Caliph al-Ma'mun (d. 218H) to the extent that they persecuted other Muslims in order to compel them to accept the doctrine of the created-ness of the Qurʾān, which says that the Qurʾān is a separate creation of God, not His divine attribute of speech that is included within His existence and subsists in His essence. The Muʿtazilah refer to themselves as 'the people of *Tawhid* and Justice'.

and entails contradictions. Indeed, it is necessary to distinguish the Lord from other things by [one's] heart and tongue, for the thing which cannot be distinguished has no reality or [positive] ontology. And this is indeed the reality of the claims of the Jahmiyyah: they do not at all affirm that there is something eternal in reality.

كَما أنَّ المُتَفَلْسِفَةَ الذين سَلَكوا مَسْلَكَ «الإمْكَانِ والوُجوبِ»، وجَعَلوا ذَلِكَ بَدَلَ «الحادِثِ والقَديمِ»، لَمْ يُثْبِتوا واجِبًا بِنَفْسِهِ البَتَّةَ، وظَهَرَ بِهَذا فَسادُ عَقْلِهِمْ، وعَظيمُ جَهْلِهِمْ، مَعَ الكُفْرِ؛

[As for] the Philosophers who took the [Avicennian] route of demonstrating [the Necessary existent] that is [known as the Argument from] Contingency and Necessity[41], considering it to be a substitute for [the argument from] Eternality and Origination, they do not [really] affirm the existence of anything that is in itself necessary. Their deficient intelligence and immense ignorance became apparent [to the people] in this way, in addition to their disbelief.

وذَلِكَ أنَّهُ يُشْهَدُ وُجودُ السَماواتِ وغَيْرِها. فَهَذِهِ الأَفْلاكُ إنْ كانَتْ قَديمَةً واجِبَةً، فَقَدْ ثَبَتَ وُجودُ المَوْجودِ القَديمِ الواجِبِ، وإنْ كانَتْ مُمْكِنَةً، أَوْ مُحْدَثَةً، فلا بُدَّ لَها مِن واجِبٍ قَديمٍ؛ فإنَّ وُجودَ المُمْكِنِ بِدُونِ الواجِبِ،

41 Ibn Taymiyyah is not referring here to what is known as the contingency argument, which is to infer the existence of the necessary Creator from the possible existence of the natural phenomena. Instead, he is criticizing the Avicennian form of the argument, which seeks to demonstrate a necessary existence without specifically leading to an Originator who created the heavens and the earth after their nonexistence [*Sharḥ al-Aṣfahāniyyah*, pp. 48-49]. Also see *Dar' Ta'āruḍ al-'Aql wa 'l-Naql* [Vol 9, pp. 113-119].

والمُحْدَثِ بِدُونِ القَديمِ= مُمْتَنِعٌ في بَدائِهِ[٤٢] العُقولِ. فَثَبَتَ وُجودُ مَوْجودٍ قَديمٍ واجِبٍ بِنَفْسِهِ عَلىٰ كُلِّ تَقْديرٍ. فَإذا كانَ ما ذَكَروهُ مِنْ نَفْيِ الصِفاتِ عَنِ القَديمِ والواجِبِ يَسْتَلْزِمُ نَفْيَ القَديمِ مُطْلَقًا ونَفْيَ الواجِبِ= عُلِمَ أَنَّهُ باطِلٌ.

For the existence of the heavens and the like is [indeed] witnessed. If these celestial spheres are [said to be] eternal and necessary, then an eternal, necessary existent will be affirmed. [But] if they are [instead] contingent and originated, then they must have a necessary, eternal [Cause]. For the existence of the contingent without the necessary, and [the existence of] the originated without the eternal, are [known to be] impossible by common sense. Therefore, the existence of an eternal existent that is in itself necessary will be affirmed either way. [Now,] since the claims of these [Philosophers] in [their] negation of all attributes from the eternal, necessary [being] necessitate the denial of anything eternal or necessary[43], their [claims] are known to be false.

وقَدْ بُسِطَ هَذا في مَواضِعَ، وبُيِّنَ أَنَّ كُلَّ مَنْ نَفىٰ صِفَةً مِمَّا أَخْبَرَ بِهِ الرَسولُ لَزِمَهُ نَفْيُ جَميعِ الصِفاتِ، فَلا يُمْكِنُ القَوْلُ بِمُوجَبِ أَدِلَّةِ العُقولِ إلا مَعَ القَوْلِ بِصِدْقِ الرَسولِ؛ فَأَدِلَّةُ العُقولِ مُسْتَلْزِمَةٌ لِصِدْقِ الرَسولِ؛

And this has been explained in [other] places; and it has been clar-

٤٢ في المطبوع: «بداية».

43 This is because it is impossible for an entity to exist without attributes. Since the Philosophers claim that the Necessary Being has no attributes at all, it means that there is nothing Eternal or Necessary.

ified [there] that anyone who negates a [divine] attribute that was affirmed by the Prophet must [also] negate all other attributes [in order to be consistent]. It is not possible to affirm the [sound] entailments of rational arguments without accepting the truthfulness of the Prophet. For the [sound] rational arguments necessitate the truthfulness of the Prophet.

فَلا يُمْكِنُ مَعَ عَدَمِ تَصْدِيقِهِ القَوْلُ بِمُوجَبِ العُقُولِ، بَلْ مَنْ كَذَّبَهُ فَلَيْسَ مَعَهُ لا عَقْلٌ ولا سَمْعٌ؛ كَما أَخْبَرَ اللهُ تَعالىٰ عَنْ أَهْلِ النَارِ: قالَ تَعالىٰ: ﴿كُلَّمَآ أُلْقِىَ فِيهَا فَوْجٌ سَأَلَهُمْ خَزَنَتُهَآ أَلَمْ يَأْتِكُمْ نَذِيرٌ ۝٨ قَالُوا۟ بَلَىٰ قَدْ جَآءَنَا نَذِيرٌ فَكَذَّبْنَا وَقُلْنَا مَا نَزَّلَ ٱللَّهُ مِن شَىْءٍ إِنْ أَنتُمْ إِلَّا فِى ضَلَٰلٍ كَبِيرٍ ۝٩ وَقَالُوا۟ لَوْ كُنَّا نَسْمَعُ أَوْ نَعْقِلُ مَا كُنَّا فِىٓ أَصْحَٰبِ ٱلسَّعِيرِ ۝١٠ فَٱعْتَرَفُوا۟ بِذَنۢبِهِمْ فَسُحْقًا لِّأَصْحَٰبِ ٱلسَّعِيرِ﴾ [الملك: ٨-١١]، وهَذا مَبْسوطٌ في غَيْرِ هَذا المَوْضِعِ.

[Indeed,] it is not possible to be consistent with the rational requirements while not believing in the Prophet. Rather, one who rejects the Prophet has neither reason nor Scripture, just as God mentions about the inhabitants of the Fire: **{Whenever a (fresh) host is flung therein, the wardens thereof ask them: Came there unto you no warner? They will say: Yes, verily, a warner came unto us; but we denied and said: "Allah has not sent down anything; you are in but a great error." And they will say: If only we had been listening or reasoning, we would not be among the dwellers in the flames. So they will acknowledge their sin; so away with the dwellers of the flames!}** This matter has been expounded in another place.

والمَقْصودُ هُنا: أنَّ المُعْتَزِلَةَ لَمّا رَأَوُا الجَهْمِيَّةَ قَدْ نَفَوْا أَسْماءَ اللهِ الحُسْنىٰ، [اسْتَعْظَموا ذَلِكَ][٤٤]، وأَقَرُّوا بالأَسْماءِ. ولَمّا رَأَوْا هَذِهِ الطَرِيقَ توجِبُ نَفْيَ الصِفاتِ: نَفَوُا الصِفاتِ؛ فَصَاروا مُتَناقِضِينَ؛ فَإِنَّ إِثْباتَ حَيٍّ، عَليمٍ، قَديرٍ، حَكيمٍ، سَميعٍ، بَصيرٍ، بِلا حَياةٍ، ولا عِلْمٍ، ولا قُدْرَةٍ، ولا حِكْمَةٍ، ولا سَمْعٍ، ولا بَصَرٍ= مُكابَرَةٌ للعَقْلِ؛ كَإِثْباتِ مُصَلٍّ بِلا صَلاةٍ، وصائِمٍ بِلا صِيامٍ، وقائِمٍ بِلا قِيامٍ، ونَحْوِ ذَلِكَ مِنَ الأَسْماءِ المُشْتَقَّةِ؛ كَأَسْماءِ الفاعِلِينَ والصِفاتِ المَعْدولَةِ عَنْها.

And the intent here is [the fact] that when the **Mu'tazilah** found the negation of God's beautiful names by the Jahmiyyah to be unacceptable, they affirmed the divine names. However, they negated [God's] **attributes** when they saw that this argument [from the Origination of Bodies] necessitates their negation. Thus, they fell into inconsistency. For it is absurd to affirm [the existence of] a 'living', 'knowing', 'powerful', 'wise', 'hearing' and 'seeing' being without [affirming the attributes of] life, knowledge, power, wisdom, hearing, and sight. [This is] like affirming [the existence of] a praying person without [affirming] the act of praying, a fasting person without the act of fasting, a standing person without the act of standing, and other similarly derived nouns, such as active participles, while avoiding [the affirmation of] the attributes [from which these nouns derive].

---

٤٤ ما بين الحاصرتين ليس في الأصل الخطي، وهي زيادة أثبتت في المطبوع ليستقيم الكلام.

ولِهَذا ذَكَروا في أُصولِ الفِقْهِ أنَّ صِدْقَ الاسْمِ المُشْتَقِّ٤٥؛ كالحَيِّ، والعَليمِ لا يَنْفَكُّ عَنْ صِدْقِ المُشْتَقِّ مِنْهُ؛ كالحَياةِ، والعِلْمِ. وذَكَروا النِزاعَ مَعَ مَنْ ذَكَروهُ مِنَ المُعْتَزِلَةِ؛ كَأبي عَلِيٍّ، وأبي هاشِمٍ.

For this reason, the [scholars] mention in *Uṣūl al-Fiqh*[46] that the truth of derived nouns, such as the 'living' and the 'knowing', cannot be separated from the truth of the [meanings] from which they are derived, such as life and knowledge. And they note that this is a point of contention with the likes of Abū 'Alī [al-Jubbā'ī] and Abū Hāshim[47] from the Mu'tazilah.

فَجاءَ ابْنُ كُلّابٍ، ومَنِ اتَّبَعَهُ؛ كالأَشْعَرِيِّ، والقَلانِسِيِّ، فَقَرَّروا أنَّهُ لا بُدَّ مِنْ إثْباتِ الصِفاتِ مُتابَعَةً للدَليلِ السَمْعِيِّ والعَقْلِيِّ، مَعَ إثْباتِ الأَسْماءِ. وقالوا: لَيْسَتْ أعْراضاً؛ لِأنَّ العَرَضَ لا يَبْقَىٰ زَمانَيْنِ، وصِفاتُ الرَبِّ باقِيَةٌ. وسَلَكوا في هَذا الفَرْقِ -وهُوَ أنَّ العَرَضَ لا يَبْقَىٰ زَمانَيْنِ- مَسْلَكاً أَنْكَرَهُ عَلَيْهِمْ جُمْهورُ العُقَلاءِ، وقالوا: إنَّهُمْ خالَفوا الحِسَّ وضَرُورَةَ العَقْلِ.

[Thereafter,] **Ibn Kullāb**[48] came [along] with those who followed

٤٥ في الأصل الخطي: «مشتق»، خطأ.

46 An Islamic science which covers the principles and methodologies through which the practical rulings of Islam are inferred from the foundational sources.

47 Abū 'Alī (d. 303 AH) and Abū Hāshim (d. 321 AH), father and son, are notable Mu'tazilī scholars. Abu al-Ḥasan al-Ash'arī was a protégé of Abu Ali before leaving I'tizāl.

48 Abu Muḥammad 'Abdullāh ibn Sa'īd ibn Kullāb (d. ~240H) was the father

him, like [Abu al-Ḥasan] al-Ashʿarī and al-Qalānisī[49], and they established that the [divine] attributes must be affirmed in addition to the names [of God], in agreement with the scriptural and rational evidence. [However,] they [also] said that these [divine attributes] are not accidents, for accidents do not endure for two instances of time[50], whereas the attributes of God are [forever] enduring [and eternal]. In establishing the [alleged] distinction [between accidents and attributes] – which is that the accidents, [unlike the attributes,] do not endure for two instances of time – they took a route that was criticized by the majority of rational minds, who noted that they contradict [both] sense perception and what is known from reason by necessity.

وَهُمْ مُوافِقونَ لِأُولَئِكَ عَلىٰ صِحَّةِ هَذِهِ الطَّرِيقَةِ – طَرِيقَةِ الأَعْراضِ – قالوا: وَهَذِهِ تَنْفِي عَنِ اللهِ أَنْ يَقومَ بِهِ حادِثٌ، وَكُلُّ حادِثٍ فَإِنَّما يَكونُ بِمَشِيئَتِهِ وَقُدْرَتِهِ. قالوا: فَلا يَتَّصِفُ بِشَيْءٍ مِنْ هَذِهِ الأُمورِ؛ لا يَتَكَلَّمُ بِمَشِيئَتِهِ وَقُدْرَتِه، وَلا يَقومُ بِهِ فِعْلٌ اخْتِيارِيٌّ يَحْصُلُ بِمَشِيئَتِهِ وَقُدْرَتِه؛ كَخَلْقِ العالَمِ، وَغَيْرِهِ.

---

of the Kullābiyyah, and the forefather of later groups of Kalām theology who came to affirm divine attributes for God, such as the Ashʿariyyah.
49 Abu al-ʿAbbās al-Qalānisī was one of the leading students of Ibn Kullāb. He wrote many books on Kalām theology.
50 These theological groups believe that accidents do not endure for two instances of time, but that every accident can exist only for a single moment before perishing necessarily, whereupon a new accident is created by God in the substance. Ibn Taymiyyah rejects this claim that an accident could not endure for two instances of time.

And these [**Kullābiyyah**] agree with the [former Jahmiyyah and Mu'tazilah] over the soundness of the argument from accidents [i.e. from the Origination of Bodies]; they accept that this [argument] does not allow for ***ḥawādith*** (originating acts) to subsist in God[51]; and since every ***ḥādith*** (originating event and act) occurs only by God's will and power, they therefore claimed that God cannot be described with any such matters [that occur at a particular moment of time **by His will and power**], i.e. He neither speaks by His will,

---

51 Ibn Taymiyyah defended using both rational and scriptural arguments that God must have always been a substrate of *ḥawādith* (events), such as divine decisions, actions, and spoken words. However, he also believed that these divine *ḥawādith* that subsist in God's essence are not creations of God, but are rather uncreated.

For Ibn Taymiyyah, the terms 'created' and 'originating' are not synonymous, as a thing can be both uncreated and with a beginning in time. In order for a thing to qualify as a creation, it must be brought into existence by an *external* agent, such that it must not be existing *within* the agent internally. For example, it is meaningful to say that a carpenter creates a chair, because the chair is an effect that lies *outside* of his existence. But it is meaningless to say that a carpenter creates his own decisions and actions, because these attributes are included *within* his existence. The cause for their *creation* must instead be something external to the carpenter, and it is none other than God who is the Creator of all things. In the same way, Ibn Taymiyyah believed that it is meaningful to say that God creates the world, but that it is meaningless to say that God creates His own attributes, including His decisions, actions and spoken words. This is because these latter divine occurrences subsist *within* God's essence and are not external to His existence. These attributes are also not made into God by an external agent, as God is independent and exists eternally without a creator. As such, these divine *ḥawādith* which arise in God's essence are neither created by God nor created by anything else, and they are therefore *uncreated* attributes, albeit ones which originate in God's essence successively by His will and power.

nor performs voluntary actions that subsist in His [essence] by will and power, such as the act of creating the world, or other [divine acts].

بَلْ مِنْهُمْ مَنْ قَالَ: لَا يَقُومُ بِهِ فِعْلٌ، بَلِ الخَلْقُ هُوَ المَخْلُوقُ؛ كَالأَشْعَرِيِّ وَمَنْ وَافَقَهُ.

In fact, some of them, such as [Abu al-Ḥasan] al-Ashʿarī and others, have claimed that there subsist no [divine] actions in God [at all], and that the act of creation is the [very] created effect [that is separate from God].

وَمِنْهُمْ مَنْ قَالَ: بَلْ فِعْلُ الرَّبِّ قَدِيمٌ أَزَلِيٌّ، وَهُوَ مِنْ صِفَاتِهِ الأَزَلِيَّةِ؛ وَهُوَ قَوْلُ قُدَمَاءِ الكُلَّابِيَّةِ، وَهُوَ الذِي ذَكَرَهُ أَصْحَابُ ابْنِ خُزَيْمَةَ لَمَّا وَقَعَ بَيْنَهُ وَبَيْنَهُمْ بِسَبَبِ هَذَا الأَصْلِ، فَكَتَبُوا عَقِيدَةً اصْطَلَحُوا عَلَيْهَا، وَفِيهَا: إِثْبَاتُ الفِعْلِ القَدِيمِ الأَزَلِيِّ.

Others claimed instead that [the Lord is to be described with actions, but that] the act of the Lord is eternal, without beginning, and is among His attributes that eternally accompany His essence [such as His attributes of power and life which are not subject to His will]. This is the statement of the **early Kullābiyyah**. And it is [also] the one mentioned by the students of Ibn Khuzaymah[52] when the dispute ensued between them and their teacher over this principle. Thus, they wrote down a creed on which they both agreed, and

---

52 Muḥammad ibn Isḥāq ibn Khuzaymah (d. 311H) was the *imām* of Nishapur in his age. He was one of the great scholars of ḥadīth, a *mujtahid*, and a prolific teacher who travelled far and wide in pursuit of knowledge and ḥadīth.

affirmed therein that the [divine] act [of God] is **eternal**.

وكانَ سَبَبُ ذَلِكَ أَنَّهُمْ كانوا كُلّابِيَّةً يَقولونَ: إِنَّهُ لا يَتَكَلَّمُ بِمَشيئَتِهِ وقُدْرَتِهِ، بَلْ كَلامُهُ المُعَيَّنُ لازِمٌ لِذاتِهِ أَزَلًا وأَبَدًا. وكانَ ابْنُ خُزَيْمَةَ وغَيْرُهُ عَلىٰ القَوْلِ المَعْروفِ للمُسْلِمينَ وأَهْلِ السُنَّةِ: إنَّ اللهَ يَتَكَلَّمُ بِمَشيئَتِهِ وقُدْرَتِهِ، وكانَ قَدْ بَلَغَهُ عَنِ الإمامِ أَحْمَدَ أَنَّهُ كانَ يَذُمُّ الكُلّابِيَّةَ، وأَنَّهُ أَمَرَ بِهَجْرِ الحارِثِ المُحَاسِبِيِّ لَمّا بَلَغَهُ أَنَّهُ عَلىٰ قَوْلِ ابْنِ كُلّابٍ. وكانَ يَقولُ: حَذِّروا عَنْ حارِثٍ الفَقيرِ؛ فإنَّهُ جَهْمِيٌّ. واشْتَهَرَ هَذا عَنْ أَحْمَدَ.

And the reason for that [dispute] was that these [students of Ibn Khuzaymah] were [from the] Kullābiyyah who say that God does not speak by His will and power, but rather that His particular spoken word accompanies His [essence] from eternity [and] forever [into the future]. [By contrast,] Ibn Khuzaymah was upon the known statement of the Muslims and Ahl al-Sunnah, that God speaks by His will and power [whenever He likes]. And it had [also] reached [Ibn Khuzaymah] that Imām Aḥmad [ibn Hanbal] used to criticize the Kullābiyyah and that he had admonished [his students] to avoid al-Hārith al-Muḥāsibī[53] when informed that he was upon the statement of Ibn Kullāb, saying [to them]: "Warn [the people] from al-Hārith, the ascetic, for he is a Jahmī".[54] This [statement] by

53 Abu ʿAbdullāh al-Ḥārith al-Muḥāsibī (d. 243H) was one of the students of Ibn Kullāb. It is said that he later regretted espousing the theology of Ibn Kullāb, returning to the more orthodox views of Ahl al-Sunnah.

54 The application of these rulings must always be guided by utilitarian calculations that seek to maximize benefit and minimize detriment to the utmost extent possible.

Aḥmad [ibn Hanbal] became well-known.

وكانَ بِنَيسابُورَ طائِفَةٌ مِنَ الجَهْمِيَّةِ والمُعْتَزِلَةِ مِمَّنْ يَقولُ٥٥: إنَّ القُرْآنَ وغَيْرَهُ مِنْ كَلامِ اللهِ مَخْلوقٌ، ويُطْلِقونَ القَوْلَ بِأنَّهُ مُتَكَلِّمٌ بِمَشيئَتِهِ وقُدْرَتِهِ، ولَكِنَّ مُرادَهُمْ بِذَلِكَ أنَّهُ يَخْلُقُ كَلامًا بائِنًا عَنْهُ قائِمًا بِغَيْرِهِ، كَسائِرِ المَخْلوقاتِ. وكانَ مِنْ هَؤُلاءِ مَنْ عَرَفَ أَصْلَ ابْنِ كُلّابٍ، فَأَرادَ التَّفْريقَ بَيْنَ ابْنِ خُزَيْمَةَ وبَيْنَ طائِفَةٍ مِنْ أَصْحابِهِ، فَأَطْلَعَهُ عَلَىٰ حَقيقَةِ قَوْلِهِمْ، فَنَفَرَ مِنْهُ. وهُمْ كانوا قَدْ بَنَوْا ذَلِكَ عَلَىٰ أَصْلِ ابْنِ كُلّابٍ، واعْتَقَدوا أَنَّهُ لا تَقومُ بِهِ الحَوادِثُ بِناءً عَلَىٰ هَذِهِ الطَّريقَةِ: طَريقَةِ الأعْراضِ.

[Now,] there existed in Nishapur a group from the Jahmiyyah and Muʿtazilah who used to say that the Qur'ān and the other words of God are creations of God, [not attributes of God]. They stated in absolute terms that "God speaks by His will and power", but they intended with this [statement] that God creates words that are separate from Himself and subsist in something/someone else[56], just like

٥٥ في المطبوع: «يقولون»، والمثبت هو ما في الأصل الخطي.

56 The fact that the Qur'ān is spoken by God contradicts the claim that it is a creation of God, as all divine attributes must be uncreated.

Ibn Taymiyyah wrote elsewhere on the uncreated nature of God's words: "The Pious Predecessors and the leading scholars of Islam unanimously agreed that God speaks with words that subsist in Himself and that His speech is uncreated. And that He wills with intentions that subsist in Himself and that His will is uncreated. They spoke out against the Jahmiyyah among the Muʿtazilah and others who claimed that the speech of God is created, or that He creates it in something distinct from Himself, such as by speaking to Moses by creating words in the air. And the Pious Predecessors and leading scholars unanimously agreed that "the Qur'ān is the speech of God, sent down, not created; it began from Him and returns to Him." By their statement: "began from Him", the Pious Predecessors meant to say that God "spoke the Qur'ān", not that He "created it in another", in contrast to the Muʿtazilah and other Jahmiyyah who [instead] claimed that the Qur'ān began from God's creations and that no words may subsist in God's essence. The Pious Predecessors did not intend to say that the speech [of God] detaches from His essence [and goes on to subsist elsewhere], for all attributes including speech are inseparable from the subjects of their attribution. Indeed, the attributes of [mere] creatures do not detach from them and move on to describe others; so how can the attribute of the [more perfect] Creator detach from Himself and move on to [describe] another?! For this reason, the Imām Aḥmad [ibn Ḥanbal] said: "The speech of God is from God, not separate from Himself", thereby responding to the Muʿtazilah and other Jahmiyyah who claimed that the speech of God is separate from Himself, [and that it is] created by Him in some bodies [that are external to His existence] ...

And the Pious Predecessors and the leading scholars of Islam have clarified in many ways the errors of the Jahmiyyah who claimed that the speech of God is created. For example, they said [to the Jahmiyyah]: If God creates His speech in a substrate, His speech will instead be an attribute of that substrate, and a name for that substrate will be derived from that attribute – just as it is the case with all other attributes, such as knowledge, power, hearing, sight, and life, and also those attributes that are not conditioned on life, such as motion, motionlessness, blackness and whiteness. For when an attribute subsists in a substrate, it will be a description of that very substrate and of nothing else, and the name derived therefrom will apply to that substrate and to nothing else ... [But] the purpose here is [only] to alert [the reader] ... to the fact that the speech and will that describe the Lord ... are not things that are separate from Him, contrary to what the Jahmiyyah and the Muʿtazilah claimed. Also, [it is to alert the reader] to the fact that if God had created His speech in a substrate, that substrate would have spoken [His words] instead. It would have been the tree that said to Moses: **{Indeed, I am God. There is no deity except Me, so worship Me}** [if these words were created in the burning bush]! Equally,

other creations. And some of them were aware of the [theological] basis of Ibn Kullāb's claim, and by that wished to cause division between Ibn Khuzaymah and some of his students. So they brought to his attention the reality of their claim, and he was repelled by it. These [students of Ibn Khuzaymah] were predicating their position on the [theological] basis of Ibn Kullab, believing that ***ḥawādith*** cannot subsist in God's essence, [which was in turn] predicated on the argument from accidents [i.e. the Argument from the Origination of Bodies].

وابْنُ خُزَيْمَةَ شَيْخُهُمْ، وهُوَ المُلَقَّبُ بِإمامِ الأَئِمَّةِ، وأَكْثَرُ النّاسِ مَعَهُ، ولَكِنْ لا يَفْهَمونَ حَقيقَةَ النِزاعِ؛ فاحْتاجوا لِذَلِكَ إلىٰ ذِكْرِ عَقيدَةٍ لا يَقَعُ فيها نِزاعٌ بَيْنَ الكُلّابِيَّةِ وبَيْنَ أَهْلِ الحَديثِ والسُنَّةِ؛ فَذَكَروا فيها: أَنَّ كَلامَ اللهِ غَيْرُ مَخْلوقٍ، وأَنَّهُ لَمْ يَزَلْ مُتَكَلِّمًا، وأَنَّ فِعْلَهُ أَيْضًا غَيْرُ مَخْلوقٍ؛ فالمَفْعولُ مَخْلوقٌ، ونَفْسُ فِعْلِ الرَبِّ لَهُ قَديمٌ غَيْرُ مَخْلوقٍ. وهَذا قَوْلُ الحَنَفِيَّةِ، وكَثيرٍ مِنَ الحَنْبَلِيَّةِ والشافِعِيَّةِ والمالِكِيَّةِ، وهُوَ اخْتِيارُ القاضي أَبي يَعْلىٰ وغَيْرِه في آخِرِ عُمُرِهِ. وبَسْطُ هَذا لَهُ مَوْضِعٌ آخَرُ. والمَقْصودُ: التَنْبيهُ علىٰ

---

the words which God causes His creations to speak would be His speech by necessity, [which is just as absurd.] God says: **{And they will say to their skins, "Why have you testified against us?" They will say, "We were made to speak by God who has made everything speak}** ... It is God who made those bodies speak. Therefore, if this speech which God creates [therein] were His own speech, [these words] would be spoken by God just like the Qur'ān. There would be no difference between His speaking and His causing of another to speak, which is clearly false." [*Sharḥ al-Aṣfahāniyyah*, pp. 11-21].

افْتِرَاقِ الأُمَّةِ بِسَبَبِ هَذِهِ الطَّرِيقَةِ.

And Ibn Khuzaymah, who was referred to as *Imām al-A'immah* (lit. the *Imām* of all *Imāms*), was their *Shaykh*. And most of the people were siding with him, but they did not understand the reality of the dispute. [For this reason,] the [parties] found it necessary to write down a creed [on which both sides agreed, one] that avoids the dispute between the Kullābiyyah and the People of Sunnah and Ḥadīth. They mentioned in [this creed] that: "The speech of God is uncreated", that "God has always been speaking", and that "The [divine] act of God is also uncreated; the [separate] effect is created, but the very act of the Lord by which He causes it is eternal and uncreated." This is the position of the Ḥanafī[57] school and many of the Ḥanbalī, Shafiʿī, and Māliki scholars. It is [also] the position chosen by Qāḍi Abu Yaʿlā towards the end of his life. The detailed explanation of these matters is mentioned in another place. [For] the purpose [here] is [only] to alert [the reader] to the division that ensued in the [Muslim] nation because of this argument.

وَلَمَّا عَرَفَ كَثِيرٌ مِنَ النَّاسِ بَاطِنَ قَوْلِ ابْنِ كُلَّابٍ، وَأَنَّهُ يَقُولُ: إِنَّ اللهَ لَمْ
يَتَكَلَّمْ بِالقُرْآنِ العَرَبِيِّ، وَإِنَّ كَلامَهُ شَيْءٌ وَاحِدٌ؛ هُوَ مَعْنَىٰ آيَةِ الكُرْسِيِّ،

---

57 Abū Ḥanīfah al-Nuʿmān ibn Thābit (d. 150H) is the first of the four *imāms* of Ahl al-Sunnah. He is the father of the Ḥanafī school of Islamic jurisprudence, the school that has the greatest number of followers within the Muslim world. He met some of the Companions of the Prophet, and is therefore considered one of the Tabiʿīn. He was known for his piety and outstanding brilliance. Because he lived in Iraq at a time when the knowledge of the ḥadīths was very limited, he came to develop the school of *rāi* which relied heavily on analogical deduction.

وآيَةِ الدَّيْنِ= عَرَفوا ما فيهِ مِنْ مُخالَفَةِ الشَّرْعِ والعَقْلِ؛ فَنَفَروا عَنْهُ، وعَرَفوا أنَّ هَؤُلاءِ يَقولونَ: إنَّهُ لا يَتَكَلَّمُ بِمَشيئَتِهِ وقُدْرَتِهِ، فَأَنْكَروهُ.

And when many of the people understood the reality of Ibn Kullāb's claim, [which is namely] that "God did not utter the Arabic[58] [wording of the] Qur'ān", and that "the speech [of God] is [instead] one [eternal] meaning, which is the very meaning of Āyat al-Kursi [2: 255][59], and [the very meaning] of the verse of debt contracts [2: 282][60], they realized the opposition [of this view] to the [prescribed] Law and [sound] reason, and thus were repelled by it. And they [also] realized that those [Kullābiyyah] were claiming that God does not speak by His will and power, and thus rejected [their claim].

وكانَ مِمَّنْ أَنْكَرَ ذَلِكَ الكَرَّامِيَّةُ، وغَيْرُ الكَرَّامِيَّةِ كَأَصْحابِ أَبي مُعاذٍ

58 The Kullābiyyah claim that the meaning of the Qur'ān is divine and uncreated, but that the wording and letter of the Qur'ān is created and not divine. Ibn Taymiyyah clarifies that both the wording/letter of the Qur'ān *and* its intended meaning are uncreated and divine, such that both subsist only in God and never in His creation.

The words of the Qur'ān subsist only in God, not in anything else, because it was God Himself who first uttered the words of the Qur'ān. Although the Angel Gabriel recited the Qur'ān to the Prophet, and the Prophet recited it to his companions, it was God's words and not theirs. This is just like the poetry of Shakespeare must remain to be his word when it is recited, and can never become the words of the reciter.

59 This is the noblest verse in the Qur'ān. The *Kursi* is an enormous Footstool that encompasses the heavens and the earth and on which God places His two blessed feet.

60 This is the longest verse of the Qur'ān. It prescribes rulings for debt contracts.

التُومَنِيِّ، وزُهَيرِ البابِيِّ، وداودَ بنِ عَلِيٍّ، وطَوائِفَ. فَصارَ كَثيرٌ مِنْ هَؤُلاءِ يَقولونَ: إنَّهُ يَتَكَلَّمُ بِمَشيئَتِهِ وقُدْرَتِهِ، فَأَنْكَروهُ، لَكِنْ يُراعِي تِلْكَ الطَريقَةِ لاعْتِقادِهِ صِحَّتَها؛ فَيَقولُ: إنَّهُ لَمْ يَكُنْ في الأَزَلِ مُتَكَلِّمًا؛ لأَنَّهُ إذا كانَ لَمْ يَزَلْ مُتَكَلِّمًا بِمَشيئَتِهِ لَزِمَ وُجودُ حَوادِثَ لا تَتَناهى، وأَصْلُ الطَريقَةِ أَنَّ هَذا مُمْتَنِعٌ؛ فَصارَ حَقيقَةُ قَوْلِ هَؤُلاءِ أَنَّهُ صارَ مُتَكَلِّمًا بَعْدَ أَنْ لَمْ يَكُنْ مُتَكَلِّمًا. فَخالَفوا قَوْلَ السَلَفِ والأَئِمَّةِ: إنَّهُ لَمْ يَزَلْ مُتَكَلِّمًا إذا شاءَ. وبَسْطُ هَذِهِ الأُمورِ لَهُ مَوْضِعٌ آخَرُ.

Among those who rejected [the claims of the Kullābiyyah] were the **Karrāmiyyah**[61], as well as others such as the students of Abu Muʿādh al-Tūmani, Zuhayr al-Bābi, Dāwūd ibn ʿAlī[62], and other groups. Many of those [groups] came to believe that God speaks by His will and power, and so they rejected [the claim that God does not speak in this way]. However, they [simultaneously] adopted the argument [from the Origination of Bodies], as they deemed it to be sound. Because of this, they claimed that God was **not speaking** eternally from the past, [but that He began to speak by His will and power at some moment in time after He was not speaking at all.] For [they argued that] if God had always been speaking when-

61 Abū ʿAbdullāh Muḥammad ibn Karrām was the father of the Kalām group known as the Karrāmiyyah. This group explicitly referred to God as a 'body' and are therefore considered from the Mujassimah. Nevertheless, they did not equate God with His creation as did some early heretics.

62 Dāwūd ibn ʿAlī (d. 270H) was a great scholar of jurisprudence and the *imām* of the Ẓāhiriyyah, a school which adheres to the apparent meanings of Scripture and avoids re-interpretations and analogical deductions. He was known for his piety and asceticism.

ever He willed, the ***ḥawādith*** (events) must be regressing infinitely [into the past], when the nature of the argument [from the Origination of Bodies] precludes [the possibility of] such [a regress]. In this way, the reality of the claims [of those groups] came to be that God [started to] speak after He was not speaking [at all], thereby contradicting the beliefs of the Pious Predecessors and leading scholars [of Islam who explicitly mentioned] that "God has always been speaking whenever He willed". The explanation of these matters is mentioned in another place.

والمَقْصودُ هُنا: أنَّ كَثيرًا مِنْ أَهْلِ النَظَرِ صارَ ما يُوجِبونَهُ مِن النَظَرِ والاسْتِدْلالِ ويَجْعَلونَهُ أَصْلَ الدينِ والإيمانِ هُوَ هَذِهِ الطَريقَةَ المُبْتَدَعَةَ في الشَرْعِ، المُخالِفَةَ للعَقْلِ، الّتي[٦٣] اتَّفَقَ سَلَفُ الأُمَّةِ وأَئِمَّتُها عَلىٰ ذَمِّها وذَمِّ أَهْلِها:

What is intended here is [to point out] that the *naẓar* and [rational] inference which many of the *Nuẓẓār* came to obligate, and considered it to be the foundation of religion and faith, was based on this innovated argument [from the Origination of Bodies], which is in contradiction to [sound] reason, and was criticized along with its proponents by the [Pious] Predecessors of the [Muslim] nation and its leading scholars.

فَذَمُّهُمْ لِلجَهْمِيَّةِ الذينَ ابْتَدَعوا هَذِهِ الطَريقَةَ أَوَّلًا مُتَواتِرٌ مَشْهورٌ، قَدْ صُنِّفَ فيهِ مُصَنَّفاتٌ. وذَمُّهُمْ للكَلامِ والمُتَكَلِّمينَ مِمَّا عُنِيَ بِهِ أَهْلُ هَذِهِ

---

٦٣ في الأصل الخطي: «الذي»، والمثبت هو مقتضىٰ السياق.

الطَرِيقَةِ؛ كَذَمِّ الشافِعِيِّ لِحَفْصٍ الفَرْدِ، الّذي كانَ عَلىٰ قَوْلِ ضِرارِ بنِ عَمْرٍو، وذَمِّ أَحْمَدَ بنِ حَنْبَلٍ لأَبي عيسىٰ مُحَمَّدِ بنِ عيسىٰ بَرْغُوثَ، الّذي كانَ عَلىٰ قَوْلِ حُسَيْنٍ النَجّارِ. وذَمِّهِما وذَمِّ أَبي يُوسُفَ ومالِكٍ وغَيْرِهِمْ لأَمْثالِ هَؤُلاءِ الّذينَ سَلَكوا هَذِهِ الطَرِيقَةِ.

[Indeed,] the [Pious Predecessors'] criticisms of the Jahmiyyah who first invented this argument is *mutawatir*[64] and well-known, for many books were authored [by these Predecessors] on the [heresy of the Jahmiyyah]. Their criticism of Kalām theology and the Kalām theologians [in general] is also directed at people who adopted this argument – such as al-Shāfiʿī's[65] criticism of Ḥafṣ al-Fard who was upon the statement of Ḍirār ibn ʿAmr, Aḥmad ibn Ḥanbal's criticism of Abū ʿĪsā Muḥammad ibn ʿIsā al-Bargūth who was upon the statement of Ḥusayn al-Najjār, and the criticism of like-minded [Kalām theologians] who adopted this argument by both [al-Shāfiʿī and Aḥmad], as well as by Abū Yusuf[66], Mālik[67] [ibn Anas], and oth-

64 A *mutawatir* report is undeniably authentic, as it is conveyed by narrators so numerous such that it is inconceivable that they have agreed on an untruth.
65 Muḥammad ibn Idrīs al-Shāfiʿī (d. 204H) is the third of the four *imāms* of Ahl al-Sunnah, and the father of the Shāfiʿī school of Islamic jurisprudence. He was one of the students of Mālik ibn Anas in Medina. He was known for his superb memory and intelligence, and was the founder of the science of *Uṣūl al-Fiqh* (i.e. the Principles of Jurisprudence). His views developed further after settling in Egypt towards the end of his life, and he is thus known for having two schools of Islamic jurisprudence.
66 Yaʿqūb ibn Ibrāhīm al-Anṣārī (d. 182H) was the student of Abū Ḥanīfah. He is said to be his most knowledgeable student, and the most dedicated to observing the ḥadīths.
67 Mālik ibn Anas (d.179H) is the second of the four *imāms* of Ahl al-Sunnah, and the father of the Māliki school of Islamic jurisprudence. He was the

ers.

وقَدْ صُنِّفَ في ذَمِّ الكَلامِ وأَهْلِهِ مُصَنَّفاتٌ أَيْضًا، وهُوَ مُتَناوِلٌ لِأَهْلِ هَذِهِ الطَّرِيقَةِ قَطْعًا. فَكانَ إِيْجابُ النَّظَرِ بِهَذا التَّفْسِيرِ باطِلًا قَطْعًا، بَلْ هَذا نَظَرٌ فاسِدٌ يُناقِضُ الحَقَّ والإيمانَ.

Moreover, many books were authored [by the Pious Predecessors] in criticism of Kalām theology and its proponents, which definitely includes the proponents of this argument [from the Origination of Bodies]. As such, to obligate *naẓar* with this [particular] interpretation is definitely pointless; this *naẓar* is indeed fallacious and conflicts with [both] factuality and Faith.

ولِهَذا صارَ مَنْ يَسْلُكُ هَذِهِ الطَّرِيقَةَ مِنْ حُذَّاقِ الطَّوائِفِ يَتَبَيَّنُ لَهُمْ فَسادُها؛ كَما ذَكَرَ مِثْلَ ذَلِكَ أَبو حامِدٍ الغَزالِيُّ، وأَبو عَبْدِ اللهِ الرازِيُّ، وأَمْثالُهُما. ثُمَّ الّذي يَتَبَيَّنُ لَهُ فَسادُها: إذا لَمْ يَجِدْ عِنْدَ مَنْ يَعْرِفُهُ مِنَ المُتَكَلِّمِينَ في أُصولِ الدِينِ غَيْرَها بَقِيَ حائِرًا مُضْطَرِبًا.

For this reason, the [leading] experts from the theological schools who adopted this argument came to realize its fallacy, as has been reported from Abū Ḥāmid al-Ghazālī[68], Abū 'Abdullāh al-Rāzī,

leading *imām* of the city of Medina, where the knowledge of the ḥadīths was most widespread. He was known for his strong memory and intelligence, his careful verification of ḥadīths, and his noble and daunting character. He compiled the *Muwaṭṭa'*, one of the first collections of ḥadīth.

68 Abū Ḥāmid Muḥammad al-Ghazālī (d. 505H) was a famous Ṣūfī scholar of the Shāfi'ī school of jurisprudence, and a student of Abu al-Ma'alī al-Ju-

and their likes. However, the one who realizes the fallacy of [this argument], but does not find other arguments [mentioned] by the Kalām theologians known to him, becomes perplexed and confused.

وَالقَائِلُونَ بِقِدَمِ العَالَمِ مِنَ الفَلاسِفَةِ، وَالمَلاحِدَةِ، وَغَيْرِهِمْ تَبَيَّنَ لَهُمْ فَسَادُها؛ فَصَارَ ذَلِكَ مِنْ أَعْظَمِ حُجَجِهِمْ عَلَىٰ قَوْلِهِمُ البَاطِلِ؛ فَيُبْطِلُونَ قَوْلَ هَؤُلاءِ أَنَّهُ صَارَ فَاعِلًا -أَوْ فَاعِلًا وَمُتَكَلِّمًا- بِمَشِيئَتِهِ بَعْدَ أَنْ لَمْ يَكُنْ، وَيُثْبِتُونَ وُجُوبَ دَوَامِ نَوْعِ الحَوَادِثِ، وَيَظُنُّونَ أَنَّهُمْ إذا أَبْطَلُوا كَلامَ أُولَئِكَ المُتَكَلِّمِينَ بِهَذا حَصَلَ مَقْصُودُهُمْ. وَهُمْ أَضَلُّ وَأَجْهَلُ مِنْ أُولَئِكَ؛ فإنَّ أَدِلَّتَهُمْ لا تُوجِبُ قِدَمَ شَيْءٍ بِعَيْنِهِ مِنَ العَالَمِ، بَلْ كُلُّ ما سِوَىٰ اللهِ فَهُوَ مُحدَثٌ⁶⁹ مَخْلُوقٌ كائِنٌ بَعْدَ أَنْ لَمْ يَكُنْ، ودَلائِلُ [ذَلِكَ]⁷⁰ كَثِيرَةٌ غَيْرُ تِلْكَ الطَرِيقَةِ، وإنْ كانَ الفَاعِلُ لَمْ يَزَلْ فَاعِلًا لِما يَشَاءُ، ومُتَكَلِّمًا بِما يَشَاءُ.

Moreover, Philosophers, atheists, and others who claim that the world is eternal, [also] realized the fallacy of this [argument]. Thus, this became one of their greatest excuses for [holding on] to their false claim [of the eternality of the world]. They invalidated the claims of those [Kalām theologians] that God became an agent [after He was not an agent], or [that God came to be] acting and speaking by His will after He was not [acting or speaking at all], and affirmed [in-

waynī. He was known for his deep sincerity, and has authored many books in various sciences, including philosophy, jurisprudence, Kalām theology, Ṣūfism, and logic. He died while studying the ḥadīth of the Prophet (may God elevate his mention).

٦٩ في المطبوع: «حادث»، والمثبت من الأصل الخطي.
٧٠ زيادة لازمة ليستقيم الكلام.

stead] that the genus of events must be eternal. And they assumed that they will have achieved their goal [in demonstrating their position] once they have invalidated the claims of those Kalām theologians. [But in truth,] they are more astray and ignorant than [their opponents]. For their arguments do not necessitate the eternality of anything in particular from the world. Rather, everything besides God is originated, created, and existing after it was once nonexistent; the evidences for this are numerous and [are] not [restricted to] the argument [from the Origination of Bodies] – even though the Creator has [indeed] been creating whatever He willed and speaking whatever He willed from the eternal past.

وصارَ كَثيرٌ مِنْ أُولَئِكَ إذا ظَهَرَ لَهُ فَسادُ أَصْلِ أُولَئِكَ المُتَكَلِّمِينَ المُبْتَدِعِينَ، ولَيْسَ عِنْدَهُ إلا قَوْلُهُمْ وقَوْلُ هَؤُلاءِ، يَميلُ إلىٰ قَوْلِ هَؤُلاءِ المَلاحِدَةِ، ثُمَّ قَدْ يُبْطِنُ ذَلِكَ، وقَدْ يُظْهِرُ لِمَنْ يَأْمَنُهُ.

And when many came to realize the fallacy of the [very] foundation of those innovating Kalām theologians, while [at the same time] they did not know of [any position] besides it and besides the statement of [atheists and Philosophers who believed in the eternality of the world], they [came to] lean towards the position of those atheists, [either] keeping this [inclination] to themselves, or disclosing it to those whom they trusted.

وابْتُلِيَ بِهَذا كَثيرٌ مِنْ أَهْلِ النَظَرِ والعِبادَةِ والتَصَوُّفِ، وصاروا يُظْهِرونَ هَذا في قالَبِ المُكاشَفَةِ، ويَزْعُمونَ أَنَّهُمْ أَهْلُ التَحْقيقِ والتَوْحيدِ والعِرْفانِ. فأَخَذوا مِنْ نَفْيِ الصِفاتِ أَنَّ صانِعَ العالَمِ لا داخِلَ العالَمِ

وَلا خَارِجَهُ، وَمِنْ قَوْلِ هَؤُلاءِ: إِنَّ العالَمَ قَدِيمٌ، وَلَمْ يَرَوْا مَوْجُودًا سِوَىٰ

العالَمِ، فَقَالُوا: إِنَّهُ هُوَ اللهُ، وقالوا: هُوَ الْوُجُودُ الْمُطْلَقُ، والْوُجُودُ واحِدٌ،

وَتَكَلَّمُوا في وَحْدَةِ الوُجُودِ، وَأَنَّهُ اللهُ، بِكَلامٍ لَيْسَ هَذا مَوْضِعَ بَسْطِهِ.

And many of the people of *naẓar*, worship, and Ṣūfism[71] were af-
flicted by these [opinions]. They came to announce these [views]
in the guise of divine inspirations, claiming that they are the people
of truth, monotheism, and gnosis. They took from the apophatic
(negative) theology [of the Jahmiyyah] the [idea] that the Maker of
the world is neither inside the world nor outside of it[72], and [they]
took] from the claims of the [Philosophers] the [idea] that the world
is eternal. And since they could not see anything in existence beside
the world, they concluded that "the world is God Himself", that
"God is absolute [universal] existence", and that "the existence is
one". They spoke of the unity of existence and that it is [none other
than] God in ways which are better discussed elsewhere.[73]

---

71 Ṣūfis first emerged in the Muslim world as a group of people in Basra who
emphasized asceticism, the fear of God, and devotion to worship. Later, Ṣūfis
developed into a variety of rituals, beliefs, and practices that spread throughout the Muslim world. Ṣūfis are of various kinds. Some are referred to as Ṣūfis
merely because of their asceticism that is within the bounds of the prescribed
Law of Islam. Others fall into innovated beliefs and practices, some consti-
tuting polytheism such as calling on the graves of saints, while others are less
serious. The later philosophical Ṣūfis fell into outright pantheism, adopting
the dangerous claim that God and His creation are one thing.
72 This negation by the Jahmiyyah entails a contradiction. A thing that is neither inside the world nor outside of it cannot have any ontological existence.
Ibn Taymiyyah defends elsewhere that God exists outside of the world and is
located above it spatially, basing this on scriptural and rational evidence.
73 Those are the late philosophical Ṣūfis like Ibn ʿArabī (d. 638H), who leaned

ثُمَّ لَمّا ظَهَرَ أنَّ كَلامَهُمْ يُخالِفُ الشَرْعَ والعَقْلَ، صاروا يَقولونَ: ثَبَتَ عِنْدَنا في الكَشْفِ ما يُناقِضُ صَريحَ العَقْلِ، ويَقولونَ: القُرْآنُ كُلُّهُ شِرْكٌ، وإنَّما التَوْحيدُ في كَلامِنا، ومَنْ أرادَ أن يَحْصُلَ لَهُ هَذا العِلْمُ اللَّدُنِّيُّ الأَعْلىٰ فَلْيَتْرُكِ العَقْلَ والنَقْلَ!

And when it became known that their statements are in opposition to the Revelation and [sound] reason, they ended up saying: "That which contradicts sound reason has been demonstrated to us through divine inspiration!" and "All of the Qur'ān is polytheism; [true] monotheism is only in what we say!" and "Whoever wishes to attain this superior, divinely-inspired knowledge, let him leave reason and Revelation [altogether]!"

وصارَ حَقيقَةُ قَوْلِهِمُ: الكُفْرَ باللهِ، وبِكُتُبِهِ، ورُسُلِهِ، وباليَوْمِ الآخِرِ، مِن جِنْسِ قَوْلِ المَلاحِدَةِ الَّذينَ يُظْهِرونَ التَشَيُّعَ. لَكِنَّ أُولَئِكَ لَمّا كانَ ظاهِرُ قَوْلِهِمْ هُوَ ذَمَّ الخُلَفاءِ أَبي بَكْرٍ[٧٤] وعُمَرَ وعُثْمانَ، صارَتْ وَصْمَةُ الرَفْضِ تُنَفِّرُ عَنْهُمْ خَلْقًا كَثيرًا لَمْ يَعْرِفوا باطِنَ أَمْرِهِمْ. وهَؤُلاءِ صاروا يَنْتَسِبونَ إلىٰ المَعْرِفَةِ والتَوْحيدِ واتِّباعِ شُيوخِ الطُرُقِ كالفُضَيْلِ، وإبْراهيمَ بنِ أَدْهَمَ، والتُسْتَرِيِّ، والجُنَيْدِ، وسَهْلِ بنِ عَبْدِ اللهِ، وأَمْثالِ هَؤُلاءِ مِمَّنْ لَهُ في الأُمَّةِ لِسانُ صِدْقٍ، فَاغْتَرَّ بِهَؤُلاءِ مَنْ لَمْ يَعْرِفْ باطِنَ أَمْرِهِمْ، وهُمْ في الحَقيقَةِ مِنْ أَعْظَمِ خَلْقِ اللهِ خِلافًا لِهَؤُلاءِ المَشايِخِ السادَةِ، ولِمَنْ هُوَ

---

towards pantheism and failed to clearly distinguish the eternally existing God from the contingently existing creations.

٧٤ في المطبوع: «كأبي بكر»، والمثبت من الأصل الخطي.

أَفْضَلُ مِنْهُمْ مِنَ السابِقِينَ الأَوَّلِينَ والأَنْبِياءِ المُرْسَلِينَ.

[In this way,] the reality of the statements [of these Ṣūfi Philosophers] amounts to [outright] disbelief in God, His books, His Prophets, and the Last Day – similar to the statements of the agnostic heretics who feign Shi'ism. However, since the apparent statement [of the latter] is that they disparage the [rightly guided] Caliphs Abū Bakr, 'Umar, and 'Uthmān (may God be pleased with them), many people were alienated by [their] rejection [of the Caliphs] without [even] realizing their [blasphemous] hidden beliefs. By contrast, the [Ṣūfi Philosophers] were attributing themselves to [mystical] knowledge, monotheism, and the following of the *Shaykhs* of Ṣūfi orders, the likes of al-Fuḍayl, Ibrāhīm ibn Adham, al-Tustari, al-Junayd, Sahl ibn 'Abdullāh, and others who have an honorable repute in the [Muslim] nation. As such, many of the people who did not know the [true] reality of the [theological] claims [of the Ṣūfi Philosophers] were deceived by them, although in reality, these [Ṣūfi Philosophers] are among the most in contradiction to [the ways and beliefs] of the aforementioned noble *Shaykhs*, as well as being in contradiction to those who are even better than them: the first forerunners [in the Faith], and the Prophets sent by God.

The Views on Love

وكانَ مِنْ أَسْبابِ ذَلِكَ أَنَّ العِبادَةَ والتَّأَلُّهَ والمَحَبَّةَ ونَحْوَ ذَلِكَ مِمّا يَتَكَلَّمُ فيهِ شُيوخُ المَعْرِفَةِ والتَّصَوُّفِ أَمْرٌ مُعَظَّمٌ في القُلوبِ، والرُّسُلُ إِنَّما بُعِثوا بِدُعاءِ الخَلْقِ إِلى أَنْ يَعْرِفوا اللهَ، ويَكونَ أَحَبَّ إِلَيْهِمْ مِنْ كُلِّ ما سِواهُ، فَيَعْبُدوهُ ويَأْلَهوهُ، ولا يَكونُ لَهُمْ مَعْبودٌ مَأْلوهٌ غَيْرُهُ.

Among the reasons which caused [people to fall for] this [deception of Ṣūfi Philosophers] was that 'worship', 'adoration', 'love', and the similar concepts that are discussed by the gnostic and Ṣūfi *shaykhs* is something that people hold in high esteem. [Indeed,] the Prophets [of God] were only sent to call the people to know God and love Him more than everything else, to worship Him [alone] and adore Him, such that they worship no other deity or god.

وقَدْ أَنْكَرَ جُمْهورُ أُولَئِكَ المُتَكَلِّمينَ أَنْ يَكونَ اللهُ مَحْبوبًا، أَو أَنَّهُ يُحِبُّ شَيْئًا، أَو يُحِبُّهُ أَحَدٌ. وهَذا في الحَقيقَةِ إِنْكارٌ لِكَوْنِهِ إِلـهًا مَعْبودًا؛ فَإِنَّ الإِلَهَ: هُوَ المَأْلوهُ الَّذي يَسْتَحِقُّ أَنْ يُؤْلَهَ ويُعْبَدَ، والتَّأَلُّهُ والتَّعَبُّدُ يَتَضَمَّنُ غايَةَ الحُبِّ بِغايَةِ الذُّلِّ.

[By contrast,] the majority of the *Kalām* theologians have denied that God may be an object of love, that He may love anything, or that anyone may love Him. In reality, this is a denial of His being a

[true] god and deity. For the *ilāh* (god) is the deity who deserves to be adored and worshipped. And [the acts of] *taalluh* and *ta'abbud* (worship) entail having the utmost love [for God] with the utmost humility.

ولَكِنْ غَلِطَ كَثيرٌ مِنْ أُولَئِكَ، فَظَنُّوا أنَّ الإلـٰـهِيَّةَ هِيَ القُدْرَةُ علىٰ الخَلْقِ، وأنَّ الإلَهَ بِمَعْنَىٰ الآلِهِ، وأنَّ العِبادَ يَأْلَهُهُمُ اللهُ، لا أَنَّهُمْ هُمْ يَأْلَهُونَ اللهَ، كَما ذَكَرَ ذَلِكَ طَائِفَةٌ مِنْهُمُ الأشْعَرِيُّ وغَيْرُهُ.

[But] many of those [Kalām theologians] were mistaken [in this regard]. They assumed that *Ilāhiyyah*[75] (divinity) is [merely] to have the power to create, and that the *ilāh* (deity) is an active participle [i.e. the one who creates, sustains, etc.], and that the act of *'alaha/yalahu'* is directed by God towards creation, rather than being directed by the creation towards God [i.e. by adoring and worshipping Him], as has been stated by some of their theologians like [Abu al-Ḥasan] al-Ash'arī and others.

وطَائِفَةٌ ثالِثَةٌ لَمّا رَأَتْ ما دَلَّ علىٰ أنَّ اللهَ يَحِبُ[٧٦] أنْ يَكُونَ مَحْبوبًا مِنْ أدِلَّةِ الكِتابِ والسُنَّةِ وكَلامِ السَلَفِ وشُيوخِ أَهْلِ المَعْرِفَةِ، صاروا يُقِرُّونَ بِأَنَّهُ مَحْبوبٌ، لَكِنَّهُ هُوَ نَفْسُهُ لا يُحِبُّ شَيْئًا إلا بِمَعْنَىٰ المَشيئَةِ، وجَميعُ الأشْياءِ مُرادَةٌ لَهُ فَهِيَ مَحْبوبَةٌ لَهُ. وهَذِهِ طَرِيقَةُ كَثيرٍ مِنْ أَهْلِ النَظَرِ والعِبادَةِ والحَديثِ، كَأَبي إِسْماعيلَ الأنْصارِيِّ، وأَبي حامِدٍ الغَزالِيِّ،

75 This term is synonymous with *Ulūhiyyah*.

٧٦ في المطبوع: «يُحِبّ»، خطأ.

وأبي بَكْرٍ بنِ العَرَبِيِّ٧٧.

And there was [yet] a third group [of theologians] who, upon seeing the evidences from the Qur'ān and Sunnah and from the words of the Predecessors and gnostic *Shaykhs* that necessitate that God is to be adored, came to admit that God is an object of love, but [nevertheless claimed] that He [Himself] does not love anything, except in the sense that He wills [for it to exist]. Because all things are willed [into existence] by God, [they argued,] they must [likewise] be loved by Him. This is the position of many of the people of *naẓar*, devotion, and Ḥadīth, such [figures] as Abū Ismā'īl al-Anṣārī[78], Abū Ḥāmid al-Ghazālī, and Abū Bakr ibn al-'Arabī[79].

وحَقيقَةُ هَذا القَوْلِ أنَّ اللهَ يُحِبُّ الكُفْرَ والفُسوقَ والعِصْيانَ، ويَرْضاهُ. وهَذا هُوَ المَشْهورُ مِنْ قَوْلِ الأشْعَرِيِّ وأصْحابِهِ، وقَدْ ذَكَرَ أبو المَعالي أنَّهُ أوَّلُ مَنْ قالَ ذَلِكَ، وكَذَلِكَ ذَكَرَ ابْنُ عَقيلٍ أنَّ أوَّلَ مَنْ قالَ إنَّ اللهَ يُحِبُّ الكُفْرَ والفُسوقَ والعِصْيانَ هُوَ الأشْعَرِيُّ وأصْحابُهُ، وهُمْ قَدْ يَقولونَ لا يُحِبُّهُ دِينًا، ولا يَرْضاهُ دِينًا، كَما يَقولونَ: لا يُريدُهُ دِينًا، أيْ: لا يُريدُ أنْ يَكونَ فاعِلُهُ مَأْجورًا، وأمَّا هَوَ نَفْسُهُ فَهُوَ مَحْبوبٌ لَهُ كَسائِرِ المَخْلوقاتِ،

---

٧٧ في الأصل الخطي: «ابن عربي».

78 Abū Ismā'īl 'Abdullāh al-Anṣārī (d. 481H) was a Ṣūfi of the Hanbali school and an expert in Qur'anic interpretation and ḥadīth. He is the author of *Manāzil al-Sā'irīn*, which was explained by Ibn al-Qayyim in his work *Madārij al-Sālikīn*.

79 Abū Bakr ibn al-'Arabī (d. 543) was a Mālikī scholar from Seville and an *imām* of Andalusia. He is not to be confused with Ibn 'Arabī, the Ṣūfi Philosopher.

فَإِنَّها عِنْدَهُمْ مَحْبوبَةٌ لَهُ؛ إِذْ كانَ لَيْسَ عِنْدَهُمْ إلا إرادَةٌ واحِدَةٌ شامِلَةٌ لِكُلِّ مَخْلوقٍ؛ فَكُلُّ مَخْلوقٍ، فَهُوَ عِنْدَهُمْ مَحْبوبٌ مَرْضِيٌّ.

And the [true] reality of this [third] statement is that God loves unbelief, defiance, and rebellion, and that He is pleased with it! This is the position that is famous from [the statement of Abu al-Ḥasan] al-Ashʿarī and his students. Abu al-Maʿālī [al-Juwaynī] mentioned that [al-Ashʿarī] was the first person to claim this [position]. Ibn ʿAqīl likewise said that the first people to claim that "God loves unbelief, defiance, and rebellion" were al-Ashʿarī and his students. They may claim that "God does not love it in a religious sense" and that "He is not pleased with it in a religious sense", just as they [also] say that "God does not will it in a religious sense". With this [expression] they intend to say that God does **not will to reward** its perpetrator – although the act, in and of itself, is loved by God, just like the rest of created things, for [all His creations] are loved by Him in their view. This is because they believe that there exists only one intention[80] that [causes] all created things into existence. In their opinion, God loves every created thing and is pleased with it, [just as He wills every created thing into existence.]

وجَماهِيرُ المُسْلِمِينَ يَعْرِفونَ أَنَّ هَذا القَوْلَ مَعْلومُ الفَسادِ بالضَرورَةِ مِنْ

80 Ibn Taymiyyah explains elsewhere that the divine will is of two kinds, not one. The first is God's creative will, which is His will to bring the creations into existence. The second is His legislative will, which is to do with the fact that He loves His commandments and wants people to obey them. These two types of will do not always coincide. For example, via His legislative will, God does not love corruption and evil people who spread it, although He decrees that many people act in this way via His creative will. [*Minhāj al-Sunnah al-Nabawiyyah*, Vol 3 pp. 156-157]

دِينِ أَهْلِ المِلَلِ، وأنَّ المُسْلِمِينَ واليَهودَ والنَصارىٰ مُتَّفِقونَ علىٰ أنَّ اللهَ لا يُحِبُّ الشِرْكَ، ولا تَكْذيبَ الرُسُلِ، ولا يَرْضىٰ ذَلِكَ، بَلْ هُوَ يُبْغِضُ ذَلِكَ ويَمْقُتُهُ ويَكْرَهُهُ؛ كَما ذَكَرَ اللهُ في سورَةِ بَني إسْرائيلَ ما ذَكَرَهُ مِنَ المُحَرَّماتِ، ثمَّ قالَ: ﴿كُلُّ ذَٰلِكَ كَانَ سَيِّئُهُۥ عِندَ رَبِّكَ مَكْرُوهًا﴾ [الإسراء: ٣٨]. وبَسْطُ هَذِهِ الأُمورِ لَهُ مَواضِعُ أُخَرُ.

[But] the [overwhelming] majority of Muslims know that this claim is necessarily known to be false from all of the faiths; for the Muslims, the Jews, and the Christians all agree that God does not love polytheism and rejection of His messengers, nor is He pleased with it. Rather, He hates and despises these [evil acts].[81] As God says in the chapter of Banī Israel [Isrā'] after mentioning various kinds of forbidden acts: **{The evil of that is ever hateful in the sight of your Lord.}** These matters have been discussed at length elsewhere.

81 Even though He wills them into creation based on some divine wisdom.

والمَقْصودُ هُنا أنَّ الّذينَ أعْرَضُوا عَنْ طَرِيقِ الرَسولِ في العِلْمِ أوِ العَمَلِ[٨٢] وَقَعُوا في الضَّلالِ والزَّلَلِ، وأنَّ أُولَئِكَ لَمّا أَوْجَبوا النظَرَ الّذي ابْتَدَعُوهُ، صارَتْ فُروعُهُ فاسِدَةً. إنْ قالُوا: إنَّ مَنْ لَمْ يَسْلُكْها كَفَرَ أو عَصَى، فَقَدْ عُرِفَ بالاضْطِرارِ مِنْ دينِ الإسْلام أنَّ الصَحابَةَ والتابِعِينَ لَهُمْ بإحْسانٍ لَمْ يَسْلُكوا طَريقَهُمْ، وهُمْ خَيرُ الأُمَّةِ. وإنْ قالوا: إنَّ مَنْ لَيْسَ عِنْدَهُ عِلْمٌ ولا بَصيرَةٌ بالإيمانِ، بَلْ قالَهُ تَقْليدًا مَحْضًا مِنْ غَيْرِ مَعْرِفَةٍ يَكونُ مُؤْمِنًا، فالكِتابُ والسُنَّةُ يُخالِفُ ذَلِكَ.

The intent here is [to demonstrate] that those [*Nuẓẓār*] who ignored the Prophetic way in knowledge and action fell into misguidance and error, and that their innovated *naẓar*, which they made [religiously] binding, led to fallacious conclusions. If they claim that those who do not follow [their innovated *naẓar*] are [either] unbelievers or sinners, then it is known by necessity in Islam that the Companions of the Prophet and their righteous followers did not follow their [invented] method, although they were, nonetheless, the best of the Muslim nation. But if they claim that people who blindly parrot [their innovated way] without having [any] insight or knowledge of the Faith are believers, then [it is also known that] the

---

٨٢ في المطبوع: «والعمل». والمثبت من الأصل الخطي.

Book and the Sunnah contradict this.

ولو أنَّهُمْ سَلَكوا طَريقَةَ الرَسولِ، لَحَفِظَهُمُ اللهُ مِنْ هَذا التناقُضِ؛ فَإنَّ ما جاءَ بِهِ الرَسولُ جاءَ مِنْ عِنْدِ اللهِ، وما ابْتَدَعُوهُ جاؤوا بِهِ مِنْ عِنْدِ غَيْرِ اللهِ، وقَدْ قالَ تَعالىٰ: ﴿وَلَوْ كَانَ مِنْ عِندِ غَيْرِ ٱللَّهِ لَوَجَدُواْ فِيهِ ٱخْتِلَٰفًا كَثِيرًا﴾ [النساء: ٨٢]

But had they followed the Prophetic way, God would have protected them from this contradiction. For whatever the Prophet brought, he brought from God. But this which they have invented, they have brought from other than God. And the exalted God says: **{If it had been from any other than God, they would have found within it much contradiction}**.

وهَؤُلاءِ بَنَوْا دِينَهُمْ علىٰ النَظَرِ، والصوفِيَّةُ بَنَوْا دِينَهُمْ علىٰ الإرادَةِ، وكِلاهُمْا لَفْظٌ مُجْمَلٌ، يَدْخُلُ فيهِ الحَقُّ والباطِلُ. فالحَقُّ: هُوَ النظَرُ الشَرْعِيُّ، والإرادَةُ الشَرْعِيَّةُ، وهُوَ[٨٣] النظَرُ فيما بُعِثَ بِهِ الرَسولُ مِنَ الآياتِ والهُدَىٰ؛ كَما قالَ: ﴿شَهْرُ رَمَضَانَ ٱلَّذِىٓ أُنزِلَ فِيهِ ٱلْقُرْءَانُ هُدًى لِّلنَّاسِ وَبَيِّنَٰتٍ مِّنَ ٱلْهُدَىٰ وَٱلْفُرْقَانِ﴾ [البقرة: ١٨٥]. والإرادَةُ الشَرْعِيَّةُ: إرادَةُ ما أَمَرَ اللهُ بِهِ ورَسولُهُ. والسَماعُ الشَرْعِيُّ: سَماعُ ما أَحَبَّ اللهُ سَماعَهُ كالقُرْآنِ. والدَليلُ الّذي يُسْتَدَلُّ بِهِ هُوَ الدَليلُ الشَرْعِيُّ، وهُوَ الّذي دَلَّ اللهُ بِهِ عِبادَهُ، وهَداهُمْ بِهِ إلىٰ صِراطٍ مُسْتَقيمٍ؛

٨٣ في المطبوع: «فالنظر الشرعي هو». والمثبت من الأصل الخطي.

And those [*Nuẓẓār*] have built their religion on *naẓar* whereas the Ṣūfis have built their religion on *irādah* (will and intention). [But] both terms are general and can refer to [both] truth and falsehood. The truth is the **prescribed** *naẓar* and the **prescribed** *irādah*. [The prescribed *naẓar*] refers to the contemplation of the verses and the guidance by which the Prophet was sent, as God says: **{The month of Ramadan in which was revealed the Qur'ān as guidance for the people, and [with] clear proofs for the guidance and the Criterion [of right and wrong]}**. [Likewise,] the prescribed *irādah* refers to intending [and willing to fulfil] what God and his Prophet have commanded. [Similarly,] the prescribed *samā'*[84] refers to listening to what God loves for us to hear, such as the Qur'ān. And the evidence that is to be used [for the demonstration of theological conclusions] is the prescribed *dalil*[85], which is the evidence by which God has demonstrated [the theological conclusions] to His servants and guided them to His straight path.

فَإِنَّهُ لَمّا ظَهَرَتِ البِدَعُ، والْتَبَسَ الحَقُّ بالباطِلِ صارَ اسْمُ النظَرِ، والدَليلِ، والسَماعِ، والإرادَةِ يُطْلَقُ علىٰ ثَلاثَةِ أُمورٍ: مِنْهُمْ: مَنْ يُريدُ بِهِ البِدْعِيَّ دُونَ الشَرْعِيِّ؛ فَيُريدونَ بالدَليلِ: ما ابْتَدَعُوهُ مِنْ الأدِلَّةِ الفاسِدَةِ، والنظَرَ فيها. ومِنَ السَماعِ والإرادَةِ: ما ابْتَدَعُوهُ مِنِ اتِّباعِ ذَوْقِهِمْ ووَجْدِهِمْ، وما تَهْواهُ أَنْفُسُهُمْ، وسَماعَ الشِعْرِ والغِناءِ الّذي يُحَرِّكُ هَذا الوَجْدَ التابعَ لِهَذِهِ الإرادَةِ النَفْسانِيَّةِ الّتي مَضْمونُها اتِّباعُ ما تَهْوَىٰ الأَنْفُسُ بِغَيْرِ هُدىً مِنَ اللهِ.

---

84 *Sama'* is listening. In Ṣūfi terminology it refers to listening to devotional hymns and songs.
85 *Dalil* is evidence.

For when religious innovations appeared[86] and the truth became mixed with falsehood, the terms '***naẓar***', '***dalīl***', '***samāʿ***' and '***irādah***' came to be used to denote three [different types of] things. Some used these [terms] to denote **innovated** matters, instead of the legislated ones. They referred by *'dalīl'* [and *'naẓar'*] to the false arguments which they invented and to the contemplation [of those arguments]. By *'samāʿ'* and *'irādah'*, they referred to the following of their tastes[87], ecstasy[88], and desires, which they introduced [into Islam as a religious practice], and [also] to their listening to poetry and singing which is a cause for that ecstasy that follows from the whim of their souls, the reality of which is following the desires of oneself without any guidance from God.

ومِنهُمْ: مَنْ يُرِيدُ مُطْلَقَ الدَلِيلِ والنَظَرِ، ومُطْلَقَ السَماعِ والإرادَةِ، مِنْ غَيرِ تَقْييدِها لا بِشَرْعِيٍّ ولا بِبِدْعِيٍّ. فَهَؤُلاءِ يُفَسِّرونَ قَوْلَهُ: ﴿ٱلَّذِينَ يَسْتَمِعُونَ ٱلْقَوْلَ﴾ [الزمر: ١٨]: بِمُطْلَقِ القَوْلِ الّذي يَدْخُلُ فيهِ القُرْآنُ والغِناءُ، ويَسْتَمِعونَ إلىٰ هَذا[٨٩] وهَذا، وأُولَئِكَ يُفَسِّرونَ الإرادَةَ بِمُطْلَقِ المَحَبَّةِ للتَأَلُّهِ[٩٠] مِنْ غَيْرِ تَقْيِيدِها بِشَرْعِيٍّ ولا بِدْعِيٍّ، ويَجْعَلونَ الجَميعَ مِنْ أَهْلِ الإرادَةِ؛ سَواءٌ عَبَدَ اللهَ بِما أَمَرَ اللهُ بِهِ ورَسولُهُ مِنَ التَوْحيدِ وطاعَةِ

86 Severe religious innovations in matters of theology became widespread after the first three or four generations of Muslims. Prior to this, Muslims were united on a theology that was both scriptural and rational.

87 The Arabic is *zauq*. The word was defined by Ṣūfis as 'creative intuition'.

88 The Arabic is *wajd*. It is defined by Ṣūfis as 'a state that occurs to the heart with ease and without effort'.

٨٩ في المطبوع: «هذه»، خطأ.

٩٠ في المطبوع: «للإله». والمثبت من الأصل الخطي.

الرَسولِ، أو كانَ عابِدًا للشَيْطانِ مُشْرِكًا، عابِدًا بالبِدَعِ. وهَؤُلاءِ أَوْسَطُهُمْ، وهُمْ أَحْسَنُ حالًا مِنَ الّذينَ قَيَّدُوا ذَلِكَ بالبِدْعِيِّ.

Others referred [by these terms] to an **absolute** [i.e. unrestricted and unconditional] *dalīl*, *naẓar*, *samāʿ* and *irādah*, without specifying whether they are prescribed [by the Law] or innovated. They understand the verse: **{Those who listen to the speech}** [39:18] to mean absolute speech which includes the Qurʾān as well as songs, and they listen to both of them. Similarly, they use the term *irādah* to refer to absolute passion for [acts of] worship, without specifying the legislated from the innovated. Thus, they consider all people to be people of [acceptable] *irāda*, whether they happen to be from those who worship God in accordance with what He and His messenger have ordained (in *Tawhid*[91] and in obedience to the Prophet), or from those who worship the devil, make partners with God, and worship by means of innovations. This [second] group is in the middle [of the classification] and are better than the [former] who exclusively used them for innovated matters.

وأمّا القِسْمُ الثالِثُ: فَهُمْ صَفْوَةُ الأُمَّةِ، وخِيارُها المُتَّبِعونَ للرَّسولِ عِلْمًا وعَمَلًا، يَدْعونَ إلىٰ النَظَرِ والاسْتِدْلالِ والاعْتِبارِ بالآياتِ والأدِلَّةِ والبَراهينِ الّتي بَعَثَ اللهُ بِها رَسولَهُ، وتَدَبُّرِ القُرْآنِ وما فيهِ مِنَ البَيانِ، ويَدْعونَ إلىٰ المَحَبَّةِ والإرادَةِ الشَرْعِيَّةِ؛ وهِيَ مَحَبَّةُ اللهِ وَحْدَهُ، وإرادَةُ

91 *Tawḥīd*, or monotheism, may be said to have three aspects. The first is the belief that God is the only Lord and Creator of all things (*Tawḥīd of Rubūbiyyah*), the second is the belief that God is the only one who is deserving of worship (*Tawḥīd of Ulūhiyyah*), and the third is the belief in the unique attributes and Names of God (*Tawḥīd of Asmāʾ and Ṣifāt*).

عِبادَتِهِ وَحْدَهُ لا شَريكَ لَهُ بِما أَمَرَ بِهِ عَلىٰ لِسانِ رَسولِهِ؛ فَهُمْ لا يَعْبُدونَ إلا اللهَ، ويَعْبُدونَهُ بِما شَرَعَ وأَمَرَ،

As for the third group, they are the elect-best of the Muslim nation who follow the Prophet in both knowledge and action. They call people to contemplate, use, and ponder on the signs, the evidences and the arguments with which God sent His Prophet, and to ponder on the Qur'ān and the expositions therein. They call to the prescribed love and *irāda*, which is to love God and to worship Him alone without partners and in accordance with His commandments that were conveyed through His Prophet. Thus, they worship none but God and worship Him in the way He has prescribed and ordained.

ويَسْتَمِعونَ ما أَحَبَّ اسْتِماعَهُ، وهُوَ قَوْلُهُ الّذي قالَ فيهِ: ﴿أَفَلَمْ يَدَّبَّرُوا۟ ٱلْقَوْلَ﴾ [المؤمنون: ٦٨]، وهُوَ الّذي قالَ فيهِ: ﴿فَبَشِّرْ عِبَادِ ١٧ ٱلَّذِينَ يَسْتَمِعُونَ ٱلْقَوْلَ فَيَتَّبِعُونَ أَحْسَنَهُۥٓ﴾ [الزمر: ١٧-١٨]؛ كَما قالَ: ﴿وَٱتَّبِعُوٓا۟ أَحْسَنَ مَآ أُنزِلَ إِلَيْكُم مِّن رَّبِّكُم﴾ [الزمر: ٥٥]. وقالَ: ﴿وَكَتَبْنَا لَهُۥ فِى ٱلْأَلْوَاحِ مِن كُلِّ شَىْءٍ مَّوْعِظَةً وَتَفْصِيلًا لِّكُلِّ شَىْءٍ فَخُذْهَا بِقُوَّةٍ وَأْمُرْ قَوْمَكَ يَأْخُذُوا۟ بِأَحْسَنِهَا﴾ [الأعراف: ١٤٥].

And they 'listen' to what God loves to be heard, which is His speech about which He says: **{Have they not pondered the Word?}**. And describing which He also says: **{So give good tidings to My servants. Who listen to the speech and follow the best of it}**, as He says: **{And follow the best of what was revealed to you from your Lord}**, and: **{And We wrote for him [Moses], upon the**

tablets, the lesson to be drawn from all things and the explanation of all things, saying: Hold it fast; and command your people to take the better [course made clear] therein}.

The Rational-Prescribed Evidence

[والله][92] سُبْحانَهُ بَيَّنَ القُدْرَةَ عَلىٰ الابْتِداءِ؛ كَقَوْلِهِ: ﴿إِن كُنتُمْ فِى رَيْبٍ مِّنَ ٱلْبَعْثِ فَإِنَّا خَلَقْنَٰكُم مِّن تُرَابٍ ثُمَّ مِن نُّطْفَةٍ ثُمَّ مِنْ عَلَقَةٍ ثُمَّ مِن مُّضْغَةٍ مُّخَلَّقَةٍ وَغَيْرِ مُخَلَّقَةٍ لِّنُبَيِّنَ لَكُمْ﴾ [الحج: ٥] الآيَةَ،

[God] has clarified that He has power to begin the creation, as He says: **{O People, if you should be in doubt about the Resurrection, then consider that indeed, We created you from dust, then from a sperm-drop, then from a clinging clot, and then from a lump of flesh, formed and unformed – that We may show you. And We settle in the wombs whom We will for a specified term, then We bring you out as a child, and then that you may reach your maturity. And among you is he who is taken in early death, and among you is he who is returned to the most decrepit old age so that he knows, after once having knowledge, nothing. And you see the earth barren, but when We send down upon it rain, it quivers and swells and grows of every beautiful kind.}**

ومِثْلُ قَوْلِهِ: ﴿وَيَقُولُ ٱلْإِنسَٰنُ أَءِذَا مَا مِتُّ لَسَوْفَ أُخْرَجُ حَيًّا ۝٦٦ أَوَلَا يَذْكُرُ ٱلْإِنسَٰنُ أَنَّا خَلَقْنَٰهُ مِن قَبْلُ وَلَمْ يَكُ شَيْـًٔا﴾ [مريم: ٦٦-٦٧] الآيَةَ،

---

٩٢ لفظ الجلالة ليس في الأصل الخطي، بل ابتدئ من «سبحانه» وذلك بعد بياض مقدار سطر.

Likewise, He says: **{And man says, "When I have died, am I going to be brought forth alive?" Does man not remember that We created him before, when he was nothing?}**.

ومِثْلُ قَوْلِهِ: ﴿وَضَرَبَ لَنَا مَثَلًا وَنَسِيَ خَلْقَهُۥ ۖ قَالَ مَن يُحْيِ ٱلْعِظَٰمَ وَهِىَ رَمِيمٌ ۝٧٨ قُلْ يُحْيِيهَا ٱلَّذِىٓ أَنشَأَهَآ أَوَّلَ مَرَّةٍ ۖ وَهُوَ بِكُلِّ خَلْقٍ عَلِيمٌ﴾ [يس: ٧٨-٧٩]، وَغَيْرُ ذَلِكَ.

And He says, among other verses: **{And he presents for Us an example and forgets his own creation. He says, "Who will give life to bones when they have rotted away?" Say, "He will give them life who produced them the first time; and He is, of all creation, Knowing."}**

فالاسْتِدْلالُ علىٰ الخالِقِ بِخَلْقِ الإنْسانِ في غايَةِ الحُسْنِ والاسْتِقامَةِ، وهِيَ طَريقَةٌ عَقْلِيَّةٌ صَحيحَةٌ. وهِيَ شَرْعِيَّةٌ دَلَّ القُرْآنُ عَلَيْها، وهَدَىٰ النّاسَ إلَيْها، وبَيَّنَها وأَرْشَدَ إلَيْها. وهِيَ عَقْلِيَّةٌ، فَإنَّ نَفْسَ كَوْنِ الإنْسانِ حادِثًا بَعْدَ أنْ لَمْ يَكُنْ، ومَوْلودًا ومَخْلوقًا مِنْ نُطْفَةٍ، ثُمَّ مِنْ عَلَقَةٍ، هَذا لَمْ يُعْلَمْ بِمُجَرَّدِ خَبَرِ الرَسولِ، بَلْ هَذا يَعْلَمُهُ النّاسُ كُلُّهُم بِعُقولِهِمْ؛ سَواءٌ أَخْبَرَ بِهِ الرَسولُ، أو لَمْ يُخْبِرْ. لَكِنَّ الرَسولَ أَمَرَ أنْ يُسْتَدَلَّ بِهِ، ودَلَّ بِهِ، وبَيَّنَهُ، واحْتَجَّ بِهِ؛ فَهُوَ دَليلٌ شَرْعِيٌّ لِأنَّ الشارِعَ اسْتَدَلَّ بِهِ، وأَمَرَ أنْ يُسْتَدَلَّ بِهِ؛ وهُوَ عَقْلِيٌّ لِأنَّهُ بالعَقْلِ تُعْلَمُ صِحَّتُهُ. وكَثيرٌ مِنَ المُتَنازِعينَ في المَعْرِفَةِ: هَلْ تَحْصُلُ بالشَرْعِ أو بالعَقْلِ= لا يَسْلُكونَهُ.

[Indeed,] inferring the existence of the Creator from the creation of man is quite excellent and proper; and it is a sound **rational** method. It is [also] a **prescribed** method which is inferred from the Qur'ān; the Qur'ān leads people to it, explains it, and guides towards it. It is rational because the very origination of man after his non-existence, his birth[93], and his creation [in stages] out of a sperm-drop and then out of a clinging clot is not known merely by the statement of the Prophet. Rather, all people know this rationally whether or not the Prophet mentions it. But the Prophet instructed us to use this as evidence, used it, clarified it, and argued by it. It is therefore both a **prescribed** method [of demonstration], because the lawgiver used it and instructed us to use it, and a **rational** method [of demonstration], because its soundness is known by reason – [although] many of the people who dispute over whether the knowledge [of theological matters] is gained through revelation or by reason do not use it.

وهُوَ عَقْلِيٌّ شَرْعِيٌّ، وكَذَلِكَ غَيْرُهُ مِنَ الأدِلَّةِ الّتي في القُرْآنِ؛ مِثْلُ الاسْتِدْلالِ بالسَّحابِ والمَطَرِ؛ هُوَ مَذْكورٌ في القُرْآنِ في غَيْرِ مَوْضِعٍ، وهُوَ عَقْلِيٌّ شَرْعِيٌّ؛ كَما قالَ تعالىٰ: ﴿أَوَلَمْ يَرَوْاْ أَنَّا نَسُوقُ ٱلْمَآءَ إِلَى ٱلْأَرْضِ ٱلْجُرُزِ فَنُخْرِجُ بِهِۦ زَرْعًا تَأْكُلُ مِنْهُ أَنْعَـٰمُهُمْ وَأَنفُسُهُمْ ۖ أَفَلَا يُبْصِرُونَ﴾ [السجدة: ٢٧]؛ فَهَذا مَرْئِيٌّ بالعُيونِ.

93 Elsewhere, when explaining why the claim that God begot a son is logically incoherent, Ibn Taymiyyah clarifies that an act of begetting involves three necessary things. First, it involves an interaction between two origins, such as two parents or flint stones. Secondly, it involves a consequent release of a part of the substance of both origins. Finally, it involves the total change of that emitted substance into a new creation. [*Majmūʿ al-Fatāwā*, Vol 17, pp. 240-249]

It is therefore a **rational-cum-prescribed** evidence, as are other evidences that were mentioned in the Qur'ān, such as the evidence from clouds and rain that was mentioned in the Qur'ān in more than one place; it is [also] a rational-cum-prescribed evidence. As God says: **{Have they not seen that We drive the water in clouds to barren land and bring forth thereby crops from which their livestock eat and they themselves? Then do they not see?}** This is seen with our eyes.

وقالَ تَعالىٰ: ﴿سَنُرِيهِمْ ءَايَـٰتِنَا فِى ٱلْـَٔافَاقِ وَفِىٓ أَنفُسِهِمْ حَتَّىٰ يَتَبَيَّنَ لَهُمْ أَنَّهُ ٱلْحَقُّ ۗ﴾، ثُمَّ قالَ: ﴿أَوَلَمْ يَكْفِ بِرَبِّكَ أَنَّهُۥ عَلَىٰ كُلِّ شَىْءٍ شَهِيدٌ﴾ [فصلت: ٥٣].فالآياتُ الّتي يُريها الناسَ حَتّىٰ يَعْلَموا أنَّ القُرْآنَ حَقٌّ هِيَ آياتٌ عَقْلِيَّةٌ؛ يَسْتَدِلُّ بِها العَقْلُ علىٰ أنَّ القُرْآنَ حَقٌّ. وهِيَ شَرْعِيَّةٌ؛ دَلَّ الشَرْعُ عَلَيْها، وأَمَرَ بِها. والقُرْآنُ مَمْلوءٌ مِنْ ذِكْرِ الآياتِ العَقْلِيَّةِ الّتي يَسْتَدِلُّ بِها العَقْلُ، وهِيَ شَرْعِيَّةٌ لِأنَّ الشَرْعَ دَلَّ عَلَيْها وأَرْشَدَ إلَيْها.

And God says: **{We will show them Our signs in the horizons and within themselves until it becomes clear to them that it is the truth. But is it not sufficient concerning your Lord that He is, over all things, a Witness?}** These signs which He shows to the people so that they know that the Qur'ān is the truth are **rational** evidences; by them does reason infer that the Qur'ān is true. And they are [also] **prescribed** evidences, [as] the [prescribed] Law directs [people] to them and instructs [them to use] them. The Qur'ān is filled with the mention of rational signs which are used by the mind in inference, and they are also **prescribed** since the [prescribed] Law leads to them and directs [people] to [use] them.

ولَكِنْ كَثيرٌ مِنَ الناسِ لا يُسَمّي دَليلًا شَرْعِيًّا إلا ما دَلَّ بِمُجَرَّدِ خَبَرِ الرَسولِ، وهُوَ اصْطِلاحٌ قاصِرٌ.

But many of the people label as **'prescribed evidence'** only those [evidences] which demonstrate [the conclusion] by the mere statement of the Prophet, [not those that additionally demonstrate it by reason]. [But] this is an inadequate convention.

ولِهَذا يَجْعَلونَ أُصولَ الفِقْهِ هُوَ لِبَيانِ الأدِلَّةِ الشَرْعِيَّةِ: الكِتابِ، والسُنَّةِ، والإجْماعِ. والكِتابُ يُريدونَ بِهِ أنْ يُعْلَمَ مُرادُ الرَسولِ فَقَطْ. والمَقْصودُ مِنْ أُصولِ الفِقْهِ: هُوَ مَعْرِفَةُ الأحْكامِ الشَرْعِيَّةِ العَمَلِيَّةِ؛ فَيَجْعَلونَ الأدِلَّةَ الشَرْعِيَّةَ: ما دَلَّتْ عَلىٰ الأحْكامِ العَمَلِيَّةِ فَقَطْ، ويُخْرِجونَ ما دَلَّ بِإخْبارِ الرَسولِ عَنْ أنْ يَكونَ شَرْعًا، فَضْلًا عَمّا دَلَّ بِإرْشادِهِ وتَعْليمِهِ. ولَكِنْ قَدْ يُسَمّونَ هَذا دَليلًا سَمْعِيًّا، ولا يُسَمّونَهُ شَرْعِيًّا، وهُوَ اصْطِلاحٌ قاصِرٌ.

And this is why they say that "*Uṣūl al-Fiqh* is to elucidate the **prescribed evidence,** that is the Book, the Sunnah, and the Consensus", referring by 'the Book' to the knowledge of the Prophet's intent only[94]. And the purpose of *Uṣūl al-Fiqh*[95] is to arrive at the

94 "Referring by the book... Prophet's intent only" This is the literal translation of the text as found in the published edition. It is the same in the manuscript, but the scribe, due to the problematic context, has written كذا (= sic) over *al-Kitāb*. There, most probably, was an omission or distortion in the exemplar manuscript from which the scribe copied.

95 An Islamic science which covers the principles and methodologies through which the practical rulings of Islam are inferred from the foundational sources.

prescribed practical rulings[96] [of Islam]. Thus, these [people] consider the **'prescribed evidence'** to be the evidence which demonstrates the practical rulings only, excluding from the **prescribed Law** [all the other kinds of] evidences that are the reports of the Prophet, let alone the [rational] evidences which he instructed and taught [when demonstrating the matters of the Faith]. But they may label these [latter evidences] as 'scriptural (*sam'ī*) evidences' instead of 'prescribed evidences', which is [also] an inadequate convention.

والأَحْكامُ العَمَلِيَّةُ أَكْثَرُ الناسِ يَقولونَ: إِنَّها تُعْلَمُ بِالعَقْلِ أَيْضًا، وإِنَّ العَقْلَ قَدْ يَعْرِفُ الحُسْنَ والقُبْحَ، فَتكونُ الأَدِلَّةُ العَقْلِيَّةُ دالَّةً عَلى الأَحْكامِ العَمَلِيَّةِ أَيْضًا. ويَجوزُ أَنْ تُسَمّى شَرعِيَّةً؛ لِأَنَّ الشَّرعَ قَرَّرَها، ووافَقَها، أَو دَلَّ عَلَيْها وأَرْشَدَ إِلَيْها؛ كَما قيلَ مِثْلُ ذَلِكَ في المَطالِبِ الخَبَرِيَّةِ كَإِثْباتِ الرَّبِّ، ووَحْدانِيَّتِهِ، وصِدْقِ رُسُلِهِ، وقُدْرَتِهِ عَلى المَعادِ: إِنَّ الشَّرعَ دَلَّ عَلَيْها وأَرْشَدَ إِلَيْها. وبَسْطُ هَذا لَهُ مَوْضِعٌ آخَرُ.

Moreover, most people say that the practical rulings [of Islam] can also be known by reason, and that reason may [independently] discern *ḥusn* (goodness, morality) and *qubḥ* (evil, immorality).[97] Thus,

---

96 These are contrasted with the prescribed rulings that pertain to knowledge.
97 Ibn Taymiyyah defined the morality of human actions in terms of their appropriateness for the human agent and their leading to his well-being and benefit. The morality of many human actions can thus be known through independent reason before coming across a Revelation from God that legislates and prohibits. That said, Ibn Taymiyyah believed that the Prophet Muḥammad (may God elevate his mention) was sent with a perfect Law (Sharī'ah) that guides human beings to the ideal human conduct, maximiz-

rational evidences can demonstrate the practical rulings [of Islam] too. These [evidences] may [also] be labeled as **'prescribed evidences'**, for the Law [of Islam] states and supports them or leads and directs people to them – just as it was said concerning the matters pertaining to knowledge, like the existence of the Lord and His Oneness, the truthfulness of His Prophets, and His ability to resurrect the dead; the [prescribed] Law leads and directs [people] to these [conclusions too]. This is explained in detail elsewhere.

---

ing their well-being and minimizing detriment to the greatest degree possible. Although human beings can independently recognize that this divine Law is morally superior, reason cannot on its own infer the details of the Law and the consequences of the human actions, such as the reward and punishment in the hereafter. [*Majmūʿ al-Fatāwā*, Vol 3, pp. 114-115].

The Argument from the Origination of Bodies *(Continued)*

والمَقْصودُ هُنا: أنَّ الأشْعَرِيَّ بَنَىٰ أُصولَ الدِينِ في «اللُمَعِ» ، و «رِسالَةِ الثغْرِ» عَلىٰ كَوْنِ الإنْسانِ مَخْلوقًا مُحْدَثًا، فَلا بُدَّ لَهُ مِنْ مُحْدِثٍ، لِكَوْنِ هَذا الدَليلِ مَذْكورًا في القُرْآنِ، فَيَكونُ شَرْعِيًّا عَقْلِيًّا. لَكِنَّهُ في نَفْسِ الأَمْرِ سَلَكَ في ذَلِكَ طَريقَةَ الجَهْمِيَّةِ بِعَيْنِها؛ وهُوَ الاسْتِدْلالُ عَلىٰ حُدوثِ الإنْسانِ بِأَنَّهُ مُرَكَّبٌ مِنَ الجَواهِرِ المُفْرَدَةِ، فَلَمْ يَخْلُ مِنَ الحَوادِثِ، وما لَمْ يَخْلُ مِنَ الحَوادِثِ فَهُوَ حادِثٌ؛

[But] the purpose here was to point out that [Abu al-Ḥasan] al-Ashʿarī[98] built his theology in his *al-Lumaʿ* and in *Risālat al-Thaghr* on [the fact] that man is created and originated and that he, therefore, requires an Originator. [He chose this method of demonstration] because it was mentioned in the Qurʾān, making it a **rational-cum-prescribed** evidence. But, in reality, he resorted to the same method of the Jahmiyyah in the explanation of this evidence, which is to infer the origination of man by [assuming] that he is composed of ***jawāhir mufradah*** (indivisible atoms).[99] Man is therefore never

---

98 Abu al-Ḥasan ʿAlī ibn Ismāʿīl al-Ashʿarī (d. 324H) is the father of the Ashʿarī school of Kalām theology. He was once an adherent of the Muʿtazilī school before changing his views and effectively preaching against the Muʿtazilah.

99 The indivisible atoms are not analogous to the modern scientific under-

void of *ḥawādith* (i.e. originating accidents, events, change)[100], and everything that is never void of *ḥawādith* is itself *ḥādith* (originated).[101]

فَجَعَلَ العِلْمَ بِكَوْنِ الإنْسانِ مُحْدَثًا، وبِكَوْنِ غَيْرِهِ مِنَ الأجْسامِ المَشْهودَةِ مُحْدَثًا إنَّما يُعْلَمُ بِهَذِهِ الطَرِيقَةِ؛ وهُوَ أنَّهُ مُؤلَّفٌ مِنَ الجَواهِرِ المُفْرَدَةِ، وهِيَ لا تَخْلو مِنِ اجْتِماعٍ وافْتِراقٍ - وتِلْكَ أعْراضٌ حادِثَةٌ - وما لَمْ يَنْفَكَّ مِنَ الحَوادِثِ، فَهُوَ مُحْدَثٌ.

In this way, al-Ashʿarī entirely predicated the knowledge of the **origination** of man and other observed bodies on this method [of demonstration that was used by the Jahmiyyah], namely that these bodies are composed of ***jawāhir mufradah*** (indivisible atoms), and [that since] these atoms are always in a state of **separation** and **combination**, which are in turn accidents that originate, and everything that is never void of originating accidents is, itself, originated; [therefore man and all other bodies must be originated.]

---

standing of atoms or even to the smaller constituents that are the subatomic particles. Indivisible atoms are instead unchanging constituents that are point-sized and have no size, volume, or mass. Kalām theologians claim that these atoms are not themselves physical, but are substances that make up physical bodies when they come together. Ibn Taymiyyah believed that the existence of such atoms is impossible.

100 Because the atoms are constantly rearranging.

101 By claiming that the genus of *ḥawādith* has a beginning, the Ashʿarī theologians reasoned that every substrate of *ḥawādith* must also be originated, as it is always accompanied by *ḥawādith* and could never have existed before they did.

وهَذِهِ الطَرِيقَةُ أَصْلُ ضَلالِ هَؤُلاءِ؛ فَإنَّهُمْ أنْكَروا المَعْلومَ بالحِسِّ والمُشاهَدَةِ والضَرورَةِ العَقْلِيَّةِ؛ مِنْ حُدوثِ المُحْدَثاتِ المَشْهودِ حُدوثُها، وادَّعَوْا أنَّهُ إنَّما يُشْهَدُ حُدوثُ أعْراضٍ لا حُدوثُ أعْيانٍ، مَعَ تَنازُعِهِمْ في الأعْراضِ. ثُمَّ قالوا: والأجْسامُ لا تَخْلُو مِنَ الأعْراضِ – وهَذا صَحيحٌ. ثُمَّ قالوا: والأعْراضُ حادِثَةٌ – فاضْطَرَبوا هُنا. ثُمَّ قالوا: وما لَمْ يَخْلُ مِنَ الحَوادِثِ فَهُوَ حادِثٌ – وهَذا أَصْلُ دِينِهِمْ، وهُوَ أَصْلٌ فاسِدٌ مُخالِفٌ للسَمْعِ والعَقْلِ، كَما قَدْ بُسِطَ في غَيْرِ هَذا المَوْضِعِ.

This method [of demonstrating the Maker's existence] is the [very] source of the [theological] errors of these [Jahmiyyah]. For they have denied what is known through sense perception, observation, and rational necessity. [They denied] the origination of things that are witnessed to originate, claiming instead that only the **accidents**[102] are observed to originate, not the **substances** – although they disputed as to what exactly constitutes an accident.[103] They then said that **"bodies are never void of accidents"**, which is correct. [But

102 Such as the arrangement, separation, and combination of atoms.

103 Both the Muʿtazilah and the Ashʿarī theologians agree that all accidents are originated and that they subsist only in created bodies, but they disagree as to what exactly constitutes an accident. The Muʿtazilah refer to all attributes as created accidents and deny that God has any divine attributes, a view which was severely criticized by the leading early scholars of Islam. By contrast, the late Ashʿarī theologians describe God with some but not all of the divine attributes that were attributed to God by the early Muslims, referring to them as divine attributes and not as accidents. They include life, knowledge, power, will, speech, hearing and sight, but exclude divine attributes that involve motion and voluntary action, referring to these latter as *ḥawādith* unfitting for attribution to God as descriptions.

then] they claimed that **"the accidents originate"**[104]; here they were inconsistent [and inconclusive]. [Finally,] they claimed that **"everything that is never void of *ḥawādith* is itself *ḥādith* (originated)"**. This [last premise] is the foundation of their theology, and it is a false foundation that contradicts both [authentic] Revelation and [sound] reason[105], as has been clarified elsewhere.

والمُتَفَلْسِفَةُ أَشَدُّ مُخالَفَةً لِلعَقْلِ والسَمْعِ مِنْهُمْ، لَكِنَّهُمْ عَرَفوا فَسادَ طَرِيقَتِهِمْ هَذِهِ العَقْلِيَّةِ، فاسْتَطالوا عَلَيْهِمْ بِذَلِكَ، وسَلَكوا ما هُوَ أَفْسَدُ مِنْها كَطَرِيقَةِ الإمْكانِ والوُجوبِ؛ كَما قَدْ بُسِطَ في مَوْضِعٍ آخَرَ؛

And the Philosophers[106] are in greater contradiction to [sound]

104 Ibn Taymiyyah mentions elsewhere that, by stating that the "accidents originate", many theologians conflated the origination of the genus of events with the origination of the particular or limited set of events. Other theologians became aware of this distinction and stressed that the genus of events must have been originated such that there must have been an absolutely first event. This in turn implies that the world was originated ex nihilo, as the world could not have preceded the first event that was possible. [*Minhāj al-Sunnah al-Nabawiyyah*, Vol 2, p 226]

105 One of the false conclusions that are necessitated by the Argument from the Origination of Bodies is that God must be motionless and incorporeal. Ibn Taymiyyah believed that a perfect God must have spatial location and measure, even though he did not describe God with terms like 'physical body' or 'substance' and refrained from using such language in both negation and affirmation. Instead, Ibn Taymiyyah restricted himself to describing God as 'above the Creation', 'upon His Throne' and to similar descriptions, for this latter vocabulary is scriptural and refers only to true meanings, unlike the former vocabulary which can equally refer to true and false meanings.

106 These are the Aristotelean philosophers that existed in the Muslim world, and they are often contrasted with the Kalām theologians. They include fig-

reason and [authentic] Revelation than [the Jahmiyyah], but they [nonetheless] realized the fallacy in the [latter's] method of demonstrating [the Maker's existence], so they condescendingly domineered over them; although they took routes [of demonstration] that are even more flawed [than those of the Jahmiyyah], such as the [Avicennian] Argument from Contingency and Necessity[107], as has been explained elsewhere.

فَلَبَّسوا هَذا البَاطِلَ بالحَقِّ الّذي جاءَ بِهِ الرَسولُ؛ وهُوَ الاسْتِدْلالُ بِحُدوثِ الإنْسانِ وغَيْرِهِ مِنَ المُحْدَثاتِ الّتي يُشْهَدُ حُدوثُها. فَصارَ في كَلامِهِمْ حَقٌّ وباطِلٌ، مِنْ جِنْسِ ما أَحْدَثَهُ أَهْلُ الكِتابِ؛ حَيْثُ لَبَّسوا الحَقَّ بالباطِلِ. واحْتاجوا في ذَلِكَ إلىٰ كِتْمانِ الحَقِّ - الّذي جاءَ بِهِ الرَسولُ - الّذي يُخالِفُ ما أَحْدَثوهُ، فَصاروا يَكْرَهونَ ظُهورَ ما جاءَ بِهِ الرُسولُ، بَلْ يَمْنَعونَ عَنْ قِراءَةِ الأَحاديثِ وسَماعِها، وقِراءَةِ كَلام السَلَفِ وسَماعِهِ. ومِنْهُمْ مَنْ يَكْرَهُ قِراءَةَ القُرْآنِ وحِفْظَهُ. والّذينَ لا يَقْدِرونَ علىٰ المَنْعِ

ures like Avicenna (d. 428H) who argued that this world is both eternal with God and dependent on His essence. Although these are described as Islamic Philosophers, they did not believe that God created this world after its nonexistence and by His will, which is one of the reasons Muslim scholars place them outside of the fold of Islam.

107 Ibn Taymiyyah is not referring here to what is known as the contingency argument, which is to infer the existence of the necessary Creator from the possible existence of the natural phenomena. Instead, he is criticizing the Avicennian form of the argument, which seeks to demonstrate a necessary existence without specifically leading to an Originator who created the heavens and the earth after their nonexistence [*Sharḥ al-Aṣfahāniyyah*, pp. 48-49]. Also see *Dar' Ta'āruḍ al-'Aql wa al-Naql* [Vol 9, pp. 113-119].

مِنْ ذَلِكَ، صاروا يَقْرَأُونَ حُروفَهُ، ولا يَعْلَمونَ حُدودَ ما أَنْزَلَ اللهُ عَلىٰ رَسولِهِ، بَلْ إِنِ اشْتَغَلُوا بِعُلومِهِ اشْتَغَلُوا بِتَفْسيرِ مَنْ يَشْرَكُهُمْ في بِدْعَتِهِمْ؛ مِمَّنْ يُحَرِّفُ الكَلِمَ؛ كَلِمَ اللهِ عَنْ مَواضِعِهِ.

Thus have they mixed this falsehood with the truth that was brought by the Prophet, which is to infer [the Maker's existence] from the origination of man and other creations that are observed to originate. So, their statements now contain [both] truth and falsehood, in a way that is similar to the innovations of the People of the Book, [for] they [too] mixed truth with falsehood. In doing so, they had to conceal part of the truth which the Prophet brought – [the parts] that contradict their inventions. As such, they came to disdain the propagation of [the guidance] that was brought by the Prophet, even preventing the people from reading and listening to the Ḥadīth and the words of the Pious Predecessors. Some [even] hate the recitation and the memorization of the Qur'ān, and those who are unable to prevent [its recitation] read its letters without understanding the precepts which God sent down upon His Prophet. Instead, should they occupy themselves with its exegesis, they will occupy themselves with the interpretations of people who share in their innovations, those who distort the words of God from their proper contexts.

Both Substances and Accidents Are Observed to Originate

والأَصْلُ العَقْلِيُّ الحِسِّيُّ الَّذي بِهِ فَارَقوا العَقْلَ والسَمْعَ، هُوَ: حُدوثُ ما يُشْهَدُ حُدوثُهُ مِثْلُ حُدوثِ الزَرْعِ والثِمارِ، وحُدوثِ الإنْسانِ وغَيْرِهِ مِنَ الحَيوانِ، وحُدوثِ السَحابِ والمَطَرِ ونَحْوِ ذَلِكَ مِنَ الأعْيانِ القائِمَةِ بِنَفْسِها= غَيْرُ حُدوثِ الأعْراضِ كالحَرَكَةِ، والحَرارَةِ، والبُرودَةِ، والضَوْءِ، والظُلْمَةِ، وغَيْرِ ذَلِكَ. بَلْ تِلْكَ الأعْيانُ الّتي يُسَمُّونَها أجْسامًا وجَواهِرَ هِيَ حادِثَةٌ؛ فَإِنَّهُ مَعْلومٌ أنَّ الإنْسانَ مَخْلوقٌ مِنْ نُطْفَةٍ، ثُمَّ مِنْ عَلَقَةٍ، ثُمَّ مِنْ مُضْغَةٍ، وأنَّ الثِمارَ تُخْلَقُ مِنَ الأشْجارِ، وأنَّ الزَرْعَ تُخْلَقُ مِنَ الحَبِّ، والشَجَرَ تُخْلَقُ مِنَ النَوَى؛

And the rational-cum-empirical foundation by [denying] which they deviated from [sound] reason and [authentic] Revelation is that: the origination of **concrete things**, such as the origination of plants, fruits, human beings, animals, clouds, rain, and other self-subsisting concrete things, is different to the origination of accidents such as motion, heat, coolness, luminosity, darkness, and the like. Indeed, the concrete things which they label as 'bodies' and 'substances' are themselves originated. For it is known that man is created from a sperm-drop, then from a clot, and then from a lump of flesh. [It is known] that fruits are created from trees, plants from grain, and [palm] trees from date seeds.[108]

قَالَ تَعالىٰ: ﴿إِنَّ ٱللَّهَ فَالِقُ ٱلۡحَبِّ وَٱلنَّوَىٰۖ يُخۡرِجُ ٱلۡحَيَّ مِنَ ٱلۡمَيِّتِ وَمُخۡرِجُ ٱلۡمَيِّتِ مِنَ ٱلۡحَيِّۚ ذَٰلِكُمُ ٱللَّهُۖ فَأَنَّىٰ تُؤۡفَكُونَ ٩٥ فَالِقُ ٱلۡإِصۡبَاحِ وَجَعَلَ ٱلَّيۡلَ سَكَنًا وَٱلشَّمۡسَ وَٱلۡقَمَرَ حُسۡبَانًاۚ ذَٰلِكَ تَقۡدِيرُ ٱلۡعَزِيزِ ٱلۡعَلِيمِ ٩٦ وَهُوَ ٱلَّذِي جَعَلَ لَكُمُ ٱلنُّجُومَ لِتَهۡتَدُواْ بِهَا فِي ظُلُمَٰتِ ٱلۡبَرِّ وَٱلۡبَحۡرِۗ قَدۡ فَصَّلۡنَا ٱلۡأٓيَٰتِ لِقَوۡمٖ يَعۡلَمُونَ ٩٧ وَهُوَ ٱلَّذِيٓ أَنشَأَكُم مِّن نَّفۡسٖ وَٰحِدَةٖ فَمُسۡتَقَرّٞ وَمُسۡتَوۡدَعٞۗ قَدۡ فَصَّلۡنَا ٱلۡأٓيَٰتِ لِقَوۡمٖ يَفۡقَهُونَ ٩٨ وَهُوَ ٱلَّذِيٓ أَنزَلَ مِنَ ٱلسَّمَآءِ مَآءٗ فَأَخۡرَجۡنَا بِهِۦ نَبَاتَ كُلِّ شَيۡءٖ فَأَخۡرَجۡنَا مِنۡهُ خَضِرٗا نُّخۡرِجُ مِنۡهُ حَبّٗا مُّتَرَاكِبٗا وَمِنَ ٱلنَّخۡلِ مِن طَلۡعِهَا قِنۡوَانٞ دَانِيَةٞ وَجَنَّٰتٖ مِّنۡ أَعۡنَابٖ وَٱلزَّيۡتُونَ وَٱلرُّمَّانَ مُشۡتَبِهٗا وَغَيۡرَ مُتَشَٰبِهٍۗ ٱنظُرُوٓاْ إِلَىٰ ثَمَرِهِۦٓ إِذَآ أَثۡمَرَ وَيَنۡعِهِۦٓۚ إِنَّ فِي ذَٰلِكُمۡ لَأٓيَٰتٖ لِّقَوۡمٖ يُؤۡمِنُونَ﴾ [الأنعام: ٩٥-٩٩].

God says: **{Indeed, God is the cleaver of grain and date seeds. He brings the living out of the dead and brings the dead out of the living. That is God; so how are you deluded? He is the cleaver of daybreak and has made the night for rest and the sun and moon for calculation. That is the determination of the Exalted in Might, the Knowing. And it is He who placed for you the stars that you may be guided by them through the**

108 Ibn Taymiyyah believed that the very substances of things change at what is today known as the molecular level. In another book, he explains that this substantial change varies in degree and intensity, mentioning a range of examples. [*Dar' Taʿārud al-ʿAql wa al-Naql*, Vol 5, pp. 195-203].

darknesses of the land and sea. We have detailed the signs for a people who know. And it is He who produced you from one soul and gave you a place of dwelling and of storage. We have detailed the signs for a people who understand. And it is He who sends down rain from the sky, and We produce thereby the growth of all things. We produce from it greenery from which We produce grains arranged in layers. And from the palm trees - of its emerging fruit are clusters hanging low. And gardens of grapevines and olives and pomegranates, similar yet varied. Look at its fruit when it yields and its ripening. Indeed in that are signs for a people who believe.}

فَهَذا الإنْسانُ والشَجَرُ والزَرْعُ المَخْلوقُ مِنْ مادَّةٍ قَدْ خُلِقَ مِنْها عَيْنٌ قائِمَةٌ بِنَفْسِها. وهَذِهِ الأعْيانُ خُلِقَتْ مِنْ مادَّةٍ هِيَ أعْيانٌ[١٠٩]، وهُوَ الجِسْمُ القائِمُ بِنَفْسِهِ، وهُوَ الجَوْهَرُ العامُّ في اصْطِلاحِهِمْ، الّذي يَقولونَ: إنَّهُ مُرَكَّبٌ مِنَ الجَواهِرِ المُفْرَدَةِ.

So, this man, tree, or plant which was created ex materia was created out of the matter as a [new] concrete, self-subsisting thing. And these concrete things were created from a matter that is [itself] a concrete thing – which is 'the self-subsisting body' and **'the general substance'** in their terminology, which they claim is composed of the indivisible atoms.[110]

١٠٩ في الأصل الخطي تأخَّرت هذه الجملة: «وهذه الأعيانُ خُلِقَت مِن مادةٍ هي أعيان» بعد قوله في السطر الآتي: «يَقولونَ إنَّه مُركَّبٌ مِنَ الجَواهِرِ المُفْرَدَةِ». ولعل هذا موضعها، وبه يستقيم السياق، وهو أهون مما في المطبوع من التغيير والزيادة في هذا الموضع.

110 The Ashʿarīyyah claim that indivisible atoms do not change into other things, but necessarily continue to exist throughout all processes of creation

[وَهُمْ يَقولونَ:][١١١] لَمْ يُخْلَقْ إلا أعْراضٌ قائِمَةٌ بِغَيْرِها، وأمّا الأعْيانُ فَهِيَ الجَواهِرُ المُفْرَدَةُ، وتِلْكَ لَمْ يُخْلَقْ مِنْها شَيْءٌ في هَذِهِ الحَوادِثِ، ولَكِنْ أُحْدِثَ فيها جَمْعٌ وتَفْريقٌ؛ فَكانَ خَلْقُ الإنْسانِ وغَيْرِهِ هُوَ تَرْكيبَ تِلْكَ الجَواهِرِ، وإحْداثَ هَذا التَرْكيبِ لا إحْداثَ تِلْكَ الجَواهِرِ.

[And they claim that] only accidents that subsist in other things are originated. As for the concrete things, [they claim that] they are the indivisible atoms [only], and none of them is created in those *ḥawādith* (i.e. originating accidents, events). Instead, it is only separation and recombination that takes place in the atoms. Thus, the creation of man and other things is a [mere] arrangement of these atoms, and it is the inception of this [particular] arrangement, not an act of originating the atoms [themselves].

وأمّا حُدوثُ تِلْكَ الجَواهِرِ فَإنَّما يُعْلَمُ بالاسْتِدْلالِ، فَيُسْتَدَلُّ عَلَيْهِ بِأنَّ الجَواهِرَ الّتي تَرَكَّبَتْ مِنْها هَذِهِ الأجْسامُ لا تَخْلو مِنِ اجْتِماعٍ وافْتِراقٍ، والاجْتِماعُ والافْتِراقُ حادِثٌ، وما لَمْ يَخْلُ مِنَ الحَوادِثِ فَهُوَ حادِثٌ. فَهَذِهِ طَريقُ هَؤُلاءِ الجَهْمِيَّةِ أَهْلِ الكَلامِ المُحْدَثِ.

As for the origination of these atoms [ex nihilo in the past], they claim to know it **by means of inference**. They infer this by [claiming] that the atoms which constitute the [physical] bodies are never void of [states of] separation and combination; and since [the states of] separation and combination are *ḥādith* (originating accidents),

---

in the natural world.

١١١ زيادة مقترحة لإقامة السياق. موضعها في الأصل الخطي: «أم».

thus, everything that was never void of *ḥawādith* (originating accidents) is itself *ḥādith* (originated).[112] This is the method of [demonstration used by] these Jahmiyyah, the proponents of the innovated *kalām* theology.[113]

وأمَّا جُمْهورُ العُقَلاءِ فيَقولونَ: بَلْ نَحْنُ نَعْلَمُ حُدوثَ هَذِهِ الأعْيانِ القائِمَةِ بِنَفْسِها، لا نَقولُ: إنَّهُ لَمْ يَحْدُثْ إلا عَرَضٌ؛ فَإنَّ هَذا القَوْلَ يَقْتَضِي أنَّ تِلْكَ الجَواهِرَ الَّتي رُكِّبَ مِنْها آدَمُ باقِيَةٌ لَمْ يَزَلْ في كُلِّ آدَمِيٍّ مِنْها شَيْءٌ. وهَذا مُكابَرَةٌ؛ فَإنَّ بَدَنَ آدَمَ لا يَحْتَمِلُ هَذا كُلَّهُ، لا يَحْتَمِلُ أنْ تَكونَ فيهِ جَواهِرُ بِعَدَدِ ذُرِّيَّتِهِ، لا سِيَّما وكُلُّ آدَمِيٍّ إنَّما خُلِقَ مِنْ مَنِيِّ أَبَوَيْهِ، وهُمْ يَقولونَ: تِلْكَ الجَواهِرُ الَّتي في مَنِيِّ الأَبَوَيْنِ باقِيَةٌ بِأَعْيانِها في الوَلَدِ.

By contrast, the majority of rational minds say: "We know [with certainty] that these self-subsisting concrete things [in the creation] are [themselves] originated, and we do not say that only the accidents are originated [in the process]". For such a claim [regarding the creation of man] would entail that the atoms which constituted Adam continue to exist [in his descendants,] such that each human has a part of them. But this is absurd, for the body of Adam could not

112 Thus, according to their line of reasoning, the physical bodies were originated ex nihilo in the past.

113 Today, many theologians seek to demonstrate the origination of the constituents of matter *ex nihilo* using scientific arguments that relate to Big Bang Cosmology. Ibn Taymiyyah mentions elsewhere that the early Muslims believed that this world was not created ex nihilo, but that it was created in the context of another created world which consisted of water vapour beneath the Throne of God. [*Minhāj al-Sunnah al-Nabawiyyah*, Vol 1, pp. 360-364]

have contained all of that; it could not have carried substances as many as his descendants,[114] especially when [it is known that] every human being was created out of the emission of his parents. [Indeed,] these [Jahmiyyah] claim that the very atoms which existed in the emission of the parents continue to exist in their child.[115]

وهُمْ يَقولونَ: إنَّ الجَواهِرَ لا تَفْنَىٰ، بَلْ تَنْتَقِلُ مِنْ حالٍ إلىٰ حالٍ. وكَثيرٌ مِنْهُمْ يَقولُ إنَّها مُسْتَغْنِيَةٌ عَنِ الرَّبِّ بَعْدَ أنْ خَلَقَها. وتَحَيَّروا فيما إذا أرادَ أنْ يُفْنِيَها: كَيْفَ يُفْنِيْها؟ كَما قَدْ ذُكِرَ في غَيْرِ هَذا المَوْضِعِ؛ إذِ المَقْصودُ هُنا التَنْبِيْهُ علىٰ أنَّ أَصْلَ الأُصولِ مَعْرِفَةُ حُدوثِ الشَيْءِ مِنَ الشَيْءِ؛ كَحُدوثِ الإنْسانِ مِنَ المَنِيِّ، فَهَؤُلاءِ ظَنّوا أنَّهُ لا يَحْدُثُ إلا عَرَضٌ[١١٦].

And these [Jahmiyyah] claim that the substances do not perish but only move from one state to another. Many of them [also] claim that these [substances] become independent of the Lord after He creates them. And they were puzzled as to how [God] may annihilate them if He so willed, as has been clarified elsewhere. For our purpose here is only to point out that the [first and] foremost foun-

114 This line of argument against the Jahmiyyah is irrelevant nowadays, as procreation is today understood to be characterized by the passing down of genetic information, not by the passing down of substance as the Jahmiyyah would have it.

115 Ibn Taymiyyah instead argues for *substantial* change in the process of conception and fetal development. The creation of a human child involves the origination of a new substance, which is the child, out of the substance of its parents, which is the emitted substance, and subsequently the nourishment from its mother.

١١٦ في المطبوع: «الأعراض». والمثبت هو ما في الأصل الخطي.

dation [of correct theology] is to know that one thing **begins to exist out of another**, such as [by] the origination of a man out of a sperm-drop. But these [Jahmiyyah] thought that only an accident originates [and thus did not accept this foundation].

ولِهَذا لَمّا ذَكَرَ أبو عَبْدِ اللهِ بنُ الخَطيبِ الرازِيُّ في كُتُبِهِ الكِبارِ والصِغارِ الطُرُقَ الدالَّةَ علىٰ إثْباتِ الصانِعِ لَمْ يَذْكُرْ طَريقًا صَحيحًا، ولا[١١٧] في كُتُبِهِ وكُتُبِ أمْثالِهِ طَريقٌ صَحيحٌ لِإثْباتِ الصانِعِ، بَلْ عَدَلوا عَنِ الطُرُقِ العَقْلِيَّةِ الّتي يَعْلَمُها العُقَلاءُ بِفِطْرَتِهِمْ، وهِيَ الّتي دَلَّتْهُمْ عَلَيْها الرُسُلُ، إلىٰ طُرُقٍ سَلَكوها مُخالِفَةٍ لِلشَرْعِ والعَقْلِ، لا سِيَّما مَنْ سَلَكَ طَريقَةَ الوُجوبِ والإمْكانِ مُتابَعَةً لابْنِ سينا؛ كالرازِيِّ، فَإنَّ هَؤُلاءِ مِنْ أفْسَدِ الناسِ اسْتِدْلالًا، كَما قَدْ ذَكَرْنا طُرُقَ عامَّةِ النُظّارِ في غَيْرِ هَذا المَوْضِعِ مِثْلِ كِتابِ «مَنْعِ تَعارُضِ العَقْلِ والنَقْلِ»، وغَيْرِ ذَلِكَ.

For this reason, when mentioning the methods of demonstrating the Maker's existence in his books, [both] expansive and concise, Abū ʿAbdullāh Ibn al-Khaṭīb al-Rāzī[118] did not mention any sound method [of demonstration]. There exist no correct methods for demonstrating the Maker's existence in his works or in the works of like-minded [Kalām theologians]. Rather, they eschewed the rational methods [of demonstration] which rational people know by their

---

١١٧ في المطبوع: «وليس». والمثبت هو ما في الأصل الخطي.

118 Fakhr al-Dīn al-Rāzī (d. 606H) is a famous late Ashʿarī theologian who authored books in Kalām and Qur'anic interpretation. He is known for bringing the Ashʿarī school closer to the views of the Philosophers, and his works are the target of many of Ibn Taymiyyah's theological criticisms.

fiṭrah, methods to which the Prophets had guided them, and instead followed other methods that contradict both [authentic] Revelation and [sound] reason. [This is] especially [true of theologians] who adopted the Avicennian Argument from Contingency and Necessity, such as al-Rāzī, for those are among the most irrational people when demonstrating [the Maker's existence]. We have mentioned the methods of the majority of the Nuẓẓār in other places, such as in the book ***Averting the Conflict between Reason and Revelation*** and others.

The Four Arguments of al-Rāzī

والمَقْصودُ هُنا: أنَّ الرازِيَّ ذَكَرَ أنَّ ما يُسْتَدَلُّ بِهِ عَلىٰ إثْباتِ الصانِعِ إمَّا حُدوثُ الأجْسامِ، وإمّا حُدوثُ صِفاتِها، وإمَّا إمْكانُها، وإمَّا إمْكانُ صِفاتِها، وذَكَرَ في بَعْضِ المَواضِعِ: وإمَّا الإحْكامُ والإتْقانُ. لَكِنَّ الإحْكامَ والإتْقانَ يَدُلُّ عَلىٰ العِلْمِ ابْتِداءً.

[Anyways,] the purpose here is to say that al-Rāzī mentioned that the existence of the Maker can be inferred from [one of four arguments]: (i) the Argument from the **Origination of Bodies**, (ii) the Argument from the **Origination of the Attributes** of bodies, (iii) the Argument from the **Contingency of Bodies**, and (iv) the Argument from the **Contingency of the Attributes** of bodies. In some places, he mentions [a fifth Argument] from the **Precision and Excellence** [in the natural world]. But [this Argument from] Precision and Excellence, prima facie, proves the knowledge [of the Maker, instead of His existence].[119]

119 Elsewhere, Ibn Taymiyyah mentions various arguments for the existence of knowledge in the Maker. God is more perfect than the knowledgeable creations He has created, and therefore has more right to possessing knowledge than they do, for He is the giver of their perfection. The precision and the intricacy in the created world also indicate supreme knowledge in its Cause. Moreover, God has a creative will, which implies that He possesses knowledge. [*Sharḥ al-Aṣfahāniyyah*, p. 396]

وَالاسْتِدْلالُ بِحُدوثِ الأَجْسامِ وإمْكانِها وإمْكانِ صِفاتِها طُرُقٌ فاسِدَةٌ؛ فَإِنَّ حُدوثَها مَبْنِيٌّ عَلىٰ امْتِناعِ حَوادِثَ لا أَوَّلَ لَها؛ وإمْكانَها مَبْنِيٌّ عَلىٰ أَنَّ ما قامَتْ بِهِ الصِفاتُ يَمْتَنِعُ أَنْ يَكونَ واجِبًا بِنَفْسِهِ، لِأَنَّهُ مُرَكَّبٌ؛ وإمْكانَ صِفاتِها مَبْنِيٌّ[١٢٠] عَلىٰ تَماثُلِها، فَلا بُدَّ لِتَخْصيصِ بَعْضِها بِالصِفاتِ مِنْ مُخَصِّصٍ. وهَٰذِهِ كُلُّها طُرُقٌ باطِلَةٌ.

The [first, third, and fourth] methods of demonstrating [the Maker's existence that are known as] the Arguments from the Origination of Bodies, the Contingency of Bodies, and the Contingency of their Attributes are [all] false methods [of demonstration]. For the Argument from the Origination of Bodies is predicated on the impossibility of an infinite regress of *ḥawādith* (events).[121] The Argument from the Contingency of Bodies is predicated on the claim that nothing that has attributes can be a necessary existent, because it is composed [from attributes and essence].[122] And the Argument

١٢٠ في المطبوع: «فإن دلالة حدوثها مبنيّة...، ودلالة إمكانها مبنيّة...، ودلالة إمكان صفاتها مبنيّة». والمثبت من الأصل الخطي.

121 Although Ibn Taymiyyah believed that an uncreated Creator must exist for the created world to exist, he also held that it is possible for every creation to be preceded by another creation in an infinite regress of events. By contrast, the Argument from the Origination of Bodies is predicated on the claim that the infinite regress of events is impossible, such that there must have been an absolutely first event that could not have been preceded by another, in turn implying an initial act of ex nihilo creation by God.

122 Proponents of this Argument from the Contingency of Bodies, also known as the Argument from Composition, seek to demonstrate the existence of a simple and Necessary existent by appealing to the multiplicity of attributes in the universe, an attribution which they refer to as a 'composition'. They argue that a thing which has multiple attributes must be composed of

from the Contingency of the Attributes of bodies is predicated on the claim that all [physical] bodies are equivalent and [that they] therefore must have a Specifier[123] who [chooses to] specify some of the bodies with [certain] attributes [while specifying the others with different attributes].[124] These are all false methods [of demonstra-

different components on which it depends. This in turn necessitates that it is dependent on another, for its components are other than it! Thus, anything which has multiple attributes must be contingent! Ibn Taymiyyah criticizes all premises of the argument and rejects the conclusion as counter-scriptural and irrational; God cannot be simple and without attributes, but is necessarily a being who is qualified with all the attributes of maximal perfection [*Sharḥ al-Aṣfahāniyyah*, pp. 62-107]. Note that this Argument from the Contingency of Bodies concludes that *all* bodies must be contingent, and is therefore not to be confused with the sound form of the contingency argument which Ibn Taymiyyah accepts and which leads to the existence of a necessary Creator being who exists above the world in a spatial sense and who is described with perfect attributes [*Sharḥ al-Aṣfahāniyyah*, pp. 303-304].

123 It is possible for physical bodies to have or lack the attributes which are possible to their existence, thus an outside Specifier is needed to determine the existence of these attributes over their nonexistence.

124 Proponents of this argument claim that all physical bodies are equivalent, meaning that all bodies are equal in regards to what is necessary, possible, and impossible for their existence. The attributes that are predicated necessarily of one body are therefore necessarily predicated of all other bodies, and the attributes that are only possibly attributed to one body (i.e. the accidents) are also possible for all other bodies, and so on. In this way, the very fact that some attribute exists in one body when no similar attribute exists in another body would imply the existence of a Specifier who chooses to specify the first body with that particular attribute while not choosing to specify the other body with a similar attribute. Ibn Taymiyyah rejected this argument because he believed that the physical bodies are not equivalent. Some of the attributes that are possible for one body can be impossible or necessary for another body. Physical bodies are not only different in their attributes but are also different

tion].

قال: وأمّا الاسْتِدْلالُ بِحُدوثِ الصِفاتِ، فَهُوَ الاسْتِدْلالُ بِحُدوثِ الأَعْراضِ. وهَذِهِ الطَريقُ أَجْوَدُ ما سَلَكوه مِنَ الطُرُقِ مَعَ أَنَّها قاصِرَةٌ؛ فَإِنَّ مَدارَها عَلىٰ أَنَّهُمْ لَمْ يَعرِفوا حُدوثَ شَيْءٍ مِنَ الأَعْيانِ، وإِنَّما عَلِموا حُدوثَ بَعْضِ الصِفاتِ. وهَذا يَدُلُّ عَلىٰ أَنَّهُ لا بُدَّ لَها مِنْ مُحْدِثٍ.

As for inferring [the Maker's existence] from the Origination of the Attributes [of bodies], it is to infer [His existence] from the origination of the accidents.[125] This argument is the best of their methods [of demonstration] although it is deficient, for it revolves around [the notion] that they do not know of the origination of anything that is concrete, but instead know the origination of some attributes.[126] And this [origination of the attributes] demonstrates that

in their very reality and substance. [*Majmūʿ al-Fatāwā*, Vol 17, pp. 244-246].

125 In the Arabic text of the published edition, the phrase "He said" is stated at the beginning of this sentence. In a footnote in that published edition, the critical editor Dr. ʿAbd al-ʿAzīz b. Ṣāliḥ al-Tuwayyan suggests that this sentence is from the statement of al-Bāqillānī in his non-extant work *Sharḥ al-Lumaʿ*, and that Ibn Taymiyyah was merely quoting him here as he did elsewhere in *Nubuwwat*. However, a closer reading of the context indicates that the sentence is probably from the words of Ibn Taymiyyah himself, not from the statement of al-Bāqillānī. The phrase "He said" may sometimes be added by scribes at specific places in the copied texts to stress that the words that follow were stated by the author (e.g. Ibn Taymiyyah).

126 When giving examples of the origination of attributes, Kalām theologians give the example of a sperm-drop that changes into a human being. Ibn Taymiyyah argued that this is not an origination of an attribute, but is an origination of an entire substance, where one concrete thing is originated out of another that is caused to perish.

they must have an Originator.

قال: وهَذا لا يَنْفي كَوْنَ المُحْدِثِ جِسْمًا، بِخِلافِ تِلْكَ الطُرُقِ.

And this [method of demonstration] does not negate the corporeality[127] of the Originator, unlike the other [three] methods.[128]

وهَذِهِ الطَرِيقُ تَدُلُّ علىٰ أنَّ الأعْراضَ - كَتَرْكيبِ الإنْسانِ - لا بُدَّ لَهُ مِنْ مُرَكِّبٍ، ولا يُنْفَىٰ بِها شَيْءٌ مِنْ قِدَمِ الأجْسامِ والجَواهِرِ، بَلْ يَجُوزُ أنْ يَكونَ جَميعُ جَواهِرِ الإنْسانِ وغَيْرِهِ قَديمَةً أَزَلِيَّةً، لَكِنْ حَدَثَتْ فيها الأعْراضُ. ويَجُوزُ أنْ يَكونَ المُحْدِثُ لِلأعْراضِ بَعْضَ أجْسامِ العالَمِ.

And although the Argument [from the Origination of Attributes] demonstrates that the accidents, such as the arrangement of a man, must have an **arranging cause**; it does not [on its own] disprove [the claim] that the [physical] bodies and substances [in the natural world] were existing eternally. Rather, [when limiting ourselves to this method of demonstration,] it will be permissible for all of the substances of the human beings and other [creations] to exist [eternally] without beginning or end, such that only the accidents would be originated therein.[129] [Also,] it will be permissible for the Origi-

127 Although Ibn Taymiyyah did not use the term 'body' in reference to God, and maintained that it is impermissible and an innovation to use this term when describing God, he still believed that God is spatially located above all things, has a tremendous spatial extent which is known only to Him, and will be seen by the believers above them when they enter Paradise. He also stressed that God is unequalled by anything in the creation.

128 The phrase "He said" is stated at the beginning of this sentence too.

129 Solely depending on the Argument from the Origination of Attributes

nator of the accidents to be one of the bodies of the [natural] world.

فَهَذِهِ الطَرِيقُ لا تَنْفِي أَنْ يَكونَ الرَبُّ بَعْضَ أَجْسامِ العالَمِ. وتِلْكَ باطِلَةٌ، مَعَ أَنَّ مَضْمونَها أَنَّ الرَبَّ لا يَتَّصِفُ بِشَيْءٍ مِنْ الصِفاتِ، فَهِيَ لا تَدُلُّ عَلىٰ صانِعٍ، وإنْ دَلَّتْ عَلىٰ صانِعٍ، فَلَيْسَ بِمَوْجودٍ، بَلْ مَعْدومٌ، أو مُتَّصِفٌ بالوُجودِ والعَدَمِ؛ كَما قَدْ بُسِطَ في غَيْرِ مَوْضِعٍ.

Thus, this argument does not disprove [the notion] of a Lord who is [merely] one of the bodies of the [natural] world[130], while the other

---

when demonstrating God's existence can give room for the false belief that the substance of this world exists co-eternally with God, which would in turn contradict Abrahamic monotheism. It may appear from such criticisms by Ibn Taymiyyah that he was against theological demonstrations that use the continuous origination of accidents and arrangements in the natural world as an evidence for the Originator. However, it should be noted that Ibn Taymiyyah actually believed that substances which have created attributes must also be originated by God. The very fact that the accidents and motions subsisting in some entity are caused by external causes is evidence for the originated nature of that entity. Even though Ibn Taymiyyah criticizes the claim that "every substrate of *ḥawādith* is originated", he nevertheless argued elsewhere that "every substrate of *ḥawādith* that are caused by another is originated". Only God's activity does not entail that the Subject of its attribution is originated, for His activity alone is not caused by an external agent. *[Majmūʿ al-Fatāwā*, Vol 6, pp. 330-332].

130 This explains why atheists find it easier to believe that life on earth was designed by extraterrestrial aliens than accept that it was created by a God who is unequalled by the creation. Atheists today describe the changes in the created world as rearrangements of already existing matter and are unable to perceive the origination of substances, which causes them to reject any divine explanation from beyond the world.

[three] arguments are false and [additionally] entail that the Lord is not described with any attributes.[131] These [three] do not [even] demonstrate [the existence of] a Maker, and even if they did demonstrate a Maker, they would demonstrate a Maker who is either without existence or described as both existent and nonexistent, as it has been clarified in detail elsewhere.

ولِهَذا يَقولُ الرازِيُّ في آخِرِ مُصَنَّفاتِهِ: «لَقَدْ تَأَمَّلْتُ الطُرُقَ الكَلامِيَّةَ، والمَناهِجَ الفَلْسَفِيَّةَ، فَما رَأَيْتُها تَشْفِي عَليلًا، ولا تَرْوِي غَليلًا، ورَأَيْتُ أَقْرَبَ الطُرُقِ طَريقَةَ القُرْآنِ؛ اقْرَأْ في الإِثْباتِ: ﴿إِلَيْهِ يَصْعَدُ ٱلْكَلِمُ ٱلطَّيِّبُ﴾ [فاطر: ١٠]، ﴿ٱلرَّحْمَٰنُ عَلَى ٱلْعَرْشِ ٱسْتَوَىٰ﴾ [طه: ٥]، واقْرَأْ في النَّفْيِ: ﴿لَيْسَ كَمِثْلِهِۦ شَيْءٌ﴾ [الشورى: ١١]، ﴿وَلَا يُحِيطُونَ بِهِۦ عِلْمًا﴾ [طه: ١١٠]». قالَ: «ومَنْ جَرَّبَ مِثْلَ تَجْرِبَتي عَرَفَ مِثْلَ مَعْرِفَتي». ولَمّا ذَكَرَ الرازِيُّ الاسْتِدْلالَ بِحُدوثِ الصِفاتِ؛ كالحَيَوانِ، والنَباتِ، والمَطَرِ، ذَكَرَ أَنَّ هَذِهِ طَريقَةُ القُرْآنِ.

For this reason, al-Rāzī admitted in the last of his works: "I have contemplated the methods of Kalām and the schools of philosophy, but I did not find them to heal the ill or satiate the parched, and I found that the best methods are the methods of the Qur'ān: Read in the affirmation [of God's attributes]: **{Unto Him good words ascend}**, **{The Most Merciful ascended the Throne}**. And read in negation: **{There is nothing equal unto Him}**, **{and they cannot**

131 The first, third and fourth arguments of Fakhr al-Dīn al-Rāzī lead to a motionless Originator, a simple Maker, and an incorporeal Specifier respectively. All three conclusions are self-refuting.

encompass Him in knowledge}." And he continued: "Whoever tries as I have tried will come to realize as I have come to realize." And when al-Rāzī mentioned the Argument from the Origination of Attributes, such as the origination of animals, plants, and rain, he admitted that it is the method of the Qur'ān.

The Qur'ān Points to Substantial Origination

ولا رَيْبَ أنَّ القُرْآنَ يُذْكَرُ فيهِ الاسْتِدْلالُ بآياتِ اللهِ؛ كَقَوْلِهِ: ﴿إِنَّ فِي خَلْقِ ٱلسَّمَٰوَٰتِ وَٱلْأَرْضِ وَٱخْتِلَٰفِ ٱلَّيْلِ وَٱلنَّهَارِ وَٱلْفُلْكِ ٱلَّتِي تَجْرِى فِي ٱلْبَحْرِ بِمَا يَنفَعُ ٱلنَّاسَ وَمَآ أَنزَلَ ٱللَّهُ مِنَ ٱلسَّمَآءِ مِن مَّآءٍ فَأَحْيَا بِهِ ٱلْأَرْضَ بَعْدَ مَوْتِهَا وَبَثَّ فِيهَا مِن كُلِّ دَآبَّةٍ وَتَصْرِيفِ ٱلرِّيَٰحِ وَٱلسَّحَابِ ٱلْمُسَخَّرِ بَيْنَ ٱلسَّمَآءِ وَٱلْأَرْضِ لَءَايَٰتٍ لِّقَوْمٍ يَعْقِلُونَ ﴿١٦٤﴾﴾. وهَذا مَذْكورٌ بَعْدَ قَوْلِهِ: ﴿وَإِلَٰهُكُمْ إِلَٰهٌ وَٰحِدٌ ۖ لَّآ إِلَٰهَ إِلَّا هُوَ ٱلرَّحْمَٰنُ ٱلرَّحِيمُ ﴿١٦٣﴾﴾، وقَبْلَ قَوْلِهِ: ﴿وَمِنَ ٱلنَّاسِ مَن يَتَّخِذُ مِن دُونِ ٱللَّهِ أَندَادًا يُحِبُّونَهُمْ كَحُبِّ ٱللَّهِ ۖ﴾ [البقرة: ١٦٣-١٦٥].

And it is without doubt that the Qur'ān mentions demonstrations that use God's signs [as evidence], such as when God says: **{Indeed, in the creation of the heavens and the earth, and the alternation of the night and the day, and the great ships which sail through the sea with that which benefits people, and the water which God sends down from the sky, thereby reviving the earth after its death, and dispersing therein all kinds of moving creatures, and His directing of the winds and the clouds controlled between heaven and earth are signs for people who reason.}** This verse is mentioned after God's words: **{And your god is one God. There is no deity worthy of worship except Him, the Entirely Merciful, the Especially Merciful}**, and before His words: **{And yet, among the people are those who take**

other than God as equals, loving them as they love God.}

لَكِنَّ القُرْآنَ لَمْ يَذْكُرْ أنَّ هَذِهِ صِفاتٌ حادِثَةٌ، وأنَّهُ لَيْسَ فيها إحْداثُ عَيْنٍ قائِمَةٍ بِنَفْسِها، بَلِ القُرْآنُ يُبَيِّنُ أنَّ في خَلْقِ الأعْيانِ القائِمَةِ بِنَفْسِها آياتٍ، ويَذْكُرُ الآياتِ في خَلْقِ الأعْيانِ والأعْراضِ؛

But the Qur'ān does not mention that these [signs] are [merely] originated attributes and do not include any self-subsisting concrete things. Rather, the Qur'ān clarifies that there are signs in the creation of the self-subsisting concrete things. It mentions the signs in [both] the creation of concrete things and [the creation of] accidents.

كَقَوْلِهِ: ﴿إِنَّ فِى خَلْقِ ٱلسَّمَٰوَٰتِ وَٱلْأَرْضِ وَٱخْتِلَٰفِ ٱلَّيْلِ وَٱلنَّهَارِ وَٱلْفُلْكِ ٱلَّتِى تَجْرِى فِى ٱلْبَحْرِ بِمَا يَنفَعُ ٱلنَّاسَ﴾، وهِيَ أعْيانٌ. ثُمَّ قالَ: ﴿وَمَآ أَنزَلَ ٱللَّهُ مِنَ ٱلسَّمَآءِ مِن مَّآءٍ﴾، والماءُ عَيْنٌ قائِمَةٌ بِنَفْسِها. وقَوْلُهُ: ﴿فَأَحْيَا بِهِ ٱلْأَرْضَ بَعْدَ مَوْتِهَا﴾؛ هُوَ ما يَخْلُقُهُ فيها مِنَ النَباتِ، وهُوَ أعْيانٌ. وكَذَلِكَ قَوْلُهُ: ﴿وَبَثَّ فِيهَا مِن كُلِّ دَآبَّةٍ﴾،

For example, God says: **{Indeed, in the creation of the heavens and the earth, and the alternation of the night and the day, and the great ships which sail through the sea with that which benefits people}**. These are concrete things. He then says: **{and the water which God sends down from the sky}**. Water is a self-subsisting concrete thing. He [then] says: **{thereby reviving the earth after its death}**. This [refers to] the plants that are created by God on the earth, which are concrete things. Likewise, He says: **{and dis-**

persing therein all kinds of moving creatures}.

وقَوْلِهِ: ﴿وَتَصۡرِيفِ ٱلرِّيَٰحِ﴾؛ فالرِياحُ أعْيانٌ، وتَصْريفُها أعْراضٌ. وقَوْلِهِ: ﴿وَٱلسَّحَابِ ٱلۡمُسَخَّرِ بَيۡنَ ٱلسَّمَآءِ وَٱلۡأَرۡضِ﴾، والسَحابُ أعْيانٌ. ﴿لَأٓيَٰتٖ لِّقَوۡمٖ يَعۡقِلُونَ﴾.

He [then] says: **{and His directing of the winds}**. The winds are concrete things, but their directed [motions] are accidents. [Lastly,] He says: **{and the clouds controlled between heaven and earth}**. Clouds are concrete things. [All of those] **{are signs for people who reason}**.

The View of Creation in Kalām and Philosophy

وَقَدْ تَقَدَّمَ أَنَّ أَصْلَ الاشْتِبَاهِ في هَذا أَنَّ خَلْقَ الشَّيْءِ مِنْ مادَّةٍ، هَلْ هُوَ خَلْقُ عَيْنٍ، أَمْ إِحْداثُ اجْتِماعٍ وافْتِراقٍ^{١٣٢} وأَعْراضٍ فَقَطْ؟ والنّاسُ مُخْتَلِفُونَ في هَذا عَلىٰ ثَلاثَةِ أَقْوالٍ:

[Now,] it has been mentioned previously that the confusion in this [matter] stems from [the question]: Does the creation of things out of matter involve the origination of concrete objects, or is it only the origination of accidents [such as the] separation and combination [of atoms]? People diverge into three groups [when answering this question].

فالقائِلونَ بالجَوْهَرِ الفَرْدِ^{١٣٣} مِنْ أَهْلِ الكَلامِ – القائِلونَ بأَنَّ الأَجْسامَ مُرَكَّبَةٌ مِنَ الجَواهِرِ الصِّغارِ الّتي قَدْ بَلَغَتْ مِنَ الصِّغَرِ إِلىٰ حَدٍّ لا يَتَمَيَّزُ مِنْها جانِبٌ عَنْ جانِبٍ – يَقولونَ: تِلْكَ الجَواهِرُ باقِيَةٌ تَنَقَّلَتْ في الحَوادِثِ، ولكِنْ تَعْتَقِبُ عَلَيْها الأَعْراضُ الحادِثَةُ.

[The first group is] the Kalām theologians who believe in the existence of the indivisible atom, those who claim that physical bodies are composed of atoms that are extremely tiny to the point that they

---

١٣٢ في الأصل الخطي: «اجتماع افتراق»

١٣٣ في المطبوع: «بالجواهر المفردة». والمثبت من الأصل الخطي.

[are dimensionless and] have no sides that are distinct from one another. [This group] claims that these [indivisible] atoms continue to exist [and are unchangeable,] moving around from one creation to another, and that only accidents originate in them successively.

وَالاسْتِدْلالُ بِالأَعْراضِ عَلىٰ حُدوثِ مايَلْزَمُهُ مِنَ الجَواهِرِ، ثُمَّ الاسْتِدْلالُ بِذَلِكَ عَلىٰ المُحْدِثِ، غَيْرُ الاسْتِدْلالِ بِحُدوثِ هَذِهِ الأَعْراضِ عَلىٰ المُحْدِثِ لَها؛ فَتِلْكَ هِيَ طَريقَةُ الجَهْمِيَّةِ المَشْهورَةُ، وهِيَ الَّتي سَلَكَها الأَشْعَرِيُّ في كُتُبِهِ كُلِّها مُتابَعَةً لِلْمُعْتَزِلَةِ، ولِهَذا قيلَ: الأَشْعَرِيَّةُ مَخانيثُ المُعْتَزِلَةِ.

Note that [the method of demonstration that] infers the origination of the substances from the [alleged origination of the genus of] accidents necessarily found in those substances, and then infers the existence of the Originator therefrom, is [a method that is very] different to [the method of] inferring the Originator's existence directly from the origination of these accidents. The [first] is the famous method [of demonstration] that is used by the Jahmiyyah, and it is the same Argument [from the Origination of Bodies] which [Abū al-Ḥasan] al-Ashʿarī uses in his books and adopts from the Muʿtazilah. For this reason, it was said that "the Ashʿarīyya are effeminate Muʿtazilah".[134]

وَأَمّا الاسْتِدْلالُ بِالحَوادِثِ عَلىٰ المُحْدِثِ، فَهِيَ الطَّريقَةُ المَعْروفَةُ لِكُلِّ أَحَدٍ، لَكِنْ تَسْمِيَةُ هَذِهِ أَعْراضًا هُوَ تَسْمِيَةُ القائِلينَ بِالجَوْهَرِ الفَرْدِ، مَعَ أَنَّ

---

134 I.e. they are merely a weaker form of Muʿtazilah, sharing most of their creedal notions.

الرَّازِيَّ تَوَقَّفَ فِي آخِرِ أَمْرِهِ فِيهِ؛ كَما ذَكَرَ ذَلِكَ فِي «نِهايَةِ العُقول». وَذَكَرَ أَيْضًا عَنْ أَبِي الحُسَيْنِ البَصْرِيِّ، وَأَبِي المَعالِي أَنَّهُما تَوَقَّفا فِيهِ.

As for the [direct method of] inferring the existence of the Originator from [the origination of] the creations [themselves], it is the [sound] method [of demonstration] that is known to all people. But to describe these [creations] as 'accidents' is [in accordance with] the descriptions of [theological] groups that believe in the existence of indivisible atoms – although al-Rāzī [himself] became undecided about the existence of these [atoms] in his last stage, as he mentions [about himself] in *Nihāyat al-ʿUqūl*. He also mentions that Abu al-Ḥusayn al-Baṣrī[135] and Abu al-Maʿālī al-Juwayni became agnostic towards their existence [in the end].

وَالمَقْصُودُ: أَنَّ القائِلِينَ بِالجَوْهَرِ الفَرْدِ يَقولونَ: إِنَّما أَحْدَثَ أَعْراضًا لِجَمْعِ الجَواهِرِ وَتَفْرِيقِها. فَالمادَّةُ الَّتِي هِيَ الجَواهِرُ المُنْفَرِدَةُ باقِيَةٌ عِنْدَهُمْ بِأَعْيانِها، وَلَكِنْ أَحْدَثَ صُوَرًا هِيَ أَعْراضٌ قائِمَةٌ بِهَذِهِ الجَواهِرِ.

[Either way,] our intent here is to clarify that those [Kalām theologians] who believe in the existence of indivisible atoms claim that God only originates accidents by combining the atoms and taking them apart. Thus, the matter which is the very indivisible atoms continues to exist in their opinion; God [only] originates new forms that subsist in these [unchanging] substances.

وَأَمَّا المُتَفَلْسِفَةُ فَيَقولونَ: أَحْدَثَ صُوَرًا فِي مَوادَّ باقِيَةٍ كَما يَقولُ هَؤُلاءِ،

---

135 Abu al-Ḥusayn al-Baṣrī (d. 436H) was one of the leading scholars of the Muʿtazilah.

لَكِنْ يَقولونَ: أَحْدَثَ صُوَرًا هِيَ جَواهِرُ في مادَّةٍ هِيَ جَوْهَرٌ، وعِنْدَهُمْ ثَمَّ مادَّةٌ باقِيَةٌ بِعَيْنِها، والصُوَرُ الجَوْهَرِيَّةُ كَصورَةِ الماءِ، والهَواءِ، والتُرابِ، والمُوَلَّداتِ تَعْتَقِبُ عَلَيْها. وهَذِهِ المادَّةُ - عِنْدَهُمْ - جَوْهَرٌ عَقْلِيٌّ، وكَذَلِكَ الصورَةُ المُجَرَّدَةُ جَوْهَرٌ عَقْلِيٌّ، ولَكِنَّ الجِسْمَ مُرَكَّبٌ مِنَ المادَّةِ والصورَةِ.

As for [the second group,] the [Aristotelian] Philosophers, they equally claim that God originates forms in an [unchanging] matter that continues to exist, but [they differ in that] they claim that the Maker originates forms that are **substantial**[136] in a matter that is a substance. According to them, the very matter continues to exist, while the substantial forms – such as the forms of water, air, earth, [fire,] and the generated forms – originate successively in the matter. This matter is according to them an intelligible substance just as the abstract form is also an intelligible substance, and the physical bodies are **composed** of [these two substances that are] the matter and the form.

ولِهَذا قَسَّموا المَوْجُوداتِ، فَقالوا: إمّا أنْ يَكونَ المَوْجودُ حالًا بِغَيْرِهِ[١٣٧]، أو مَحَلًّا، أو[١٣٨] مُرَكَّبًا مِنَ الحالِّ والمَحَلِّ، أو لا هَذا ولا هَذا. فالحالُّ في غَيْرِهِ هُوَ الصورَةُ، والمَحَلُّ هُوَ المادَّةُ، والمُرَكَّبُ مِنْهُما هُوَ الجِسْمُ، وما

136 As its name implies, the *substantial* form is a substance. Ibn Taymiyyah rejected the claim that forms can be substantial as he believed that the form of a thing is necessarily an attribute.

١٣٧ في الأصل الخطي: «لغيره»، خطأ.
١٣٨ «أو» ليست في الأصل الخطي.

لَيْسَ كَذَلِكَ إِنْ كانَ مُتَعَلِّقًا بِالجِسْمِ فَهُوَ النَّفْسُ، وإلا فَهُوَ العَقْلُ. وهَذا التَّقْسيمُ فيهِ خَطَأٌ كَثيرٌ مِنْ وُجوهٍ، لَيْسَ هَذا مَوْضِعَها؛ إِذِ المَقْصودُ أَنَّهُمْ يَقولونَ أَيْضًا: إِنَّهُ لَمْ يُحْدِثْ جِسْمًا قائِمًا بِنَفْسِهِ، بَلْ إِنَّما أَحْدَثَ صورَةً في مادَّةٍ باقِيَةٍ.

For this reason, they categorize existents by saying: "An existent is either (i) subsisting in another, (ii) a substrate, (iii) a compound of both the substrate and what subsists, or (iv) none of the above." [They explain that] the existent which subsists in another is the **form**, the substrate is the **matter**, and the existent which is composed of both is the **physical body**. Anything else is [either] a **soul**[139] if it is associated with the physical body, or an **intellect** if it is not [associated with it]. This classification contains many errors from various aspects[140], but the explanation of this is not for this place. For our purpose [here] is only to clarify that these Philosophers equally say that the Maker does not originate self-subsisting bodies, and that He only originates forms in a matter which continues to exist.

ولا رَيْبَ أَنَّ الأَجْسامَ بَيْنَها قَدْرٌ مُشْتَرَكٌ في الطُّولِ والعَرْضِ والعُمْقِ،

---

139 Although Ibn Taymiyyah believed that the human soul is radically different to the human body, he argued that souls are concrete and spatially located existents which have attributes and can be physically seen. The human being is the totality of the two separable entities that are the human body and the human soul.

140 Ibn Taymiyyah argued that all ontological existents divide into self-subsisting concrete things and attributes that subsist in these concrete things. Nothing exists in reality beyond these two categories [*Majmūʿ al-Fatāwā*, Vol 2, p 495].

وهُوَ المِقْدارُ المُجَرَّدُ الّذي لا يَخْتَصُّ بِجِسْمٍ بِعَيْنِهِ. ولَكِنَّ هذا المِقْدارَ المُجَرَّدَ هُوَ في الذِهْنِ، لا في الخارِجِ؛ كالعَدَدِ المُجَرَّدِ، والسَطْحِ المُجَرَّدِ، والنُقْطَةِ المُجَرَّدَةِ، وكالجِسْمِ التَعْليمِيِّ؛ وهُوَ الطَويلُ العَريضُ العَميقُ الّذي لا يَخْتَصُّ بِمادَّةٍ بِعَيْنِها. فَهَذِهِ المادَّةُ المُشْتَرَكَةُ الّتي أَثْبَتوها هِيَ في الذِهْنِ، ولَيْسَ بَيْنَ الجِسْمَيْنِ في الخارِجِ شَيْءٌ اشْتَرَكا فيهِ بِعَيْنِهِ، فَهَؤُلاءِ جَعَلوا الأَجْسامَ مُشْتَرِكَةً في جَوْهَرٍ عَقْلِيٍّ، وأُولَئِكَ جَعَلوها مُشْتَرِكَةً في الجَواهِرِ الحِسِّيَّةِ.

Now, it is without doubt that physical bodies have in common a measure of length, width, and depth, and [that] this is an abstract measurement that is not specific to any [one] physical body in particular. But this abstract measure exists only **in the mind**, not outside [in the external world]. [This is] similar to the abstract number, the abstract geometric surface or point, and the [three-dimensional] mathematical body [made up] of height, width and depth [which is] not specific to any [one] material [thing] in particular. In the same way, this [abstract] matter that is shared [by all physical bodies] and which is claimed by the Philosophers to exist [ontologically] exists only in the mind. There is no particular thing in the external world which two [distinct] bodies share [ontologically]. Thus, these [Philosophers] have [incorrectly] claimed that physical bodies share in an **intelligible substance** [i.e. the matter], whereas those [former Kalām theologians] have claimed that the physical bodies share in **empirical substances** [i.e. the indivisible atoms].

وهَؤُلاءِ قالوا: إذا خَلَقَ كُلَّ شَيْءٍ مِنْ شَيْءٍ، فَإِنَّما أُحْدِثَتْ صورَةٌ، مَعَ أَنَّ

المادَّةَ باقِيَةٌ بِعَيْنِها، لَكِنْ أُفْسِدَتْ صورَةٌ وكُوِّنَتْ صورَةٌ. ولِهَذا يَقولونَ عَنْ ما تَحْتَ الفَلَكِ: عالَمُ الكَوْنِ والفَسادِ. ولِهَذا قالَ ابْنُ رُشْدٍ: «إنَّ الأجْسامَ المُرَكَّبَةَ مِنَ المادَّةِ والصورَةِ هِيَ في عالَمِ الكَوْنِ والفَسادِ، بِخِلافِ الفَلَكِ؛ فَإنَّهُ لَيْسَ مُرَكَّبًا مِنْ مادَّةٍ وصورَةٍ عِنْدَ الفَلاسِفَةِ». قال: «وإنَّما ذَكَرَ أنَّهُ مُرَكَّبٌ مِنْ هَذا وهَذا: ابْنُ سينا».

And these Philosophers claim that only a form originates when things are created out of others. The very matter continues to exist, but one form is destroyed and another is generated. For this reason, they refer to the sub-lunar[141] world as 'the world of generation and destruction'. This is why Ibn Rushd (Averroes)[142] said: "The physical bodies that are composed of matter and form are only those which exist in the world of generation and destruction, unlike the celestial spheres [i.e. the moon and what lies beyond], for those [heavenly bodies] are not composed of matter and form according to the [Aristotelean] Philosophers, [but are unchangeable]." And he continued: "The one who [first] claimed that [the celestial spheres] are composed of matter and form was Avicenna."

وهَؤُلاءِ، وهَؤُلاءِ تَحَيَّروا في خَلْقِ الشَّيْءِ مِنْ مادَّةٍ؛ كَخَلْقِ الإنْسانِ مِنَ

141 Aristotelean philosophers believe that the generation of the forms in the matter occurs only in the terrestrial sphere that lies below the moon. As for the moon and everything above it, they believe that it is an eternal and unchanging material called the aether.

142 Ibn Rushd (d. 595H) was a famous Aristotelean philosopher from Muslim Spain who authored books in Islamic jurisprudence, philosophy, and medicine.

النُّطْفَةِ، والحَبِّ مِنَ الحَبِّ، والشَّجَرَةِ مِنَ النَّواةِ، وظَنّوا أَنَّ هَذا لا يَكونُ إلا مَعَ بَقاءِ أَصْلِ تِلْكَ المادَّةِ؛ إِمّا الجَواهِرِ عِنْدَ قَوْمٍ، وإِمّا المادَّةِ المُشْتَرَكَةِ عِنْدَ قَوْمٍ.

And both parties [the Kalām theologians and the Philosophers] were puzzled by the creation of things out of matter, such as the creation of a man out of a sperm-drop, grain out of grain, and trees out of seeds. They thought that this cannot be the case unless the **basis** of that matter continues to exist, whether it is the indivisible atoms according to one group or the shared [abstract] matter according to the other group.

وهُمْ في الحَقيقَةِ يُنْكِرونَ أَنْ يَخْلُقَ اللهُ شَيْئًا مِنْ شَيْءٍ؛ فَإِنَّهُ عِنْدَهُمْ لَمْ يُحْدِثْ إلا الصّورَةَ الَّتي هِيَ عَرَضٌ عِنْدَ قَوْمٍ، أَوْ جَوْهَرٌ عَقْلِيٌّ عِنْدَ قَوْمٍ. وكِلاهُما لَمْ يُخْلَقْ مِنْ مادَّةٍ، والمادَّةُ عِنْدَهُمْ باقِيَةٌ بِعَيْنِها، لَمْ تُخْلَقْ ولَمْ يُخْلَقْ مِنْها شَيْءٌ¹⁴³.

[But] in actual fact, both [parties] deny that God creates one thing **out of another**. For they claim that He originates only **forms** which are either accidents according to one group or intelligible substances [i.e. substantial forms] according to the other group. [But] neither [the accidents nor the substantial forms] are created out of matter. The matter according to them continues to exist; it was neither [newly] created [i.e. in this new creation] nor anything was created out of it.

---

١٤٣ في المطبوع: «لم يخلق ولن يخلق منها شيء». والمثبت من الأصل الخطي.

وقَدْ ذَكَروا في قَوْلِهِ: ﴿أَمْ خُلِقُواْ مِنْ غَيْرِ شَيْءٍ﴾ [الطور: ٣٥] ثَلاثَةَ أُمورٍ: قالَ ابْنُ عَبّاسٍ والأَكْثَرونَ: أَمْ خُلِقوا مِنْ غَيْرِ خالِقٍ، وهُوَ الّذي ذَكَرَهُ الخَطّابِيُّ. وقالَ الزَجّاجُ وابْنُ كَيْسانَ: «أَمْ خُلِقوا عَبَثًا وسُدىً، فَلا يُبْعَثونَ، ولا يُحاسَبونَ، ولا يُؤْمَرونَ، ولا يُنهَوْنَ؛ كَما يُقالُ[١٤٤]: فَعَلْتُ هَذا مِنْ غَيْرِ شَيْءٍ؛ أيْ: لِغَيْرِ عِلَّةٍ». وقِيلَ: أَمْ خُلِقوا مِنْ غَيْرِ مادَّةٍ؛ أيْ: مِنْ غَيْرِ أَبٍ وأُمٍّ. ثُمَّ مِنْ هَؤُلاءِ مَنْ قالَ: فَهُمْ كالجَمادِ. ومِنْهُمْ مَنْ قالَ: كالسَمَاواتِ؛ ظَنًّا مِنْهُ أَنَّها خُلِقَتْ مِنْ غَيْرِ مادَّةٍ. ذَكَرَ الأَرْبَعَةَ أبو الفَرَجِ. وذَكَرَ البَغَوِيُّ الوَجْهَيْنِ الأَوَّلَيْنِ.

And [Muslim scholars] have mentioned three [interpretations] for the verse in which God says: **{Were they created from nothing?}** (i) Ibn ʿAbbās and most [of the scholars] explained that it means: "Where they created **without a Creator**?"[145] This [first] interpretation is the one mentioned by al-Khaṭṭābī.[146] (ii) Al-Zajjāj and Ibn Kaysān understood it as: "Were they created aimlessly and **without purpose**, i.e. without ever being resurrected [on the Last Day] and judged, and without being commanded [in this life] what to do and what not to do?" [For the Arabs] say: "I did this *from* nothing", with the intention of saying: "I did it without any [final] cause". (iii) Some understood it as: "Were they created **without [prior] matter**?", i.e. "without a father and a mother?" Some added "and

١٤٤ في المطبوع: «يقولون»، وفي الأصل الخطي: «يقول»، ولعلّ الصواب ما أثبت.

145 Ibn Taymiyyah mentions elsewhere that this first interpretation is the correct one.

146 Abu Sulaymān Ḥamad ibn Muḥammad al-Khaṭṭabī (d. 388H) was a Shafiʿī scholar of ḥadīth and jurisprudence.

are thus like inanimate objects?", while (iv) others added "like the heavens?", for they assumed that the heavens were created without prior matter. Abu al-Faraj[147] mentioned all four [interpretations], and al-Baghawī[148] mentioned the first two.

والّذي ذكَرْناهُ مِنْ قَوْلِ أُولَئِكَ المُتَكَلِّمِينَ والفَلاسِفَةِ مَعْنىً آخَرُ؛ وهُوَ أنَّ مَنْ قالَ: المادَّةُ باقِيَةٌ بعَيْنِها، وإنَّما حَدَثَ عَرَضٌ، أو صورَةٌ، وذَلِكَ لَمْ يُخْلَقْ مِنْ غَيْرِهِ، ولَكِنْ أُحْدِثَ في المادَّةِ الباقِيَةِ، فَلا يَكونُ اللهُ خَلَقَ شَيْئًا مِنْ شَيْءٍ؛ لِأنَّ المادَّةَ عِنْدَهُمْ لَمْ تُخْلَقْ.

But the meaning [of creation] which we have [here] ascribed to those Kalām theologians and Philosophers is a [totally] different meaning. It is that they claim [that] the very matter [in the natural world] continues to exist and [that] only an accident or a form originates. Those [accidents and forms] are not created out of another but are originated in [this] matter that continues to exist. Thus, God would not be creating anything out of another [in their opinion], for the matter according to them is not created.

أمّا المُتَفَلْسِفَةُ: فَعِنْدَهُمُ المادَّةُ قَديمَةٌ أَزَلِيَّةٌ باقِيَةٌ بِعَيْنِها.

As for the Philosophers, [it is because] they believe that the very mat-

147 He is the well-known Ḥanbalī scholar Ibn al-Jawzī (d. 597H). He was a skilled orator and preacher who wrote books on Qur'anic interpretation, ḥadīth, history, and preaching. His work being cited by Ibn Taymiyyah is *Zād al-Masīr* in which he compiles all the various different exegetic statements said in each and every verse or set of verses.

148 A Shāfi'ī scholar of Qur'anic interpretation (d. 516H). His tafsir *Ma'ālim al-Tanzīl* is well-known.

ter is eternal, without beginning, and will continue to exist [forever].

وَأمّا الْمُتَكَلِّمونَ: فَالجَواهِرُ عِنْدَهُمْ مَوْجودَةٌ، ما زالَتْ مَوْجودَةً. لَكِنْ مَنْ قالَ إِنَّها حادِثَةٌ مِنْ أَهْلِ الْمِلَلِ وغَيْرِهِمْ قالوا: يُسْتَدَلُّ عَلَىٰ حُدوثِها بِالدَّليلِ، لا أَنَّ خَلْقَها مَعْلومٌ لِلناسِ؛ فَهُوَ عِنْدَهُمْ مِمّا يُسْتَدَلُّ عَلَيْهِ بِالأَدِلَّةِ الدَّقيقَةِ الخَفِيَّةِ، مَعَ أَنَّ ما يَذْكُرونَهُ مُنْتَهاهُ إِلَىٰ أَنَّ ما لا يَخْلو عَنِ الحَوادِثِ فَهُوَ حادِثٌ. وهُوَ دَليلٌ باطِلٌ. فَلا دَليلَ عِنْدَهُمْ عَلَىٰ حُدوثِها.

As for the Kalām theologians, [it is because] they believe that the [indivisible] atoms continue to exist [throughout the processes of creation] and [that they] are always existing. Nevertheless, those [among them who are] from religious groups and others who believe that these atoms were originated [in the distant past] claim that their origination can be known through [rational] arguments, not that it is self-evident to all people. Thus, it is from those things that are demonstrated through sophisticated arguments in their opinion. But the furthest they [are able to] argue is that **every substrate that was never void of *ḥawādith* (events and change) is originated**, which is a false argument. Thus, they have no [dependable] evidence for [the claim] that the [indivisible atoms] were originated [in the past].

وإِذا كانَتْ لَمْ تُخْلَقْ إِذْ خُلِقَ الإِنْسانُ، بَلْ هِيَ باقِيَةٌ في الإِنْسانِ، والأَعْراضُ الحادِثَةُ لَمْ تُخْلَقْ مِنْ مادَّةٍ، فَإِذا خُلِقَ الإِنْسانُ لَمْ يُخْلَقْ مِنْ شَيْءٍ؛ لا جَواهِرُهُ، ولا أَعْراضُهُ. وعَلَىٰ قَوْلِهِمْ ما جَعَلَ اللهُ مِنَ الماءِ كُلَّ شَيْءٍ حَيٍّ،

ولا خَلَقَ كُلَّ دابَّةٍ مِنْ ماءٍ، ولا خَلَقَ آدَمَ مِنْ تُرابٍ، ولا ذُرِّيَّتَهُ مِنْ نُطْفَةٍ، بَلْ نَفْسُ الجَواهِرِ التُرابِيَّةِ باقِيَةٌ بِعَيْنِها لَمْ تُخْلَقْ حينَئِذٍ، ولَكِنْ أُحْدِثَ فيها أعْراضٌ، أو صورَةٌ حادِثَةٌ، وتِلْكَ الأعْراضُ لَيْسَتْ مِنَ التُرابِ. فَلَمّا خُلِقَ آدَمُ، لَمْ يُخْلَقْ شَيْءٌ مِنْ تُرابٍ.

Now, if these [atoms] are not created when man is created but instead continue to exist in the man, and [if the] originated accidents are [additionally] not created out of matter, then man will not be created out of anything when he is created, neither his substances nor his accidents. [Thus,] according to the opinions [of the Kalām theologians and the Philosophers], God neither makes **{every living thing out of water}**, nor creates **{every animal out of water}**, nor created Adam **{out of dust}**, nor [created] his children **{out of a sperm-drop}**. Rather, [both parties believe that] the very substances in the dust continue to exist and are not created in the process [of man's creation]. Either accidents are caused to exist therein, or an originated form. [But] these accidents are not [originated] out of dust. It so follows that nothing was created out of dust when Adam was created!

وكَذَلِكَ النُّطْفَةُ جَواهِرُها باقِيَةٌ؛ إمّا الجَواهِرُ المُنْفَرِدَةُ، وإمّا المادَّةُ. والحادِثُ هُوَ عَرَضٌ، أو صورَةٌ في مادَّةٍ، ولا هَذا ولا هَذا خُلِقَ مِنْ نُطْفَةٍ.

Likewise, [both parties believe that] the substances in the sperm-drop continue to exist, whether they are indivisible atoms [according to one group] or [substantial] matter [according to the other group]. The originated thing is [only] the accident or the substantial form [that subsists] in the matter. [But] neither is created out of a sperm-drop!

وَلَيْسَ قَوْلُهُمْ: إِنَّهُ لَمْ يُخْلَقْ مِنْ مَادَّةٍ، مَعْنَاهُ أَنَّ الخَالِقَ أَبْدَعَهُ لا مِنْ شَيْءٍ،

وَأَنَّهُمْ قَصَدُوا بِهَا تَعْظِيمَ الخَالِقِ، بَلِ الإِنْسَانُ لا رَيْبَ أَنَّهُ جَوْهَرٌ قَائِمٌ

بِنَفْسِهِ، وَعِنْدَهُمْ ذَلِكَ القَائِمُ بِنَفْسِهِ مَا زَالَ مَوْجُودًا، لَمْ يُخْلَقْ إِذْ خُلِقَ

الإِنْسَانُ. وَالجَوْهَرُ الحَامِلُ لِصُورَتِهِ مَا زَالَ مَوْجُودًا أَيْضًا؛ فَلَمْ يُخْلَقْ

عِنْدَ هَؤُلاءِ إِلا عَرَضٌ¹⁴⁹، وَعِنْدَ هَؤُلاءِ إِلا صُورَةٌ مُجَرَّدَةٌ.

[Note that] by claiming that man "is not created out of matter", the [Kalām theologians and Philosophers] do not intend to revere God by saying that He creates man out of nothing. Rather, man is undoubtedly a self-subsisting substance, but this substance has always existed in their opinion; it is not created when man is created. Likewise, the substantial [matter] which carries his form has always existed [according to the Philosophers]. Thus, only an accident is created according to those [Kalām theologians], and only an abstract form is created according to those [Philosophers].

وَكِلاهُمَا لَيْسَ هُوَ الإِنْسَانَ، بَلْ صِفَةٌ لَهُ، أَوْ صُورَةٌ لَهُ. هَذَا هُوَ المَخْلُوقُ

عِنْدَهُمْ بِخَلْقِ¹⁵⁰ الإِنْسَانِ فَقَطْ.

But neither [the accident nor the form] are the man himself. They are instead his attribute or his image. Only this is created of the man in their opinion.

---

١٤٩ في المطبوع: «الأعراض». والمثبت من الأصل الخطي.

١٥٠ في المطبوع: «يخلق»، خطأ.

وقَدْ قالَ تَعالىٰ: ﴿أَوَلَا يَذْكُرُ ٱلْإِنسَٰنُ أَنَّا خَلَقْنَٰهُ مِن قَبْلُ وَلَمْ يَكُ شَيْـًٔا﴾ [مريم: ٦٧]، وقالَ تَعالىٰ: ﴿وَقَدْ خَلَقْتُكَ مِن قَبْلُ وَلَمْ تَكُ شَيْـًٔا﴾ [مريم: ٩]. فَقَدْ أَمَرَ الإنْسانَ أنْ يَتَذَكَّرَ أنَّ اللهَ خَلَقَهُ ولَمْ يَكُ شَيْئًا. والإنْسانُ إذا تَذَكَّرَ إنَّما يَذْكُرُ أنَّهُ خُلِقَ مِنْ نُطْفَةٍ. وعِنْدَهُمْ ما زالَ جَواهِرُ الإنْسانِ شَيْئًا، وذَلِكَ الشَّيْءُ باقٍ، وإنَّما حَدَثَ أعْراضٌ لِتِلْكَ الأشْياءِ.

And the exalted God has said: **{Does man not remember that We created him before, when he was nothing?}** And said: **{I created you before, while you were nothing.}** Thus, He has instructed man to remember that He has created him after his **nonexistence**. And in doing so, man only remembers that he was created out of a sperm-drop. But according to the [Jahmiyyah], the substances in man are always **something** [prior to his creation]. This thing continues to exist, and only accidents are originated for these things.

ومَعْلومٌ أنَّ تِلْكَ الأعْراضَ وَحْدَها لَيْسَتْ هِيَ الإنْسانَ؛ فَإنَّ الإنْسانَ مَأْمورٌ، مَنْهِيٌّ، حَيٌّ، عَليمٌ، قَديرٌ، مُتَكَلِّمٌ، سَميعٌ، بَصيرٌ، مَوْصوفٌ بالحَرَكَةِ والسُكونِ. وهَذِهِ صِفاتُ الجَواهِرِ، والعَرَضُ لا يُوصَفُ بِشَيْءٍ؛

But it is known that these accidents are not on their own the man. For man is [a concrete thing that is] instructed and warned, living, knowing, powerful, speaking, hearing, seeing, and described with movement and stillness. [All of] these are attributes that describe **substances**, for attributes are not described with attributes.[151]

151 Man is therefore a substance, not an accident.

لا سِيَّما وهُمْ يَقولونَ: العَرَضُ لا يَبْقَىٰ زَمانَيْنِ. فالمَخْلوقُ - عَلَىٰ قَوْلِهِمْ - لا يَبْقَىٰ زَمانَيْنِ، بَلْ يَفْنَىٰ عَقِبَ ما يُخْلَقُ.

This is especially true given their claim that accidents do not endure for two [consecutive] instances of time. For according to this opinion of theirs, the created thing [i.e. the human being] would not endure for two instances of time [if it were an accident], but would perish straight after it is created.[152]

152 If the human being is defined as an accident and not as a substance, it would follow according to the opinion of the Ashʿarīyyah that this same human being does not exist for two moments of time. This is because they believe that accidents do not endure for two consecutive instances of time, but that every accident can exist only for a single moment before perishing necessarily, whereupon a new accident is created by God in the substance.

The Kalām View is Incompatible with Re-creation

وَلِهَذا اضْطَرَبوا في المَعادِ؛ فَإِنَّ مَعْرِفَةَ المَعادِ مَبْنِيَّةٌ عَلىٰ مَعْرِفَةِ المَبْدَأِ، والبَعْثَ مَبْنِيٌّ عَلىٰ الخَلْقِ.

And this explains the inconsistency [of the Jahmiyyah] in regards to the Resurrection. For knowing [the possibility of] the Resurrection is predicated on [first] knowing the origin, and [the knowledge of] re-creation is predicated on [first knowing] the [reality of] creation.

فَقالَ بَعْضُهُمْ: هُوَ تَفْريقُ تِلْكَ الأَجْزاءِ، ثُمَّ جَمْعُها، وهِيَ باقِيَةٌ بِأَعْيانِها. وقالَ بَعْضُهُمْ: بَلْ يُعْدِمُها، ويُعْدِمُ الأَعْراضَ القائِمَةَ بِها، ثُمَّ يُعيدُها، وإذا أَعادَها فَإِنَّهُ يُعيدُ تِلْكَ الجَواهِرَ الّتي كانَتْ باقِيَةً، إلىٰ أَنْ حَصَلَتْ في هَذا الإِنْسانِ.

Some of them claimed that the Resurrection is to combine those parts [i.e. the indivisible atoms in the man] after causing them to disperse [after his death], [claiming] that these very parts will continue to exist [after his death]. Others claimed that the Maker [will] cause these parts to perish [into nothingness] along with their accidents before re-creating them [ex nihilo later], [and they said] that He [will] re-create these very same atoms that continued to exist until they ended up in the human being.

فَلِهَذا اضْطَرَبوا لَمّا قيلَ لَهُمْ: فالإِنْسانُ إذا أَكَلَهُ حَيَوانٌ آخَرُ، فَإِنْ أُعيدَتْ

تِلْكَ الجَوَاهِرُ مِنَ الأَوَّلِ، نَقَصَتْ مِنَ الثَّاني، وبِالعَكْسِ.

For this reason, they were dumbfounded when asked: If a human being were eaten by another animal [and thus his atoms became part of the animal's body], wouldn't the atoms be lacking in the animal[153] if they are resurrected as part of the human being, and vice versa?

أمَّا عَلَى قَوْلِ مَنْ يَقُولُ: إِنَّها تُفَرَّقُ ثُمَّ تُجْمَعُ، فَقِيلَ لَهُ: تِلْكَ الجَوَاهِرُ إِنْ جُمِعَتْ لِلآكِلِ، نَقَصَتْ مِنَ المَأْكُولِ، وإِنْ أُعِيدَتْ لِلمَأْكُولِ، نَقَصَتْ مِنَ الآكِلِ.

As for the first group which claimed that the parts are caused to separate and combine, it was said to them: If these atoms are returned to the predator, they will be subtracted from the preyed [man]. But if they are returned to the preyed [man], they will be subtracted from the predator.

وأمَّا الّذي يَقُولُ: تُعْدَمُ ثُمَّ تُعَادُ بِأَعْيانِها، فَقِيلَ لَهُ: أَتُعْدَمُ لَمَّا أَكَلَها الآكِلُ، أَمْ قَبْلَ أَنْ يَأْكُلَها؟ فَإِنْ كانَ بَعْدَ أَنْ أَكَلَها، فَإِنَّها تُعَادُ في الآكِلِ، فَيَنْقُصُ المَأْكُولُ. وإِنْ كانَ قَبْلَ الأَكْلِ، فالآكِلُ لَمْ يَأْكُلْ إلا أَعْرَاضًا، لَمْ يَأْكُلْ جَوَاهِرَ، وهَذا مُكَابَرَةٌ. ١٥٤

---

153 Animals will also be resurrected on the Day of Resurrection. The Prophet Muḥammad (may God elevate his mention) stated in the authentic ḥadīth that was narrated by Muslim: "Rights will be given to their due on the Day of Resurrection, to the point that the hornless sheep would be avenged from the horned sheep."

١٥٤ في المطبوع: «فهذا مكابرة». والمثبت هو ما في الأصل الخطي.

As for the others who claimed that the parts [of the man] are annihilated [into nothingness] before being re-created [ex nihilo later], they were asked: Do these parts annihilate [into nothingness] after they are consumed by the animal or beforehand? If they are annihilated after consumption, they will be re-created in the preying [animal] and the preyed [man] will be lacking. But if they are annihilated beforehand, then the consuming [animal] will have only eaten accidents and not substances, which is absurd.

ثُمَّ إنَّ المَشْهورَ أنَّ الإنْسانَ يَبْلَىٰ ويَصيرُ تُرابًا كَما خُلِقَ مِنْ تُرابٍ، وبِذَلِكَ أَخْبَرَ اللهُ. فَإنْ قِيلَ: إنَّهُ إذا صارَ تُرابًا عُدِمَتْ تِلْكَ الجَواهِرُ؛ فَهُوَ لَمَّا خُلِقَ مِنْ تُرابٍ عُدِمَتْ أيْضًا تِلْكَ الجَواهِرُ. فَكَوْنُهُمْ يَجْعَلونَ الجَواهِرَ باقِيَةً في جَميعِ الاسْتِحالاتِ - إلا إذا صارَ تُرابًا - تَناقُضٌ بَيِّنٌ، ويَلْزَمُهُمْ عَلَيْهِ الحَيَوانُ المَأْكولُ، وغَيْرُ ذَلِكَ.

Furthermore, it is commonly known that man perishes and becomes [part of the] earth [when he dies], just as he was [once] created out of it. And this is [also] what God mentions [in the Qur'ān]. Thus, if it is said that these atoms [in the man] perish when he becomes [part of] the earth, then [it should equally be said that] the atoms [in the earth] perish when he is created out of the earth. It is a clear inconsistency to make the atoms perpetually existent in all cases of *istiḥālah* (substantial change) but not when man becomes [a part of] the earth. This [inconsistency] is also inevitable for them in the case of the preyed animal and other examples.

وكَأَنَّ هَذا الضَلالَ أَصْلُهُ[١٥٥] ضَلالُهُمْ في تَصَوُّرِ الخَلْقِ الأَوَّلِ، والنَشْأَةِ الأُولَىٰ الّتي أَمَرَهُمُ الربُّ أنْ يَتَذَكَّروها ويَسْتَدِلّوا بها علىٰ قُدْرَتِهِ علىٰ الثانِيَةِ. قالَ تَعالىٰ: ﴿أَفَرَءَيْتُم مَّا تُمْنُونَ ۝٥٨ ءَأَنتُمْ تَخْلُقُونَهُۥٓ أَمْ نَحْنُ ٱلْخَـٰلِقُونَ ۝٥٩ نَحْنُ قَدَّرْنَا بَيْنَكُمُ ٱلْمَوْتَ وَمَا نَحْنُ بِمَسْبُوقِينَ ۝٦٠ عَلَىٰٓ أَن نُّبَدِّلَ أَمْثَـٰلَكُمْ وَنُنشِئَكُمْ فِى مَا لَا تَعْلَمُونَ ۝٦١ وَلَقَدْ عَلِمْتُمُ ٱلنَّشْأَةَ ٱلْأُولَىٰ فَلَوْلَا تَذَكَّرُونَ﴾ [الواقعة: ٥٨-٦٢].

It is as though the root of their error [here] is their error in conceiving of the initial Creation, [the origin] which God has called them to remember and use as an evidence for His power [to create them] for a second [time]. God says: **{Have you seen that which you emit? Do you create it or are We the Creator? We have decreed death among you, and We are not to be outdone. In that We will change your likenesses and produce you in that which you do not know. And verily you have known the first creation, so will you not reflect?}**

والفَلاسِفَةُ أَجْوَدُ تَصَوُّرًا في هَذا المَوْضِعِ؛ حَيْثُ قالوا: تَفْسُدُ الصورَةُ الأُولَىٰ وهِيَ جَوْهَرٌ، وتَحْدُثُ صورَةٌ أُخْرىٰ. فَإنَّ هذا أَجْوَدُ مِنْ أنْ يُقالَ: يَزولُ عَرَضٌ ويَحْدُثُ عَرَضٌ. ولَكِنَّ الفَلاسِفَةَ غَلِطوا في تَوَهُّمِهِمْ أنَّ هُناكَ مادَّةً باقِيَةً بِعَيْنِها، وإنَّما تَفْسُدُ صورَتُها.

And the Philosophers [are able to] better conceive of this matter [of Resurrection than the Kalām theologians], for they claim that one

---

١٥٥ في المطبوع: «أصل»، وهو خطأ يقلب المعنىٰ، والتصحيح من الأصل الخطي.

[**substantial**] form is destroyed and another is generated. For this claim [that substances are originated] is better than the [previous] claim that only an accident vanishes and another is originated. However, the Philosophers are mistaken in assuming that the matter continues to exist and that only its form is destroyed.

والحَقُّ أنَّ المادَّةَ الّتي مِنْها يُخْلَقُ الثاني تَفْسُدُ وتَسْتَحيلُ وتَتَلاشَىٰ، ويُنْشِئُ اللهُ الثانِيَ ويَبْتَدِيهُ، ويَخْلُقُهُ[١٥٦] مِنْ غَيْرِ أنْ يَبْقَىٰ مِنَ الأوَّلِ شَيْءٌ؛ لا مادَّةٌ، ولا صورَةٌ، ولا جَوْهَرٌ، ولا عَرَضٌ.

And the truth is that the matter out of which the second thing is created is destroyed, totally changes, and ceases to exist. God originates the second thing and brings it into existence [such that] nothing of the first thing continues to exist, neither its matter nor its form, and neither a substance nor an accident.

فَإذا خَلَقَ اللهُ الإنْسانَ مِنَ المَنِيِّ، فالمَنِيُّ اسْتَحالَ وصارَ عَلَقَةً، والعَلَقَةُ اسْتَحالَتْ وصارَتْ مُضْغَةً، والمُضْغَةُ اسْتَحالَتْ إلىٰ عِظامٍ وغَيْرِ عِظامٍ. والإنْسانُ بَعْدَ أنْ خُلِقَ، خُلِقَ كُلُّهُ: جَواهِرُهُ وأعْراضُهُ، وابْتَدَأَهُ اللهُ ابْتِداءً؛ كَما قالَ تَعالىٰ: ﴿ٱلَّذِىٓ أَحْسَنَ كُلَّ شَىْءٍ خَلَقَهُۥ ۖ وَبَدَأَ خَلْقَ ٱلْإِنسَٰنِ مِن طِينٍ ۝٧ ثُمَّ جَعَلَ نَسْلَهُۥ مِن سُلَٰلَةٍ مِّن مَّآءٍ مَّهِينٍ﴾ [السجدة: ٧-٨]، وقالَ تَعالىٰ: ﴿أَوَلَا يَذْكُرُ ٱلْإِنسَٰنُ أَنَّا خَلَقْنَٰهُ مِن قَبْلُ وَلَمْ يَكُ شَيْـًٔا﴾ [مريم: ٦٧].

---

١٥٦ في المطبوع: «يخلق». والمثبت من الأصل الخطي.

Thus, when God creates a man out of semen, the semen **totally changes** and becomes a clinging clot, and [then] that clot totally changes becoming a lump of flesh. The lump then totally changes into bones and other things. After man is created, he is originated entirely, both his substances and his accidents. God will have brought him into existence and begun his creation [after his nonexistence], as He says: **{That is the Knower of the unseen and the witnessed, the Exalted in Might, the Merciful, Who perfected everything which He created and began the creation of man from clay. Then He made his seed from a draught of despised fluid}**. And says: **{Does man not remember that We created him before, when he was nothing?}**

فالإنْسانُ مَخْلوقٌ، خَلَقَ اللهُ جَواهِرَهُ وأعْراضَهُ كُلَّها مِنَ المَنِيِّ؛ مِنْ مادَّةٍ اسْتَحالَتْ، لَيْسَتْ باقِيَةً بَعْدَ خَلْقِهِ كَما تَقولُ المُتَفَلْسِفَةُ أنَّ هُناكَ مادَّةً باقِيَةً.

Thus man is created; God creates [both] his substances and his accidents entirely out of semen from a matter that totally changes and does not continue to exist [in the man] after his creation, contrary to the belief of the Philosophers that there is matter that continues to exist.

Creation in Kalām and Philosophy *(Continued)*

ولَفْظُ المادَّةِ مُشْتَرَكٌ، فالجُمْهورُ يُريدونَ بِهِ: ما مِنْهُ خُلِقَ، وهُوَ أَصْلُهُ وعُنْصُرُهُ. وهَؤُلاءِ يُريدونَ بالمادَّةِ: جَوْهَرٌ باقٍ، وهُوَ مَحَلٌّ لِلصورَةِ الجَوْهَرِيَّةِ. فَلَمْ يُخْلَقْ عِنْدَهُمُ الإنْسانُ مِنْ مادَّةٍ، بَلِ المادَّةُ باقِيَةٌ، وأُحْدِثَتْ[١٥٧] صورَتُهُ فيها؛ كَما أَنَّ الصُوَرَ الصِناعِيَّةَ -كَصورَةِ الخاتَمِ، والسَريرِ، والثِيابِ، والبُيوتِ، وغَيْرِ ذَلِكَ- إِنَّما أَحْدَثَ الصانِعُ صورَتَهُ العَرَضِيَّةَ في مادَّةٍ لَمْ تَزَلْ مَوْجودَةً ولَمْ تَفْسُدْ، ولَكِنْ حُوِّلَتْ مِنْ صِفَةٍ إِلىٰ صِفَةٍ.

'Matter' is an ambiguous term [that can mean different things]. The majority of the people use it to refer to the [prior existent] out of which a thing is created, which is its origin and element. [But] those [Philosophers] refer by 'matter' to an unchangeable substance in which [they say] the **substantial** form[158] exists. Thus, according to their opinion, man is not created **out of** matter. The matter continues to exist and only the form of the man is originated in the matter – in a way analogous to how the manufactured forms (like the forms of a ring, bed, dress and house) are originated by the man-

١٥٧ في المطبوع: «وأحدث». والمثبت من الأصل الخطي.

158 As its name implies, the *substantial* form is a substance, not an attribute. Ibn Taymiyyah rejected the claim that forms can be substantial.

ufacturer as accidental forms[159] in a material that continues to exist and is not destroyed [i.e. gold, wood, cloth, etc.]; the material [here] is only changed from one shape to another.

فَهَكَذَا تَقُولُ الجَهْمِيَّةُ المُتَكَلِّمَةُ المُبْتَدِعَةُ: إِنَّ اللهَ أَحْدَثَ صورَةً عَرَضِيَّةً في مادَّةٍ باقِيَةٍ لَمْ تَفْسُدْ؛ فَيَجْعَلونَ خَلْقَ الإِنْسانِ بِمَنْزِلَةِ عَمَلِ الخاتَمِ، والسَرِيرِ، والثَوْبِ.

Likewise, the heretical Kalām theologians from the Jahmiyyah claim that God originates **accidental** forms in a continuously existing matter that is not destroyed in the process [of creation]. Thus, they make the creation of a man like [the human act of] forging a ring, making a bed, and knitting a dress.[160]

والمُتَفَلْسِفَةُ تَقولُ أَيْضًا: إِنَّ مادَّتَهُ باقِيَةٌ لَمْ تَفْسُدْ؛ كَمادَّةِ الصورَةِ الصِناعِيَّةِ، لَكِنْ يَقولونَ: إِنَّهُ أَحْدَثَ صورَةً جَوْهَرِيَّةً. وهُمْ قَدْ يَخْلِطونَ ولا يُفَرِّقونَ بَيْنَ الصُوَرِ العَرَضِيَّةِ والجَوْهَرِيَّةِ؛ فَإِنَّهُمْ يُسَمُّونَ صورَةَ الإِنْسانِ صورَةً في مادَّةٍ، وصورَةَ الخاتَمِ صورَةً في مادَّةٍ؛

And the Philosophers equally say that the matter of the man continues to exist and is not destroyed, just like the material of a manufactured form [continues to exist]. However, they say that the Maker originates a **substantial form** [that is the form of the man]. They

---

159 An *accidental* form is an attribute.

160 Ibn Taymiyyah believed that both the man's substance and his accidental form are originated in the process of his creation. It is not just the form that originates as in the case of forging a ring.

may also conflate accidental forms with substantial forms and fail to distinguish between the two, for they equally refer to the form of a man and the form of a ring as 'forms in matter'.

فَيَكونُ خَلْقُ الإنْسانِ عِنْدَ هَؤُلاءِ وهَؤُلاءِ مِنْ جِنْسِ ما يُحْدِثُهُ الناسُ في الصُوَرِ مِنَ المَوادِّ، ويَكونُ خَلْقُهُ بِمَنْزِلَةِ تَرْكيبِ الحائطِ مِنَ اللَبِنِ. ولِهَذا قالَ مَنْ قالَ مِنْهُمْ: إنَّهُ يَسْتَغْنِي عَنِ الخالِقِ بَعْدَ الخَلْقِ، كَما يَسْتَغْنِي الحائِطُ عَنِ البَنّاءِ.

Thus, according to both parties [the Philosophers and the Kalām theologians], the creation of a man [by God] is of the same class as the reshaping of materials by man; the act of creating man is like the act of arranging a wall from bricks. For this reason, some of them have claimed that a man becomes independent of the Creator after creation just like a wall becomes independent of its builder.

والأشْعَرِيَّةُ عِنْدَهُمْ أنَّ البَنّاءَ والخَيّاطَ وسائِرَ أَهْلِ الصَنائِعِ لَمْ يُحْدِثوا في تِلْكَ المَوادِّ شَيْئًا؛ فَإنَّ القُدْرَةَ المُحْدَثَةَ عِنْدَهُمْ لا تَتَعَلَّقُ إلا بِما هُوَ في مَحَلِّها، لا خارِجًا عَنْ مَحَلِّها، ويَقولونَ: إنَّ تِلْكَ المَصْنوعاتِ كُلَّها مَخْلوقَةٌ للهِ، لَيْسَ لِلإنْسانِ فيها صُنْعٌ. وخَلْقُ اللهِ عَلىٰ أَصْلِهِمْ: هُوَ إحْداثُ أعْراضٍ فيها كَما تَقَدَّمَ. فَيُنْكِرونَ ما يَصْنَعُهُ الإنْسانُ، وهُوَ في الحَقيقَةِ مِثْلُما يَجْعَلونَهُ مَخْلوقًا[١٦١] لِلرَحْمَنِ.

١٦١ في الأصل الخطي: «مخلوقة».

And the Ashʿarīyyah[162] believe that the builder, the tailor, and all the other [kinds of human] manufacturers do not cause anything in the materials. For they believe that the power that is created [in man] is only associated with that which subsists in its substrate [i.e. the man]; it has no association with anything that exists outside [of the man]. [Thus,] they say that all manufactured things are created by God, but are not made by man [in any way].[163] [But] as previously stated, [the Ashʿarīyyah] define God's act of creation as an act of originating the accidents in the matter.[164] Thus, they deny the [act

162 The Ashʿarīyyah is the school of Kalām theology that is attributed to Abu al-Ḥasan al-Ashʿarī.

163 The Ashʿarī theologians negate human agency altogether and claim that God is the only agent in existence, as they believe that the existence of human and natural agency would compromise God's omnipotence and His creation of all things. Their position here is the opposite of that of the Muʿtazilah who claim that God does not create all things in the world and that human beings create their own actions. Ibn Taymiyyah rejected both the Ashʿarī and Muʿtazili positions as counter-scriptural and irrational. Instead, he defended that the correct position is that of early Muslims who believed in human and natural agency while also making it subordinate to God's agency and placing it under His creative will. According to this view, God creates plants by means of rain and earth, burning by means of fire, and human designs by means of human agents and builders. The existence of these causes in the created world does not compromise God's omnipotence, for they only act if He wills and as a consequence of His act of creation. Thus, for Ibn Taymiyyah, the middle path of Ahl al-Sunnah involves the acceptance of the fact that there do exist other agents apart from God, but that they do not act together with God, for God is the only independent Agent in existence. This is in line with the ḥadīth which mentions that: "God is the Creator of every maker and his creation". [*Minhāj al-Sunnah al-Nabawiyyah*, Vol 3, pp 7-339]

164 Such as by causing new arrangements in the substances, or by separating and combining the atoms.

of] manufacturing by man, which is in actual fact similar to [their understanding of] creation which they attribute to the Merciful [God].

وهُمْ لا يَشْهَدونَ لِلرَحْمَنِ إحْداثًا ولا إفْناءً، بَلْ إنَّما يُحْدِثُ عِنْدَهُمُ الأعْراضَ، وهِيَ تَفْنَىٰ بِأنْفُسِها، لا بِإفْنائِهِ، وهِيَ تَفْنَىٰ عَقِبَ إحْداثِها؛ وهَذا لا يُعْقَلُ.

[For] they [the Ashʿarīyyah] do not testify that the Merciful God originates [substances] and causes [others] to perish. Only the accidents are originated in their opinion. And [they believe that] the accidents perish **by themselves**, not by an act of annihilation by God, and [that] they perish right after they are originated, [which] is an irrational position.

وهُمْ حائِرونَ: إذا أرادَ أنْ يُعْدِمَ الأجْسامَ، كَيْفَ يُعْدِمُها؟ والمَشْهورُ عِنْدَهُمْ أنَّها تُعْدَمُ بِأنْفُسِها إذا لَمْ يَخْلُقْ لَها أعْراضًا. فالعَرَضُ يَفْنَىٰ عِنْدَهُمْ بِنَفْسِهِ، والجَوْهَرُ يَفْنَىٰ بِنَفْسِهِ إذا لَمْ يُخْلَقْ لَهُ عَرَضٌ بَعدَ عَرَضٍ. هَذا في الإفْناءِ.

They are [also] puzzled as to how God may annihilate [created] bodies should He will. They famously answer that bodies perish by themselves when God does not create accidents for them. Thus, they believe that the accidents perish by themselves, and that the substance also perishes by itself when God does not create in it one accident after another [in succession]. This is [their opinion] regarding the **act of annihilation**.

وأمّا في الإحْداثِ: فَإنَّهُمْ اسْتَدَلُّوا علىٰ حُدوثِها بِدَليلٍ باطِلٍ، لو كانَ صَحيحًا لَلَزِمَ حُدوث كُلِّ شَيْءٍ مِنْ غَيرِ مُحْدِثٍ.

As for [their views on] the **act of creation**, they infer that [all] bodies were originated [in the past] using a false argument[165], an argument which would entail that everything was originated without an Originator if it were true.

فَحَقيقَةُ أَصْل أَهْلِ الكَلام المُتَّبعينَ لِلجَهْمِيَّةِ: أنَّهُ لا يُحْدِثُ شَيْئًا، ولا يُفْنِي شَيْئًا، بَلْ يَحْدُثُ كُلُّ شَيْءٍ بِنَفْسِهِ، ويَفْنىٰ بِنفْسِهِ، ويَلْزَمُهُمْ جوازُ أنْ يَكونَ الربُّ مُحْدِثًا أيْضـًا بلا مُحْدَثٍ. وهَذِهِ الأُصولُ هي[١٦٦] أُصولُ دِينِهِمُ العَقْلِيَّةُ الّتي بِها يُعارِضونَ الكِتابَ والسُنَّةَ والمَعْقولاتِ الصَريحَةَ، وهِيَ في الحَقيقَةِ لا عَقْلٌ ولا سَمْعٌ؛ كَما حَكىٰ [اللهُ][١٦٧] عَنْ مَنْ قالَ: ﴿لَوْ كُنَّا نَسۡمَعُ أَوۡ نَعۡقِلُ مَا كُنَّا فِيٓ أَصۡحَٰبِ ٱلسَّعِيرِ﴾ [الملك: ١٠].

Thus, the reality of the theological foundation of these Kalām theologians who follow the Jahmiyyah is that God neither originates nor annihilates anything, but that everything originates and annihilates by itself. Also, it entails that it is permissible for God to have [always]

---

165 This is the Argument from the Origination of Bodies which was mentioned in a previous chapter. The argument concludes that the world came into being ex nihilo by the agency of an Originator who was motionless from eternity, and therefore implies that God began to create without a reason. For Ibn Taymiyyah, this contradicts the very principle of causality on which the arguments for God's existence ought to be predicated.

١٦٦ في الأصل الخطي بعده: «الأصول»، وهو تكرار حصل سهوًا.

١٦٧ لفظ الجلالة مثبت في المطبوع، وليس في الأصل الخطي.

been an Originator when there was no originated thing [or another for an eternal past].[168] These foundations are the rational principles of their theology by which they contradict the Book, the Sunnah, and sound reason. In truth, they are neither rational nor scriptural principles, but are just like the opinions of those whom [God] has described as saying: **{"If only we had been listening or reasoning, we would not be among the dwellers in the flames."}**

168 Here, Ibn Taymiyyah is criticizing the belief that God must have been on His own since eternity until the world came into existence, i.e. that God could not have been creating one thing after another since eternity. He points out that such a God is not always an Originator, but that He becomes 'the Creator' when the first created effect is originated.

The True Meaning of Creation

وَالخَلْقُ يَشْهَدُونَ إحْداثَ اللهِ لِما يُحْدِثُهُ، وإفْناءَهُ لِما يُفْنِيهِ؛ كالمَنِيِّ الَّذِي اسْتَحالَ وفَنِيَ وتَلاشَى، وأَحْدَثَ مِنْهُ هَذا الإنْسانَ؛ وكالحَبَّةِ الَّتِي فَنِيَتْ واسْتَحالَتْ، وأَحْدَثَ مِنْها الزَّرْعَ؛ وكالهَواءِ الَّذِي اسْتَحالَ وفَنِيَ، وحَدَثَ مِنْهُ النارُ أو الماءُ؛ وكالنارِ الَّتِي اسْتَحالَتْ، وحَدَثَ مِنْها الدُّخانُ. فَهُوَ – سُبْحانَهُ – دائِمًا يُحْدِثُ ما يُحْدِثُهُ ويُكَوِّنُهُ، ويُفْنِي ما يُفْنِيهِ ويُعْدِمُهُ.

[Now] the people witness that God originates what He brings into existence and annihilates what He removes out of existence, such as the semen which has totally changed, perished, annihilated, and [served as the matter] out of which God originated this man, and such as the grain which perished, totally changed, and [served as the matter] out of which God originated the plant. Also, [they witness] the air to change and perish into fire or water, and the [burning] fire to change into smoke. For He – exalted is He – is always originating what He wills to originate and bring into existence, and annihilating what He wills to destroy and remove out of existence.

وَالإنْسانُ إذا ماتَ وصارَ تُرابًا فَنِيَ وعُدِمَ، وكَذَلِكَ سائِرُ ما عَلى الأَرْضِ؛ كَما قالَ: ﴿كُلُّ مَنْ عَلَيْها فانٍ﴾ [الرحمن: ٢٦]، ثُمَّ يُعِيدُهُ مِنَ التُّرابِ كَما خَلَقَهُ ابْتِداءً مِنَ التُّرابِ، ويَخْلُقُهُ خَلْقًا جَدِيدًا. ولَكِنْ لِلنَّشْأةِ الثانِيَةِ أَحْكامٌ

وصِفاتٌ لَيْسَتْ لِلأُولَىٰ. فَمَعْرِفَةُ الإِنْسانِ بِالخَلْقِ الأَوَّلِ، وما يَخْلُقُهُ مِنْ بَنِي آدَمَ وغَيْرِهِمْ مِنَ الحَيَوانِ، وما يَخْلُقُهُ مِنَ الشَّجَرِ والنَّباتِ والثِّمارِ، وما يَخْلُقُهُ مِنَ السَّحابِ والمَطَرِ وغَيْرِ ذَلِكَ= هُوَ أَصْلٌ لِمَعْرِفَتِهِ بِالخَلْقِ والبَعْثِ، بِالمَبْدَأِ والمَعادِ.

And when man has died and become [part of the] earth, he will have totally perished and ceased to exist, just like all others upon the earth will. God says: **{Everyone upon it will perish}**. God will then resurrect him out of the earth just as He created him out of it before; He will create him anew. But [this] second Creation will have specifications and features which the first [one] did not. [Indeed,] the human knowledge of the first Creation and [how] God has created the Sons of Adam and the animals, the trees and the fruits, the clouds and the rain, is a **basis** to knowing the fact of Creation and the Resurrection, the origins and the return [to God].

وإِنْ لَمْ يَعْرِفْ أَنَّ اللهَ يَخْلُقُهُ كُلَّهُ مِنَ المَنِيِّ: جَواهِرَهُ وأَعْراضَهُ، وإِلّا فَما عَرَفَ أَنَّ اللهَ خَلَقَهُ. ومَنْ ظَنَّ أَنَّ جَواهِرَهُ لَمْ يَخْلُقْها إِذْ خَلَقَهُ، بَلْ جَواهِرُ المَنِيِّ وجَواهِرُ ما يَأْكُلُهُ ويَشْرَبُهُ باقِيَةٌ بِعَيْنِها فيهِ، لَمْ يَخْلُقْها، أَو أَنَّ مادَّتَهُ الَّتِي تَقومُ بِها صورَتُهُ لَمْ يَخْلُقْها إِذْ خَلَقَهُ، بَلْ هِيَ باقِيَةٌ أَزَلِيَّةٌ أَبَدِيَّةٌ= لَمْ يَكُنْ قَدْ عَرَفَ أَنَّهُ مَخْلوقٌ مُحْدَثٌ.

[For] if man does not know that God creates him in his entirety out of semen, both his substances and his accidents, he will not know that God has created him. And whoever believes [as Kalām theologians do] that his substances [i.e. atoms] are not created in the process of his creation, but that the substances in the semen and those in his food and drink continue to exist,[169] or [believes as the Philosophers do] that the matter in which his form subsists is not created in the process of his creation but continuously and eternally exists without beginning or end, has not known that he is created and originated.

وَالعُلَمَاءُ يُنْكِرونَ عَلَىٰ مَنْ يَقولُ إِنَّ رُوحَ الإِنْسانِ قَديمَةٌ أَزَلِيَّةٌ مِنَ المُنْتَسِبِينَ إِلَىٰ الإِسْلام. وهَؤُلاءِ الَّذينَ يَقولونَ إِنَّ مادَّةَ جِسْمِهِ باقِيَةٌ بِعَينِها، وهِيَ أَزَلِيَّةٌ أَبَدِيَّةٌ، أَبْعَدُ عَنِ العَقْلِ والنَّقْلِ مِنْهُمْ. وأُولَئِكَ أَنْكَروا عَلَيهِمْ حَيثُ قالوا: الإِنْسانُ مُرَكَّبٌ مِنْ قَديمٍ ومُحْدَثٍ؛ مِنْ لاهوتٍ قَديمٍ، وناسوتٍ مُحْدَثٍ. و هَؤُلاءِ جَعَلوهُ مُرَكَّبًا مِنْ مادَّةٍ قَديمَةٍ أَزَلِيَّةٍ، وصورَةٍ مُحْدَثَةٍ، وجَعَلوا القَديمَ الأَزَلِيَّ فيهِ أَخَسَّ ما فيهِ، وهُوَ المادَّةُ؛ فَإِنَّها عِنْدَهُمْ أَخَسُّ المَوْجوداتِ، وهِيَ قَديمَةٌ أَزَلِيَّةٌ. وأُولَئِكَ جَعَلوا القَديمَ الأَزَلِيَّ أَشْرَفَ ما فيهِ وهِيَ النَّفْسُ الناطِقَةُ. وكِلْتا الطائِفَتَينِ وإِنْ كانَ ضالًّا؛ فالشَّريفُ العالِي أَوْلَىٰ بِالقِدَمِ مِنَ الخَسيسِ السافِلِ، وهَذا أَوْلَىٰ بِالحُدوثِ.

[Moreover,] the [Muslim] scholars denounce claimants to Islam who hold that the human soul is eternal and without beginning. But those [Philosophers] who claim that the very matter of the hu-

---

169 Ibn Taymiyyah believed that the substances in the natural world change at what is today known as the molecular level. Scientists today are convinced that the components of molecules do not change substantially in the processes of chemical change, and thus may find it difficult to accept the intuitive position he is defending.

man body continues to exist without beginning or end are farther away from reason and Revelation. The [former people] are criticized [by the Muslim scholars] for claiming that the human being is composed of an eternal [part] and an originated [part]: an eternal divine [component] and an originated human [component]. [But] the latter [Philosophers] claim that the human being is composed of eternal matter and originated form, thus considering the inferior of his components, i.e. matter, to be eternal, for matter is according to them the lowest of existents and is also eternally existing; whereas the former deem the nobler component, which is the rational soul, to be eternal. Although both parties have gone astray [in claiming that something exists eternally with God], the nobler component is worthier of being eternal than the inferior one, which is, in turn, worthier of being originated.

وأمّا المُتكلِّمَةُ الجَهْمِيَّةُ: فَهُمْ لا يَتصَوَّرونَ ما يَشْهَدونَهُ مِنْ حُدوثِ هَذِهِ الجَواهِرِ في جَواهِرَ أُخرَ مِنْ مادَّةٍ، ثُمَّ يَدَّعونَ أنَّ الجَواهِرَ جَميعَها أُبْدِعَتِ ابْتِداءً لا مِنْ شَيْءٍ. وهُمْ لَمْ يَعْرِفوا قَطُّ جَوْهرًا أُحْدِثَ لا مِنْ شَيْءٍ، كَما لَمْ يَعْرِفوا عَرَضًا أُحْدِثَ لا في مَحَلٍّ.

As for the Jahmiyyah from the Kalām theologians, they are unable to conceive of this [fact of creation] which they witness [before them, namely] that substances originate in [place of] other substances [and] out of matter. They then claim that all substances were originated in the beginning ex nihilo[170], although they do not know of

170 The Kalām theologians are not only saying that the world was originated after its nonexistence, but are additionally saying that this world was originated out of no prior matter. According to Ibn Taymiyyah, this view is neither in

a single substance that was originated ex nihilo just as they do not know of a single accident that was originated not in a substrate.

وحَقيقَةُ قَوْلِهِمْ أنَّ اللهَ لا يُحْدِثُ شَيْئًا مِنْ شَيْءٍ؛ لا جَوْهَرًا، ولا عَرَضًا؛ فَإِنَّ الجَواهِرَ كُلَّها أُحْدِثَتْ لا مِنْ شَيْءٍ، والأعْراضَ كَذَلِكَ.

And the reality of their claim is that God does not originate anything out of another, neither substances nor accidents. For [they claim that] all substances are originated ex nihilo, and so are all accidents [i.e. originated ex nihilo].

والمَشْهودُ المَعْلومُ لِلناسِ إنَّما هُوَ إحْداثُهُ لِما يُحْدِثُهُ مِنْ غَيْرِهِ، لا إحْداثًا مِنْ غَيْرِ مادَّةٍ، ولِهَذا قالَ تَعالىٰ: ﴿وَقَدْ خَلَقْتُكَ مِن قَبْلُ وَلَمْ تَكُ شَيْـًٔا﴾ [مريم: ٩]، ولَمْ يَقُلْ: خَلَقْتُكَ لا مِنْ شَيْءٍ، وقالَ تعالىٰ: ﴿وَٱللَّهُ خَلَقَ كُلَّ دَآبَّةٍ مِّن مَّآءٍ﴾ [النور: ٤٥]، ولَمْ يَقُلْ: خَلَقَ كُلَّ دابَّةٍ لا مِنْ شَيْءٍ، وقالَ تَعالىٰ: ﴿وَجَعَلْنَا مِنَ ٱلْمَآءِ كُلَّ شَىْءٍ حَىٍّ﴾ [الأنبياء: ٣٠].

[But] what is witnessed and known to people is that God creates things out of others; not that He creates things out of no [prior] matter. This is why the exalted God says: **{I created you before, while you were nothing}**, but does not say: I created you out of nothing. And this is why He says: **{God created every animal out of water}**, but does not say that He created animals out of nothing. Likewise, God says: **{We made every living thing out of water}**.

---

line with Scripture nor demonstrated by sound reason and empirical observation. It is also unnecessary for holding the belief that God is the Creator of all things and that only He is eternal.

وهَذا هُوَ القُدْرَةُ الّتي تُبْهِرُ العُقولَ؛ وهُوَ أنْ يَقْلِبَ حَقائِقَ المَوْجوداتِ فَيُحِيلَ الأوَّلَ ويُفْنِيَهُ ويُلاشِيَهُ، ويُحْدِثَ شَيْئًا آخَرَ؛ كَما قالَ: ﴿فَالِقُ ٱلْحَبِّ وَٱلنَّوَىٰ ۖ يُخْرِجُ ٱلْحَىَّ مِنَ ٱلْمَيِّتِ وَمُخْرِجُ ٱلْمَيِّتِ مِنَ ٱلْحَيِّ ۚ﴾ [الأنعام: ٩٥]، يُخْرِجُ[١٧١] الشَجَرَةَ الحَيَّةَ والسُنْبُلَةَ الحَيَّةَ مِنَ النَواةِ والحَبَّةِ المَيِّتَةِ، ويُخْرِجُ النَواةَ المَيِّتَةَ والحَبَّةَ المَيِّتَةَ مِنَ الشَجَرَةِ والسُنْبُلَةِ الحَيَّةِ؛ كَما يُخْرِجُ الإنْسانَ الحَيَّ مِنَ النُطْفَةِ المَيِّتَةِ، والنُطْفَةَ المَيِّتَةَ مِنَ الإنْسانِ الحَيِّ.

And this is the power [of God] which amazes the intellects [of men]. It is [His] power to turn the realities of existents [into others], totally changing one thing, annihilating it, causing it to perish, and originating something else. As He says: **{God is the cleaver of grain and date seeds. He brings the living out of the dead and brings the dead out of the living.}** He brings living trees and spikes out of dead date seeds and grain, and brings dead seeds and grain out of living trees and spikes. Similarly, He creates a living man out of dead sperm and dead sperm out of a living man.

وعِنْدَهُمْ لا يُخْرِجُ حَيًّا مِنْ مَيِّتٍ، ولا مَيِّتًا مِنْ حَيٍّ؛ فَإنَّ الحَيَّ والمَيِّتَ إنَّما [هُوَ][١٧٢] الجَوْهَرُ القائِمُ بِنَفْسِهِ؛ فَإنَّ الحَياةَ عَرَضٌ لا يَقومُ إلا بِجَوْهَرٍ. والعَرَضُ نَفْسُهُ لا يَقومُ بِعَرَضٍ آخَرَ، وإنْ كانَ العَرَضُ يُوصَفُ بِأنَّهُ حَيٌّ؛ كَما يُقالُ: قَدْ أَحْيَيْتَ العِلْمَ والإيمانَ، وأَحْيَيْتَ الدِينَ، وأَحْيَيْتَ السُنَّةَ

---

١٧١ في المطبوع: «ويخرج». والمثبت من الأصل الخطي.

١٧٢ ما بين الحاصرتين ليست في الأصل الخطي، وهي زيادة لازمة أثبتت في المطبوع.

وَالعَدْلَ؛ كَما يُقالُ: أَماتَ¹⁷³ البِدْعَةَ. فَهَؤُلاءِ عِنْدَهُمْ لا يُخْرِجُ جَوْهَرًا
مِنْ جَوْهَرٍ، ولا عَرَضًا مِنْ عَرَضٍ؛ فَلا يُخْرِجُ حَيًّا مِنْ مَيِّتٍ، ولا مَيِّتًا مِنْ
حَيٍّ، بَل الجَوَاهِرُ الَّتِي كانَتْ في المَيِّتِ هِيَ بِعَيْنِها باقِيَةٌ كَما كانَتْ، ولَكِنْ
أَحْدَثَ فيها حَياةً لَمْ تَكُنْ. وتِلْكَ الحَياةُ لَمْ تَخْرُجْ مِنْ مَيِّتٍ؛ فَما أُخْرِجَ
عِنْدَهُمْ حَيٌّ مِنْ مَيِّتٍ، ولا مَيِّتٌ مِنْ حَيٍّ،

[But] according to those [Kalām theologians], God does not bring anything living out of anything dead. For indeed, the **living** or **dead** thing is the self-subsisting **substance**, [not the attribute of life or death]. [The attribute of] life is an accident, [meaning that] it subsists only in the substance [and not on its own in isolation]. And that very accident cannot subsist in another accident; although an accident may be described as living [in a strictly figurative sense], such as when it is said: "You have revived knowledge and Faith", "You have revived the religion, the Sunnah and justice", or that "one has killed heresy". [Now,] those [Kalām theologians] believe that God does not bring a substance into existence out of another substance nor an accident into existence out of another accident.[174] It so

---

١٧٣ في الأصل الخطي: «أمه».

174 In addition to believing that God creates substances out of substances and accidents out of accidents, Ibn Taymiyyah believed that God is able to create substances out of accidents and vice versa. This is contrasted with the position of Kalām theologians who believed that it is impossible for attributes to change into physical objects.

An example of a substance that is created out of another substance is the creation of a tree out of the earth and a man out of semen. An example of an accident that is created out of another accident is the color of a fruit that changes. As for accidents that change into substances, Ibn Taymiyyah's student Ibn al-Qayyim al-Jawziyyah mentions examples of these in his poem

follows that He neither brings a living thing out of a dead thing nor a dead thing out of a living thing. Instead, the very substances in the dead thing continue to exist in the living thing without change; only life is originated in the substance, and that life is not originated out of a dead thing. Thus, according to their opinion, nothing living is brought out of anything dead, and nothing dead is brought out of anything living.

ولِهَذا يُنْكِرونَ أنْ يَقْلِبَ اللهُ جِنْسًا إلىٰ جِنْسٍ آخَرَ، ويَقولونَ: الجَواهِرُ كُلُّها جِنْسٌ واحِدٌ؛ فَإذا خَلَقَ النُطْفَةَ إنْسانًا، لَمْ يَقْلِبْ عِنْدَهُمْ جِنْسًا إلىٰ جِنْسٍ، بَلْ نَفْسُ الجَواهِرِ هِيَ باقِيَةٌ كَما كانَتْ.

And this is why they deny that God may turn [a thing of] one genus into [another thing of] a different genus and [instead] claim that all

---

known as *'al-Nūniyyah'*. According to authentic ḥadīth reports, the attribute of death which now subsists in the deceased will be changed by God into a black-and-white ram that will be sacrificed in a place between the Paradise and the Hellfire after all the people settle in their final destinations. Also, the deeds of human beings will be turned into physical objects that will be weighed in a physical scale on the Day of Judgement. Furthermore, the Qur'ān will come in the form of a pale man, and the second and third chapters of the Qur'ān will come as two clouds or two flocks of birds that will plead for their reciter on the Day of Judgement. [*Al-Kāfiyyah al-Shāfiyyah*, Vol 3 pp. 1028-1033]. In this last example where it is mentioned that the Qur'ān will come in physical form, the ḥadīth is not referring to the very Qur'ān which is the word of God, for that is a divine attribute that can never change into a creation. Instead, as stressed by Aḥmad ibn Ḥanbal, the ḥadīth refers to our act of reciting the Qur'ān, which is a human act that subsists in the human reciter. That act will be turned into a physical form just like the rest of our deeds.

jawāhir (atoms) are of the same genus.[175] For example, when God creates man from a sperm-drop, He does not turn one class into another. Rather, the very same *jawāhir* (atoms) continue to exist without change.

وخاصِّيَّةُ الخَلْقِ إنَّما هِيَ بِقَلْبِ جِنْسٍ إلىٰ جِنْسٍ، وهَذا لا يَقْدِرُ عَلَيْهِ إلا اللهُ؛ كَما قالَ تَعالىٰ: ﴿يَـٰٓأَيُّهَا ٱلنَّاسُ ضُرِبَ مَثَلٌ فَٱسْتَمِعُوا۟ لَهُۥٓ ۚ إِنَّ ٱلَّذِينَ تَدْعُونَ مِن دُونِ ٱللَّهِ لَن يَخْلُقُوا۟ ذُبَابًا وَلَوِ ٱجْتَمَعُوا۟ لَهُۥ ۖ وَإِن يَسْلُبْهُمُ ٱلذُّبَابُ شَيْـًٔا لَّا يَسْتَنقِذُوهُ مِنْهُ ۚ ضَعُفَ ٱلطَّالِبُ وَٱلْمَطْلُوبُ ﴿٧٣﴾ مَا قَدَرُوا۟ ٱللَّهَ حَقَّ قَدْرِهِۦٓ ۗ إِنَّ ٱللَّهَ لَقَوِىٌّ عَزِيزٌ﴾ [الحج: ٧٣-٧٤].

[But in actual fact,] the defining feature of the creative agency [of God] is to turn one [thing of some] genus into another genus. None can do this but God, just as He says: **{O people, an example is presented, so listen to it. Indeed, those you invoke besides God will never create as much as a fly, even if they gathered together for that purpose. And if the fly should steal away from them a tiny thing, they could not rescue it from it. So weak are both the seeker and the sought! They have not appraised God with due appraisal. Indeed, God is Powerful and Exalted in Might.}**

ولا رَيْبَ أنَّ النَخْلَةَ ما هِيَ مِنْ جِنْسِ النَواةِ، ولا السُنْبُلَةَ مِنْ جِنْسِ الحَبَّةِ، ولا الإنْسانَ مِنْ جِنْسِ المَنِيِّ، ولا المَنِيَّ مِنْ جِنْسِ الإنْسانِ. وهُوَ يُخْرِجُ هَذا مِنْ هَذا، وهَذا مِنْ هَذا؛ فَيُخْرِجُ كَلَّ جِنْسٍ مِنْ جِنْسٍ آخَرَ بَعيدٍ عَنْ

175 Meaning that all physical bodies are equivalent.

مُماثَلَتِهِ، و﴿هَٰذَا خَلْقُ ٱللَّهِ فَأَرُونِي مَاذَا خَلَقَ ٱلَّذِينَ مِن دُونِهِۦ ۚ﴾ [لقمان: ١١].

And it is without doubt that neither trees are of the same substance as date seeds, nor spikes of the same substance as grain, nor man of the same substance as semen, nor semen of the same substance as man. Yet God creates this out of that and that out of this, hence bringing each substance out of another very different one. And **{This is the creation of God. So show Me that which those beside Him have created}**.

وهُوَ سُبْحانَهُ إذا جَعَلَ الأبْيَضَ أَسْوَدَ، أَعْدَمَ ذَلِكَ البَياضَ، وجَعَلَ مَوْضِعَهُ السَوادَ، كما أنَّهُ[١٧٦] [في] الأجْسامِ يُعْدِمُ تِلْكَ المادَّةَ، فَيُحِيلُها ويُلاشِيها، ويَجْعَلُ مِنْها هَذا المَخْلوقَ الجَديدَ، ويَخْلُقُ الضِدَّ مِنْ ضِدِّهِ؛ كَما جَعَلَ مِنَ الشَجَرِ الأخْضَرِ نارًا، فَإذا حَكَّ الأخْضَرَ بالأخْضَرِ، سَخَّنَ ما يُسَخِّنُهُ بالحَرَكَةِ، حَتّىٰ يَنقَلِبَ نَفْسُ الأخْضَرِ فَيَصِيرَ نارًا. وعَلَىٰ قَوْلِهِمْ ما جَعَلَ فيهِ نارًا، بَلْ تِلْكَ الجَواهِرُ باقِيَةٌ بِعَيْنِها، وأُحْدِثَ فيها عَرَضٌ لَمْ يَكُنْ.

And when He makes a white thing black, He removes that whiteness and makes blackness[177] in its place, [turning one accident into

١٧٦ في الأصل الخطي: «لا أن»، ولعل فيه تصحيفًا أو سقطًا، والمثبت يستقيم به السياق.

177 Color is not defined by Muslim theologians as the light that is separate from the object and is reflected by its surface. Instead, color refers to an attribute that subsists in the surface of the colored object, one that involves the reflection of certain colors of light and absorbing others. For example, blackness is a property subsisting in the surface which involves the absorption of all the colors of light in the spectrum.

another accident] – akin to [how when He changes] the body [itself,] He annihilates that matter, causes it to change and perish, and makes this newly created thing out of it, creating one thing out of its opposite. [This is] such as when He creates fire out of green trees. For when the green [tree] is rubbed against a green [tree], heat comes out of this motion, until the very green [tree] changes into a [burning] fire. [But] according to those [Kalām theologians], He does not make fire in the tree. Instead, the very substances [of the tree] continue to exist and [only] an accident which did not exist is originated therein.

وخَلْقُ الشَيْءِ مِنْ غَيْرِ جِنْسِهِ أبْلَغُ في قُدْرَةِ القادِرِ الخالِقِ سُبْحانَهُ وتَعالى[١]؛ كَما وَصَفَ نَفْسَهُ بِذَلِكَ في قَوْلِهِ: ﴿قُلِ ٱللَّهُمَّ مَٰلِكَ ٱلْمُلْكِ تُؤْتِى ٱلْمُلْكَ مَن تَشَآءُ وَتَنزِعُ ٱلْمُلْكَ مِمَّن تَشَآءُ وَتُعِزُّ مَن تَشَآءُ وَتُذِلُّ مَن تَشَآءُ ۖ بِيَدِكَ ٱلْخَيْرُ ۖ إِنَّكَ عَلَىٰ كُلِّ شَىْءٍ قَدِيرٌ (٢٦) تُولِجُ ٱلَّيْلَ فِى ٱلنَّهَارِ وَتُولِجُ ٱلنَّهَارَ فِى ٱلَّيْلِ ۖ وَتُخْرِجُ ٱلْحَىَّ مِنَ ٱلْمَيِّتِ وَتُخْرِجُ ٱلْمَيِّتَ مِنَ ٱلْحَىِّ ۖ وَتَرْزُقُ مَن تَشَآءُ بِغَيْرِ حِسَابٍ﴾ [آل عمران: ٢٦-٢٧].

And creating a thing out of an altogether different substance **more strongly** indicates the power of the Omnipotent Creator – exalted is He – [than creating it out of nothing], just as He has described Himself in saying: **{Say, "O God, Owner of Sovereignty, You give sovereignty to whom You will and You take sovereignty away from whom You will. You honor whom You will and You humble whom You will. In Your hand is all good. Indeed, You are over all things Competent. You cause the night to enter the day, and You cause the day to enter the night; and You**

bring the living out of the dead, and You bring the dead out of the living. And You give provision to whom You will without account."}

ولِهَذا قالَ لِلمَلائِكَةِ: ﴿إِنِّي خَٰلِقُۢ بَشَرًا مِّن طِينٍ ۝٧١ فَإِذَا سَوَّيۡتُهُۥ وَنَفَخۡتُ فِيهِ مِن رُّوحِي فَقَعُواْ لَهُۥ سَٰجِدِينَ﴾ [ص: ٧١-٧٢]، وقالَ: ﴿أَلَمۡ نَخۡلُقكُّم مِّن مَّآءٍ مَّهِينٍ ۝٢٠ فَجَعَلۡنَٰهُ فِي قَرَارٍ مَّكِينٍ ۝٢١ إِلَىٰ قَدَرٍ مَّعۡلُومٍ ۝٢٢ فَقَدَرۡنَا فَنِعۡمَ ٱلۡقَٰدِرُونَ﴾ [المرسلات: ٢٠-٢٣].

And for this reason did God say to the angels: **{"Indeed, I am about to create a human being out of clay. So when I have proportioned him and breathed into him of My spirit, then fall down to him in prostration."}**[178] And say: **{Did We not create you out of a fluid disdained. Which We laid up in a safe abode. For a known term? Thus We determined it. So how excellent are We to determine!}**

ولِهَذا امْتَنَعَ اللَعِينُ؛ كَما قالَ تَعالىٰ: ﴿وَإِذۡ قُلۡنَا لِلۡمَلَٰٓئِكَةِ ٱسۡجُدُواْ لِأٓدَمَ فَسَجَدُوٓاْ إِلَّآ إِبۡلِيسَ قَالَ ءَأَسۡجُدُ لِمَنۡ خَلَقۡتَ طِينًا﴾ [الإسراء: ٦١]، وقالَ: ﴿لَمۡ أَكُن لِّأَسۡجُدَ لِبَشَرٍ خَلَقۡتَهُۥ مِن صَلۡصَٰلٖ مِّنۡ حَمَإٖ مَّسۡنُونٖ﴾ [الحجر: ٣٣].

---

178 Elsewhere, Ibn Taymiyyah compares God's act of creation by means of natural causes with His direct act of creation without efficient means, such as His creation of Adam out of dust with His two hands. He argues that neither type of creation entails that God depends on an outside cause for His act. [*Bayān Talbīs al-Jahmiyyah*, Vol 3 p. 235].

And for this reason did the accursed [Satan] refuse [to prostrate[179] to Adam]. God says: **{And mention when We said to the angels, "Prostrate to Adam," and they prostrated, except for Iblis. He said, "Should I prostrate to one You created from clay?"}** And Iblīs also said: **{"Never would I prostrate to a human whom You created out of clay from an altered black mud."}**

وأيْضًا: فَكَوْنُ الشَيْءِ مَخْلوقًا مِنْ مادَّةٍ وعُنْصُرٍ أَبْلَغُ في العُبودِيَّةِ مِنْ كَوْنِهِ خُلِقَ لا مِنْ شَيْءٍ، وأَبْعَدُ عَنْ مُشابَهَةِ الرُبوبِيَّةِ؛ فَإِنَّ الرَبَّ هُوَ أَحَدٌ، صَمَدٌ، لَمْ يَلِدْ، ولَمْ يُولَدْ، ولَمْ يَكُنْ لَهُ كُفُوًا أَحَدٌ؛ فَلَيْسَ لَهُ أَصْلٌ وُجِدَ مِنْهُ، ولا فَرْعٌ يُحْصُلُ عَنْهُ. فَإِذا كانَ المَخْلوقُ لَهُ أَصْلٌ وُجِدَ مِنْهُ، كانَ بِمَنْزِلَةِ الوَلَدِ لَهُ، وإذا خُلِقَ لَهُ شَيْءٌ آخَرُ، كانَ بِمَنْزِلَةِ الوالِدِ، وإذا كانَ والِدًا ومَوْلودًا كانَ أَبْعَدَ عَنْ مُشابَهَةِ الرُبوبِيَّةِ والصَمَدِيَّةِ؛ فَإِنَّهُ خَرَجَ مِنْ غَيْرِهِ، ويَخْرُجُ مِنْهُ غَيْرُهُ؛

Furthermore, a thing that is created out of [a prior] matter or element **more strongly** indicates its servitude to its Lord and is **farther away** from being equal to its Lord [than a thing created ex nihilo]. This is because the Lord alone is the **One**, **Self-sufficient** Master who **neither begets nor is born** and who has **no equivalent**. Thus, He does not exist out of an origin and nothing [at all] produces out of Him. [For] if a created thing begins to exist out of

179 This prostration to Adam was a form of salutation and greeting. God would never command His creations to prostrate in worship of other creations, as polytheism is immoral and is the greatest injustice. Greeting by prostration was permissible before Islam but was prohibited in the Sharīʿah.

an origin, that origin will be like[180] its father, and if another thing is created out of it, that [other] will be like a son. And if it is both a father and a son, it will be **farther away** from being like the Independent[181] Lord, for it will have come out of another, and another

180 *Material conditions* are not synonymous with *efficient causes*. In other words, not all things that originate out of materials are begotten or caused by them; for instance, Adam was created out of dust directly but was not caused or begotten by it [*Majmūʿ al-Fatāwā*, Vol 17, p 266]. This subtle distinction between efficient causes and material conditions can help reconcile the position of causal finitism with Ibn Taymiyyah's view that material conditions regress indefinitely into the infinite past.

Ibn Taymiyyah argues that no created *cause* or *agent* can act or produce effects on its own without assisting conditions. This implies that every *effect* of nature is created by God out of at least two created causes or origins, be those causes natural, human, or unseen such as angelic causes. It makes sense to say that a human child is begotten by its parents as there existed two prior origins from which God created the child. But it does not make sense to say that Adam was begotten or caused by the dust, as he came into being out of a *single* material origin.

Note that although Ibn Taymiyyah states that the material condition from which Adam was created was singular, he also implies in the same book that this material condition could not have been homogenous and non-composite, but that it must have been mixed with water. He writes: "Nothing can be created from pure dust that is not mixed with anything." [*Majmūʿ al-Fatāwā*, Vol 17, p 262]. This statement by Ibn Taymiyyah seems to indicate that he believed that it is impossible for a material condition that is not composed of more than one part to change into a new creation unless it is combined with another material component. In this way, the multiplicity in the material world and its composition from various constituents is a necessary aspect of the fact that it changes substantially and is subject to annihilation, whether or not the material condition is assumed to have an efficacy in the process.

181 Ibn Taymiyyah is here referring to the divine name *'Al-Ṣamad'*, which translates as 'the Self-sufficient Master on whom all things depend' and 'the

will have come out of it.

لا سِيَّما إذا كانَتِ المادَّةُ الّتي خُلِقَ مِنْها مَهِينَةً؛ كَما قالَ تَعالىٰ: ﴿أَلَمْ نَخْلُقكُّم مِّن مَّآءٍ مَّهِينٍ﴾ [المرسلات: ٢٠]، وقالَ تَعالىٰ ﴿فَلْيَنظُرِ ٱلْإِنسَٰنُ مِمَّ خُلِقَ ۝٥ خُلِقَ مِن مَّآءٍ دَافِقٍ ۝٦ يَخْرُجُ مِنۢ بَيْنِ ٱلصُّلْبِ وَٱلتَّرَآئِبِ ۝٧ إِنَّهُۥ عَلَىٰ رَجْعِهِۦ لَقَادِرٌ ۝٨ يَوْمَ تُبْلَى ٱلسَّرَآئِرُ ۝٩ فَمَا لَهُۥ مِن قُوَّةٍ وَلَا نَاصِرٍ﴾ [الطارق: ٥-١٠].

This [servitude] is especially true if the thing is created out of a disdained matter, as the exalted God says: **{Did We not create you out of a fluid disdained?}** And says: **{So let man observe from what he was created. He was created out of a gushing fluid. Emerging from between the backbone and the ribs. Indeed, God is Able to return him to life. On that Day when secrets will be put on trial, Then will he have no might nor any helper.}**[182]

Perfect being who deserves maximal perfection in all respects'. This holy name also indicates that God is not hollow or in need of food and drink. With greater reason, it indicates that God is not divisible or composed of separate components, such as atoms or persons. [*Majmū' al-Fatāwā*, Vol 17, p 238].

182 One of the valid interpretations of this verse is that the 'backbone' refers to the loins of the man, whereas the 'ribs' refer to the chest of the woman. The language here also allows the two terms to serve as indicants for the man and the woman in their entirety, with the semen emerging from between them during intercourse. The verse cautions people that God has power to re-create them out of the earth and gather them for a Day of Judgement, just as He is able to create them now from the most amazing and difficult of places.

وفي الْمُسْنَدِ عَنْ بُسْرِ بْنِ جَحَّاشٍ قَالَ: «بَصَقَ رَسُولُ اللهِ ﷺ فِي كَفِّهِ، فَوَضَعَ عَلَيْهَا إِصْبَعَهُ، ثُمَّ قَالَ: يَقُولُ اللهُ تَعَالىٰ: ابْنَ آدَمَ أَنَّىٰ تُعْجِزُنِي، وقَدْ خَلَقْتُكَ مِنْ مِثْلِ هٰذِهِ؟! حَتّىٰ إِذَا سَوَّيْتُكَ وعَدَلْتُكَ، مَشَيْتَ بَيْنَ بُرْدَيْنِ ولِلْأَرْضِ مِنْكَ وَئِيدٌ، فَجَمَعْتَ، ومَنَعْتَ، حَتّىٰ إِذَا بَلَغَتِ التَّرَاقِيَ، قُلْتَ أَتَصَدَّقُ، وأَنّىٰ أَوَانُ الصَّدَقَةِ؟!».

And in the *Musnad* of Aḥmad ibn Ḥanbal, it is narrated by Busr ibn Jaḥḥāsh that the Prophet (may God elevate his mention) spat in his palm and placed his finger on it and said: God says: {**O Son of Adam, do you think you can escape Me when I have created you out of something like this? By the time I have proportioned and balanced you, you are walking [haughtily] in two lavish garments, thumping the ground, and accumulating wealth while withholding from charity. But when your soul reaches your throat, you say: "I shall give charity!" But how would that be possible at that moment?!**}

وكَذٰلِكَ إِذَا خُلِقَ فِي مَحَلٍّ مُظْلِمٍ وضَيِّقٍ؛ كَمَا خُلِقَ الْإِنْسَانُ فِي ظُلُمَاتٍ ثَلَاثٍ، كَانَ أَبْلَغَ فِي قُدْرَةِ الْقَادِرِ، وأَدَلَّ عَلىٰ عُبُودِيَّةِ الْإِنْسَانِ، وذُلِّهِ لِرَبِّهِ، وحاجَتِهِ إِلَيْهِ.

Moreover, a thing that is created in a dark and confined space, as man is created in the three darknesses [of his mother's womb][183], more strongly indicates the power of the Omnipotent God and more obviously indicates its servitude, humility, and dependence on

---

183 As referred to in the Qur'ān, 39:6.

its Lord.

وقَدْ يَقولُ العَرَبُ [إذا عَيَّروا] الرَّجُلَ[١٨٤]: ما لَكَ أَصْلٌ ولا فَصْلٌ! والإنْسانُ[١٨٥] أَصْلُهُ التُرابُ، وفَصْلُهُ الماءُ المَهينُ.

And the Arabs may say when they insult a man: "You have neither a [noble] origin nor a [noble] issue!" Although the origin of man is dust and his issue is the despised fluid.

ولِهَذا لَمّا خُلِقَ المَسيحُ مِنْ غَيْرِ أَبٍ، وَقَعَتْ بِهِ الشُبْهَةُ لِطائِفَةٍ، وقالوا: إنَّهُ ابْنُ اللهِ، مَعَ أَنَّهُ لَمْ يُخْلَقْ إلا مِنْ مادَّةٍ مِنْ[١٨٦] أُمِّهِ، ومِنَ الرُوحِ الَّذي[١٨٧] نَفَخَ فيها؛ كَما قالَ تَعالىٰ: ﴿وَمَرْيَمَ ٱبْنَتَ عِمْرَٰنَ ٱلَّتِىٓ أَحْصَنَتْ فَرْجَهَا فَنَفَخْنَا فِيهِ مِن رُّوحِنَا﴾ [التحريم: ١٢]، [وقالَ تَعالىٰ:][١٨٨] ﴿فَتَمَثَّلَ لَهَا بَشَرًا سَوِيًّا ﴿١٧﴾ قَالَتْ إِنِّىٓ أَعُوذُ بِٱلرَّحْمَٰنِ مِنكَ إِن كُنتَ تَقِيًّا ﴿١٨﴾ قَالَ إِنَّمَآ أَنَا۠ رَسُولُ رَبِّكِ لِأَهَبَ لَكِ غُلَٰمًا زَكِيًّا﴾ [مريم: ١٧-١٩]؛

And for this reason, when Christ was created without a father, it sowed misapprehension into (the hearts of) some people, who began to claim that he is a [begotten] son of God, although he was only created out of his mother's substance and the breath that was breathed into her [by the angel].[189] As God says: **{And Mary the**

١٨٤ في الأصل الخطي: «وقد قيل المعرب الرجل»، والمثبت يستقيم به السياق.
١٨٥ في المطبوع: «ولكنّ الإنسان»، والمثبت من الأصل الخطي.
١٨٦ «من» سقطت من المطبوع، وهي في الأصل الخطي.
١٨٧ في الأصل الخطي والمطبوع: «التي»، والمثبت أقرب إلىٰ الصواب.
١٨٨ ما بين الحاصرتين ليس في الأصل الخطي.
189 These are the two causes for the conception of Jesus. Ibn Taymiyyah

daughter of ʿImrān, who guarded her chastity; so We blew therein by [the agency of] Our spirit [Gabriel].} [And He says:] **{Then We sent to her Our Spirit [Gabriel], and he assumed for her the likeness of a perfect man. She said, "Indeed, I seek refuge in the Most Merciful from you, if you should be fearing of God." He said, "I am only the messenger of your Lord to bestow on you a pure boy."}**

فَما خُلِقَ مِنْ غَيْرِ مادَّةٍ تَكونُ[١٩٠] كالأبِ لَهُ، قَدْ يُظَنُّ فيهِ أَنَّهُ ابْنُ اللهِ، وأنَّ اللهَ خَلَقَهُ مِنْ ذاتِهِ. فَلِهَذا كانَتِ الأَنْبِياءُ مَخْلوقَةً مِنْ مادَّةٍ، لَها أُصولٌ، ومِنْها فُروعٌ، لَها والِدٌ ومَوْلودٌ. والأَحَدُ الصَمَدُ: لَمْ يَلِدْ، ولَمْ يُولَدْ، ولَمْ يَكُنْ لَهُ كُفُواً أَحَدٌ.

[Indeed,] a thing which is created out of no [prior] matter that acts like its father could be mistaken [by some people] as a [begotten] son of God[191] and that God created it out of His own essence. And

---

clarifies elsewhere that Jesus would not have been called 'the *son* of Mary' if he were created out of only one origin. A son is necessarily born out of two created origins, although in this case Jesus was created miraculously without a father.

١٩٠ في الأصل الخطي: «يكون».

191 It is impossible for God to beget a son for many reasons. An act of begetting entails the existence of a partner or an origin that acts *together* with God, which would contradict God's oneness and independent agency. It is also impossible for God to beget a son for other reasons such as His indivisible and eternal nature: Nothing of God's essence breaks free or changes into a creation, which is what begetting a son entails. Moreover, the claim that God begot a son contradicts monotheism, for a son of God would have to be a god like its father.

this is why Prophets were created out of matter and had both origins and offspring, fathers and sons, whereas the One, Self-sufficient God does not beget, is not begotten, and has no equal.

وحُدوثُ الشَيْءِ لا مِنْ مادَّةٍ قَدْ يُشْبِهُ حُدوثَهُ مِنْ غَيْرِ رَبٍّ خالِقٍ، وقَدْ يُظَنُّ أنَّهُ حَدَثَ مِنْ ذاتِ الرَبِّ؛ كَما قِيلَ مِثْلُ ذَلِكَ في المَسيحِ، والمَلائِكَةِ أنَّها بَناتُ اللهِ، لَمّا لَمْ يَكُنْ لَها أَبٌ[١٩٢]، مَعَ أنَّها مَخْلوقَةٌ مِنْ مادَّةٍ؛ كَما ثَبَتَ في الصَحيحِ: «صَحيحِ مُسْلِمٍ» عَنْ عائِشَةَ: أنَّ النَبِيَّ ﷺ قالَ: «خُلِقَتِ المَلائِكَةُ مِنْ نورٍ، وخُلِقَ الجانُّ مِنْ مارِجٍ مِنْ نارٍ، وخُلِقَ آدَمُ مِمّا وُصِفَ لَكُمْ».

Also, things originating ex nihilo are somewhat similar to things originating without an Originator[193], and they may also be mistaken as originating out of God's essence, just as it was wrongly thought about Christ and the angels; [the angels] were [incorrectly] said to be daughters of God because they had no fathers, although they were [surely] created out of matter. For it is recorded in *Ṣaḥīḥ Muslim* that 'Ā'ishah narrated that the Prophet (may God elevate his mention) said: "Angels were created out of light, jinn were created out of a smokeless flame of fire, and Adam was created out of that which

١٩٢ في الأصل الخطي: «أبا».

193 A person who believes that all natural phenomena must have prior material conditions and natural causes has a stronger conviction in the universality of the principle of causality than someone who believes that the prior materials are not necessary conditions. Such a person should therefore have more reason to believe that these originating phenomena must have an eternal Originator who brings them into existence.

has been described to you[194]."

وَلَمَّا ظَنَّ طَائِفَةٌ أَنَّهَا لَمْ تُخْلَقْ مِنْ مَادَّةٍ، ظَنُّوا أَنَّهَا قَدِيمَةٌ أَزَلِيَّةٌ.

And when a group of people assumed that the angels were not created out of matter, they [incorrectly] thought that they are eternal and without beginning.

---

194 It is described in the Qur'ān in several places that Adam was created out of dust.

The Impossibility of Creation Ex Nihilo

وأيْضًا فالدَليلُ الّذي احْتَجَّ بِهِ كَثيرٌ مِنَ الناسِ عَلىٰ أنَّ كُلَّ حادِثٍ لا يَحْدُثُ إلا مِنْ شَيْءٍ، أو في شَيْءٍ؛ فَإنْ كانَ عَرَضًا لَمْ[195] يَحْدُثْ إلا في[196] مَحَلٍّ، وإنْ كانَ عَيْنًا قائِمَةً بِنَفْسِها لَمْ يَحْدُثْ إلا مِنْ مادَّةٍ، فَإنَّ الحادِثَ إنَّما يَحْدُثُ إذا كانَ حُدوثُه مُمْكِنًا، وكانَ يَقْبَلُ الوُجودَ والعَدَمَ، فَهُوَ مَسْبوقٌ بِإمْكانِ الحُدوثِ وجَوازِهِ، فَلا بُدَّ لَهُ مِنْ مَحَلٍّ يَقومُ بِهِ هَذا الإمْكانُ والجَوازُ.

Also, [there exists] the [Aristotelean] argument which many people use [to demonstrate] that every originating thing originates *out of* something or *in* something: If it is an accident, it originates only in a substrate, and if it is a self-subsisting concrete thing, it originates only out of matter. For an originating thing will originate only if its origination was possible and only if it accepted both existence and nonexistence. It is therefore preceded by the possibility and the permissibility of its origination. [But] there must exist a [prior] substrate in which this possibility and permissibility subsist.

وقَدْ تَنازَعوا في هَذا: هَلِ الإمْكانُ صِفَةٌ خارِجِيَّةٌ، لا بُدَّ لَها مِنْ مَحَلٍّ، أو

---

١٩٥ في المطبوع: «لا». والمثبت من الأصل الخطي.
١٩٦ في الأصل الخطي: «من»، والمثبت أولىٰ.

هِيَ حُكْمٌ عَقْلِيٌّ لا يَفْتَقِرُ إِلىٰ غَيرِ الذِهْنِ؟ والتَحْقيقُ: أَنَّهُ نَوْعانِ:

And people disputed over whether the possibility [of things] is an ontologically[197] existing **attribute** and must [therefore] subsist in some place, or is simply a rational judgement that does not depend on anything beyond the mind. The truth of the matter is that the possibility [of things] is of two kinds: [epistemic possibility and extra-mental possibility].

فالإمْكانُ الذِهْنِيُّ: وهُوَ تَجْويزُ الشَيْءِ، أو عَدَمُ العِلْمِ بامْتِناعِهِ؛ مَحَلُّهُ الذِهْنُ.

As for epistemic possibility, it is to allow for [the existence of] something [without knowing that it is actually possible], or to be ignorant of whether [or not] it is impossible. This [kind] exists in the mind [and not in the external world.]

والإمْكانُ الخارِجِيُّ المُتَعَلِّقُ بالفاعِلِ، أوِ المَحَلِّ؛ مِثْلُ أنْ تَقولَ: يُمْكِنُ القادِرُ أنْ يَفْعَلَ، والمَحَلُّ مِثْلُ أنْ تَقولَ: هَذِهِ الأَرْضُ يُمْكِنُ أنْ تُزْرَعَ، وهَذِهِ المَرْأَةُ يُمْكِنُ أنْ تَحْبَلَ= هَذا لا بُدَّ فيهِ[١٩٨] مِنْ مَحَلٍّ خارِجِيٍّ،

As for the extra-mental possibility[199] [of things], which is related to

197 Ontologically existing things are things that exist outside our minds and in reality. Those may either be concrete things or attributes of concrete things. Ontological things are contrasted with things that are mind-dependent, those existing in knowledge and conception.

١٩٨ في المطبوع: «وهذا لا بدّ له». والمثبت من الأصل الخطي صواب.

199 Extra-mental possibility may be understood as 'metaphysical possibility'. A thing is extra-mentally or metaphysically possible iff it is actually possible

an agent or a substrate, such as [the possibility that is related to an agent] when one says: "It is possible for an able agent to act", or [the possibility that is related to] a substrate when one says: "It is possible for this earth to be planted" and "it is possible for this woman to become pregnant with a child" – this [kind of possibility] must have

---

for it to occur, such that it is actually the case that its occurrence entails no impossibility whatsoever. Note that by "impossibility", we are not merely referring to strict logical contradictions such as things that both exist and do not exist, or are both moving and motionless (i.e. A and not A), but rather to the broader sense of impossibility that includes the incompatibility of propositions with the laws of metaphysics, such laws as "the cause precedes its effect temporally" or "a thing cannot exist without its concomitants".

Ibn Taymiyyah held that the mere conceivability of a thing is not enough to know that it is extra-mentally possible. This is because, in order to know that some proposition X is extra-mentally possible, one must be certain of the universality of the negative proposition: "No impossibility is entailed by X". But we are not omniscient and therefore cannot discount all potential contradictions in a given proposition by way of conception, and thus we cannot attain certainty in the universal negation in this way. Instead, in order to know that X is extra-mentally possible such that it entails no impossibility at all, one must have either (i) evidence for the existence of X, (ii) evidence for the existence of something that is similar to X, or (iii) evidence for the existence of something that is closer to impossibility than X. Otherwise, if the evidence is not available, one should withhold judgement on whether X is extra-mentally possible (unless, of course, one has infallible scriptural information that indicates that X is possible). This withholding of judgement amounts to affirming that X is merely "epistemically" possible; which is to say: "For all we know, X could be possible".

Ibn Taymiyyah mentions the example of the Resurrection of the dead. In many verses of the Qur'ān, God demonstrates the extra-mental possibility of the Resurrection by referring to our initial creation as evidence. [*Dar' Ta'āruḍ al-'Aql wa al-Naql*, Vol 1, pp. 30-32].

a substrate which exists ontologically.

فَإذا قِيلَ عَنِ الرَبِّ: يُمْكِنُ أنْ يَخْلُقَ؛ فَمَعْناهُ أَنَّهُ يَقْدِرُ عَلىٰ ذَلِكَ، ويَتَمَكَّنُ مِنْهُ. وهَذِهِ صِفَةٌ قائِمَةٌ بِهِ.

For example, when it is said that "it is possible for the Lord to create", the meaning is that He has **power** and is **able** to do so. Such a possibility is an [ontologically existing] attribute that subsists in His essence.

وإذا قِيلَ: يُمْكِنُ أنْ يَحْدُثَ حادِثٌ؛ فَإنْ قِيلَ يُمْكِنُ حُدوثُهُ بِدُونِ سَبَبٍ حادِثٍ، فَهُوَ مُمْتَنِعٌ، وإذا كانَ الحُدوثُ لا بُدَّ لَهُ مِنْ سَبَبٍ حادِثٍ؛ فَذاكَ السَبَبُ إنْ كانَ قائِمًا بِذاتِ الرَبِّ، فَذاتُهُ قَديمَةٌ أَزَلِيَّةٌ، واخْتِصاصُ ذَلِكَ الوَقْتِ بِقِيامِ مَشيئَةٍ، أوْ تَمامِ تَمَكُّنٍ، ونَحْوِ ذَلِكَ، لا يَكونُ إلا لِسَبَبٍ قَدْ أَحْدَثَهُ قَبْلَ هَذا في غَيْرِهِ، فَلا يَحْدُثُ حادِثٌ مُبايِنٌ إلا مَسْبوقًا بِحادِثٍ مُبايِنٍ لَهُ.

And if it is said that "it is possible for some creation to originate", then, if it is said that it is possible for this origination [to occur] without a cause that occurs [before it], that will be impossible. And since the origination must have a cause that occurred [before it, we say:] If that cause subsisted in the essence of the Lord, then [it is also known that] the essence of the Lord is eternal and without beginning, and therefore that the specification of that [specific] time with the occurrence of a decision, the fulfillment of power, and the like, can never be without a reason[200] which [the Lord] had originated before in something else. Thus, every creation that is separate [from the Lord] is preceded by [the origination of] another creation that is separate from the Lord.

فالحُدوثُ مَسْبوقٌ[٢٠١] بإمْكانِهِ، ولا بُدَّ لإمْكانِهِ مِنْ مَحَلٍّ، ولِهَذا لَمْ يَذْكُرِ اللهُ قَطُّ أنَّهُ أَحْدَثَ شَيْئًا إلا مِنْ شَيْءٍ.

Thus, the origination [of things] is preceded by its possibility. And for that possibility, there must exist a substrate. And this is why God only mentions [in the Qur'ān] that He creates things out of others[202], [not ex nihilo.]

---

200 The Arabic word is *sabab*, which is usually translated as 'cause'. More generally, it denotes something that leads to another.

٢٠١ في المطبوع: «مسبوقًا»، خطأ. والتصحيح من الأصل الخطي.

202 Omnipotence is to have power over everything that is *possible*, and thus the omnipotence of God would not be challenged if creating things without prior materials is impossible. Impossibilities and are not 'things' to begin with, and they are therefore excluded from God's omnipotence and divine power that is mentioned in Qur'anic verses such as: **{God has power over all things}**.

This point can be elaborated further by pointing out that the existence of something without its necessary conditions is impossible and entails a contradiction. Consider the following question: "Is it possible for God to originate a human's actions without originating his power first?" Rational minds accept that this is impossible, for the human power is a necessary condition for the existence of the human act. In much the same way, it can be argued that God originates a tree only after originating its material conditions. Neither example would undermine the omnipotence of God and His maximal perfection.

Note that the impossibility of creation ex nihilo would entail an infinite regress of conditions or of secondary causes at the most, not a regress of de-

والّذي يَقولُ: إنَّ جِنْسَ الحَوادِثِ حَدَثَتْ لا مِنْ شَيْءٍ، هُوَ كَقَوْلِهِمْ: إنَّها حَدَثَتْ بِلا سَبَبٍ حادِثٍ، مَعَ قَوْلِهِمْ إنَّها كانَتْ مُمْتَنِعَةً، ثُمَّ صارَتْ مُمْكِنَةً مِنْ غَيْرِ تَجَدُّدِ سَبَبٍ، بَلْ حَقيقَةُ قَوْلِهِمْ أنَّ الرَبَّ صارَ قادِرًا بَعْدَ أنْ لَمْ يَكُنْ، مِنْ غَيْرِ تَجَدُّدِ شَيْءٍ يُوجِبُ ذَلِكَ. وهَذِهِ الأُمورُ كُلُّها مِنْ أقْوالِ الجَهْمِيَّةِ: أَهْلِ الكَلامِ المُحْدَثِ المُبْتَدَعِ المَذْمومِ، وهُوَ بَناءً عَلى قَوْلِهِمْ: إنَّهُ تَمْتَنِعُ حَوادِثُ لا أَوَّلَ لَها. وهَؤُلاءِ وأَمْثالُهُمْ غَلِطوا فيما جاءَ بِهِ الشَرْعُ، وأَخْبَرَتْ بِهِ الرُسُلُ؛ كَما غَلِطوا في المَعْقولاتِ...

And the claim of those [theologians] who say that the genus of creations has originated ex nihilo is similar to the claim of one who says that they have originated without any originating cause, in addition to their claim that they were once impossible before becoming possible without a reason.[203] In fact, the reality of their claim is

pendencies. The creations of God would be conditioned on preceding things which serve as material conditions for their existence and without which their coming into existence would be impossible, but it would not follow that there is a regress of creators or originators in the materials. Also note that it would not follow that the world is fully deterministic if creation without prior matter is impossible. God will still be choosing to create these particular creations instead of others out of the materials, and He will still be able to intervene in the world through the creation of miracles. This is not the only possible world which God is able to create; it is in the perfect power of God to create completely different worlds out of matter.

203 Ibn Taymiyyah accepts that the possibility of the origination of each *particular* creation is not permanent and that it originates. However, he also argues that the origination of this possibility must be due to prior reasons and causes that are prepared by God, which implies the infinite regress of material conditions and of God's created effects.

that God became powerful after having been powerless without the occurrence of anything which caused this [to happen]. All of these are [consequences of] the claims of the Jahmiyyah, the proponents of innovated and blameworthy Kalām, and they are predicated on their [initial] claim that it is impossible for events to regress into the past[204]. These [Jahmiyyah] and their counterparts were mistaken in regards to what the [prescribed] Law has brought and the Prophets have conveyed[205], just as they were mistaken in regards to the rational judgements...

---

204 If the regress of events is said to be impossible, God's act must be said to be impossible from the infinite past. This in turn would imply that His act cannot become possible at a later time and into the infinite future. This is because such a change from the state of impossibility to the state of possibility must have a cause, such as a divine act or decision. But since the regress of events was said to be impossible, no act or decision that causes this change could have existed prior to the change. Thus, a God whose act of creation is impossible from the eternal past must forever remain powerless in the future, which clearly contradicts His necessary perfection and the fact of creation.

205 One of the few scriptural evidences that can be understood to contradict Ibn Taymiyyah's position on the impossibility of creation without prior matter is a ḥadīth in *Ṣaḥīḥ al-Bukhārī* (3191) which mentions that the Prophet Muḥammad (may God elevate his mention) said to a group of Yemenites who asked him about the creation of this world: "God was, and there was nothing with Him". Ibn Taymiyyah points out that the Prophet went on to say in that same ḥadīth: "And His Throne was on the water. And He wrote everything in the Reminder. And [then] He created the heavens and the earth", thus indicating that the Throne and the water were already in existence prior to the creation of this world when there was nothing "with" God. Furthermore, Ibn Taymiyyah answers that the more accurate narration of that same incident is the ḥadīth in *Ṣaḥīḥ al-Bukhārī* (7418) where it is recorded that the Prophet said instead: "God was, and there was nothing *before* Him..." [*Majmūʿ al-Fatāwā*, Vol 18, p. 216].

بيان
تلبيس الجهمية

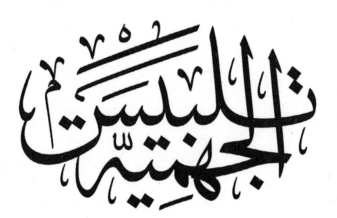

الدليل على استحالة المادة

On the Argument for the Creation of Matter

The Indivisible Atom

فَصْلٌ: وأَصْلُ هَؤُلاءِ المُتَكَلِّمِينَ مِنَ الجَهْمِيَّةِ المُعْتَزِلَةِ ومَنْ وافَقَهُمُ الّذي بَنَوْا عَلَيْهِ هَذا هُوَ مَسْأَلَةُ الجَوْهَرِ الفَرْدِ، فَإِنَّهُمْ ظَنّوا أَنَّ القَوْلَ بِإِثْباتِ الصانِعِ وبِأَنَّهُ خَلَقَ السَمَاواتِ والأَرْضَ وبِأَنَّهُ يُقِيمُ القِيامَةَ ويَبْعَثُ الناسَ مِنَ القُبورِ لايَتِمُّ إلا بِإِثْباتِ الجَوْهَرِ الفَرْدِ، فَجَعَلوهُ أَصْلاً لِلإِيمانِ باللهِ واليَوْمِ الآخِرِ.

SECTION: The [existence of the **conceptually**] **indivisible atom** [i.e. point-sized atom] is the foundation on which Kalām theologians – the Muʿtazilah, Jahmiyyah, and others[206] who agreed with them – have predicated this matter [of theology]. For they have [falsely] assumed that the belief in the Maker's existence, that He has created the heavens and the earth, brings the world to an end, and resurrects people out of their graves, is [all] incomplete without first affirming the existence of the indivisible atom. Thus, they have made it a basis for faith in God and the Last Day.

أَمّا جُمْهورُ المُعْتَزِلَةِ ومَنْ وافَقَهُمْ كَأَبي المَعالي وذَوِيْهِ فَيَجْعَلونَ الإيمانَ

206 These others are mainly the Ashʿarī theologians.

باللهِ تَعالىٰ لايَحْصُلُ إلا بِذَلِكَ. وكَذَلِكَ الإيمانُ باليَوْمِ الآخِرِ، إذْ كانوا يَقولونَ: لايُعْرَفُ ذَلِكَ إلا بِمَعْرِفَةِ حُدوثِ العالَمِ، ولايُعْرَفُ حُدوثُهُ إلا بِطَرِيقَةِ الأعْراضِ. وطَريقَةُ الأعْراضِ مَبْنِيَّةٌ علىٰ أنَّ الأجْسامَ لاتَخْلو مِنْها، وهَذا لَمْ يُمْكِنْهُم أنْ يُثْبِتوهُ إلا بالأكْوانِ الّتي هِيَ الاجْتِماعُ والافْتِراقُ والحَرَكَةُ والسُكونُ. فَعَلىٰ هَذِهِ الطَريقَةِ اعْتَمَدَ أوَّلُوهُمْ وآخِرُوهُمْ.

As for the majority of the Muʿtazilah and those who agreed with them, like Abu al-Maʿāli [al-Juwaynī] and his adherents, they consider that the belief in God and the Last Day cannot be realized without first affirming the existence of this atom. For they claim that the knowledge [of God and the Last Day] is predicated on first knowing that the world was originated [ex nihilo], and that the knowledge of its origination is predicated on the argument from accidents, an argument that is [in turn] predicated on [the claim] that bodies are never void of [originating] accidents. But this latter they could not affirm without first affirming that all bodies are [constantly] in four modes of being: (i) **combination**, (ii) **separation**, (iii) **motion** and (iv) **stillness**. This is the method on which both the early and the late [Jahmiyyah] rely –

حَتّىٰ القائِلينَ بِأنَّ الجَواهِرَ لا تَخْلو عَنْ كُلِّ جِنْسٍ مِنْ أجْناسِ الأعْراضِ، وعَنْ جَميعِ أضْدادِهِ إنْ كانَ لَهُ أضْدادٌ، وإنْ كانَ لَهُ ضِدٌّ واحِدٌ لَمْ يَخْلُ الجَوْهَرُ عَنْ أَحَدِ الضِدَّيْنِ، وإنْ قُدِّرَ عَرَضٌ لا ضِدَّ[٢٠٧] لَهُ لَمْ يَخْلُ الجَوْهَرُ عَنْ قَبولِ واحِدٍ مِنْ جِنْسِهِ إذا لَمْ يَمْنَعْ مانِعٌ مِنْ قَبولِهِ، فَإنَّ هَذا

٢٠٧ في الأصل الخطي والمطبوع: «جنس»، خطأ.

أَبْلَغُ الأَقْوالِ، وهُوَ قَوْلُ أَصْحابِ الأَشْعَرِيِّ ومَنْ وافَقَهُمْ كالقاضي أَبِي بَكْرٍ والقاضي أَبِي يَعْلىٰ وأَبِي المَعالي الجُوَيْنِيِّ وأَبِي الحَسَنِ الزاغُونيِّ وغَيْرِهِمْ. فَإِنَّهُ لَمْ يُمْكِنْهُمْ أَنْ يُثْبِتوا أَنَّ الجِسْمَ لا يَخْلو مِنَ الأَعْراضِ إلا بالأَكْوانِ.

[This includes] even those who claim that substances are never void of any one of the categories of accidents. Or [that substances are never void] of all opposite [accidents] if the accident [is said to] have [numerous] opposites. And [that] if an accident [is said to] have [only] one opposite, the substances cannot be void of both of the two opposites. Or, [alternatively,] if an accident is assumed to be without an opposite, the substances cannot be void of one [accident] from the [same] category, provided that nothing prevents the [substance] from accepting [its attribution] – for this statement is at the extreme. And it is the position of the students of [Abu al-Ḥasan] al-Ashʿarī and those who agreed, like Qaḍī Abū Bakr [al-Bāqillānī], Qaḍī Abū Yaʿlā, Abu al-Maʿālī al-Juwaynī, Abu al-Ḥasan al-Zāghūnī, and others. Indeed, these [Kalām theologians] could not affirm that bodies are never void of [originating] accidents without [affirming] the [four] **modes of being**.

ثُمَّ عِنْدَ التَحْقيقِ لَمْ يُمْكِنْهُمْ أَنْ يُثْبِتوا ذَلِكَ إلا بالاجْتِماعِ والافْتِراقِ، فَإِنَّ مِنْهُمْ مَنْ يَقولُ: السُكونُ أَمْرٌ عَدَمِيٌّ، ومِنْهُمْ مَنْ يَقولُ: الكَوْنُ الّذي هُوَ الحَرَكَةُ والسُكونُ إِنَّما يَلْزَمُ إذا كانَ الجِسْمُ في مَكانٍ، فَأَمّا إذا لَمْ يَكُنْ في مَكانٍ فَيَجوزُ خُلُوُّهُ عَنِ الحَرَكَةِ والسُكونِ، كَما يَقولُهُ طَوائِفُ كالّذينَ قالوا ذَلِكَ مِنَ الكَرّامِيَّةِ. فَآلَ الأَمْرُ بِهَذِهِ الطَريقَةِ إلىٰ الاجْتِماعِ والافْتِراقِ،

وعَلىٰ ذَلِكَ اعْتَمَدَ أبو المَعالي وغَيْرُهُ مِنَ الأشْعَرِيَّةِ، وعَلىٰ ذَلِكَ اعْتَمَدَ مُحَمَّدُ بنُ الهَيْصَمِ وغَيْرُهُ مِنَ الكَرّامِيَّةِ.

But after examining the matter, they could only affirm this [accompaniment of originating accidents] by [affirming the first two modes of being:] **combination** and **separation**. For some of them have claimed that stillness is [a] negative [attribute][208], and others have claimed that the modes of motion and stillness are only necessitated if the physical body exists in [relation to] a place, [and that] it may be void of both motion and stillness if it did not exist in a place, as it was claimed by some of the groups like the people among the Karrāmiyyah who take this position. Thus, this method [of demonstrating the Maker's existence] came to rest on [demonstrating that all physical bodies are constantly in the two states of] **combination** and **separation**. Abu al-Maʿālī and others from the Ashʿarīyyah relied on this very method. Muḥammad ibn al-Hayṣam and others from the Karrāmiyyah relied on this method [too].

ومَعْلومٌ أنَّ قَبولَ الاجْتِماعِ والافْتِراقِ لَمْ يُمْكِنْهُمْ [أنْ يُثْبِتوهُ][٢٠٩] حَتّىٰ يُثْبِتوا أنَّ الجِسْمَ يَقْبَلُ الاجْتِماعَ والافْتِراقَ، وذَلِكَ مَبْنِيٌّ علىٰ أنَّهُ مُرَكَّبٌ مِنَ الأجْزاءِ الّتي هِيَ الجَواهِرُ المُنْفَرِدَةُ. فَصارَ الإقْرارُ بالصانِعِ مَبْنِيًّا عِنْدَ هَؤُلاءِ المُتَكَلِّمِينَ علىٰ إثْباتِ الجَوْهَرِ الفَرْدِ.

But it is known that the [Kalām theologians] could not affirm that physical bodies are always combining and separating [i.e. rearranging from within] without first affirming that all bodies are subject

208 A negative attribute is the mere absence of some positive attribute.

٢٠٩ زيادة لازمة ليستقيم الكلام.

to assembly and disassembly. And this was predicated on the existence of [conceptually] indivisible atoms that [are said to] constitute the physical bodies. Thus, the belief in the Maker's existence became predicated by those Kalām theologians on the existence of the **indivisible atom**.

ثُمَّ الّذينَ ذَكَروا أنَّ لَهُمْ طَريقًا إلىٰ إثْباتِ الصانِعِ غَيْرَ هَذِهِ كَأبي عَبْدِ اللهِ الرازيِّ وغَيْرِهِ – وهُوَ الّذي عَلَيْهِ أبو الحَسَنِ الأشْعَرِيُّ وغَيْرُهُ مِنَ الحُذّاقِ – قالَ مَنْ قالَ مِنْ هَؤُلاءِ: إنَّ إثْباتَ المَعادِ مَوْقوفٌ علىٰ ثُبوتِ الجَوْهَرِ الفَرْدِ. وهَذا قَوْلُ أبي عَبْدِ اللهِ الرازيِّ وغَيْرِهِ، وهُوَ مُخَلَّصٌ مِمَّنْ جَعَلَهُ الأصْلَ في الإيمانِ باللهِ، فَجَعَلَهُ هُوَ الأصْلَ في الإيمانِ بالمَعادِ، مَعَ كَوْنِهِ يَجْعَلُهُ أصْلًا في نَفْيِ الصِفاتِ الّتي يُنْكِرُها كَما سَيَأْتي بيانُهُ.

Moreover, many of the [theologians] who claim to have routes other than this [argument from the Origination of Bodies] for demonstrating the Maker's existence, [figures] such as Abū ʿAbdullāh al-Rāzī and others – which is also the position of Abu al-Ḥasan al-Ashʿarī and other experts – ended up saying: The affirmation of the **Resurrection** is conditional on the affirmation of the indivisible atom. This is the position of Abū ʿAbdullāh al-Rāzī and others, and it is taken from [the claims of] those [theologians] who consider the [indivisible atom] to be a basis for the belief in God; he thus makes it a basis for the belief in the Resurrection. Additionally, he considers it to be a basis for the negation of the [divine] attributes which he rejects, as is explained [later].

قالَ في بَعْضِ أكْبَرِ كُتُبِهِ الكَلامِيَّةِ الّذي سَمّاهُ «نِهايَةَ العُقولِ»: «في الأصْلِ

السابِعَ عَشَرَ: اعْلَمْ أَنَّ مُعْظَمَ الكَلامِ في المَعادِ إنَّما يَكونُ مَعَ الفَلاسِفَةِ، وَلَهُمْ أُصولٌ يُفَرِّعونَ شُبَهَهُمْ عَلَيها. فَيَجِبُ عَلَينا إيرادُ تِلْكَ الأُصولِ أَوَّلًا ثُمَّ الخَوْضُ بَعْدَها في المَقْصودِ. فَلا جَرَمَ رَتَّبْنا الكَلامَ في هَذا الأَصْلِ عَلىٰ أَقْسامٍ ثَلاثَةٍ. القِسْمُ الأَوَّلُ: في المُقَدِّماتِ، وفيهِ ثَمانُ مَسائِلَ. المَسْأَلَةُ الأُولىٰ: في الجُزْءِ الّذي لا يَتَجَزَّأُ.

Al-Rāzī states in one of his largest works on Kalām, which he called *Nihāyat al-ʿUqūl*: "On the seventeenth principle. Know that most of the discussion on [the topic of] the Resurrection is with the Philosophers. They have their [own] foundations on which they base their misconceptions. As such, we must first mention these foundations before engaging [them to prove] the intended conclusion. We arrange the discussion on the [seventeenth] principle into three sections. The first section is on the premises, and it contains eight questions. The first question is on the **indivisible atom**.

ولا شَكَّ أَنَّ الأَجْسامَ الّتي نُشاهِدُها قابِلَةٌ لِلانْقِساماتِ. فالانْقِساماتُ الّتي يُمْكِنُ حُصولُها فيها إمّا أَنْ تَكونَ مُتَناهِيَةً أو لا تَكونُ. فَيَخْرُجُ مِنْ هَذا التَقْسيمِ أَقْسامٌ أَرْبَعَةٌ، أَوَّلُها: أَنْ تَكونَ الانْقِساماتُ حاصِلَةً وتَكونَ مُتَناهِيَةً. وثانيها: أَنْ تَكونَ حاصِلَةً وتَكونَ غَيْرَ مُتَناهِيَةٍ. وثالِثُها: أَنْ لا تَكونَ حاصِلَةً ولكِنْ ما يُمْكِنُ حُصولُهُ مِنْها يَكونُ مُتَناهِيًا. ورابِعُها: أَنْ لا تَكونَ حاصِلَةً ولكِنْ ما يُمْكِنُ حُصولُهُ مِنْها يَكونُ غَيْرَ مُتَناهٍ. فالأَوَّلُ مَذْهَبُ جُمْهورِ المُتَكَلِّمينَ، والثاني مَذْهَبُ النَظَّامِ، والثالِثُ مَذْهَبُ

بَعْضِ الْمُتَأَخِّرِينَ، وَالرابِعُ مَذْهَبُ الفَلاسِفَةِ.

[Now,] it is without doubt that the bodies we observe [in the natural world] **accept** division. The divisions which may occur in them are either **finite** or **infinite**. From this, four categories arise. The first is [the claim] that the divisions are [both] actualized and finite. The second is that the divisions are actualized and infinite. The third is that the divisions are not actualized, but that [the divisions] which can be actualized therefrom are finite. And the fourth is that the divisions are not actualized, but that [the divisions] which can be actualized therefrom are infinite. The first is the position of the majority of the Kalām theologians. The second is the position of al-Naẓẓām[210]. The third is the position of some of the late [theologians]. And the fourth is the position of the Philosophers.

فَنَخْلُصُ مِنْ هَذا أَنَّ الْخِلافَ بَيْنَنا وَبَيْنَ الفَلاسِفَةِ في هَذِهِ المَسْأَلَةِ يَقَعُ في مَقامَيْنِ. أَحَدُهُما: أَنَّ الجِسْمَ مَعَ كَوْنِهِ قابِلًا لِلانْقِساماتِ، هَلْ يُعْقَلُ أَنْ يَكونَ واحِدًا؟ ثانيهما: أَنَّهُ بِتَقْديرِ أَنْ يَكونَ واحِدًا، هَلْ يُعْقَلُ أَنْ يَكونَ قابِلًا لِلانْقِساماتِ الغَيْرِ مُتَناهِيَةٍ؟»

From this, we conclude that our dispute with the Philosophers is over two things. The first is whether it is conceivable for bodies to be **singular** if they accept division[211]. The second is whether, assuming

---

210 Abū Isḥāq Ibrāhīm ibn Sayyār (d. 220H) was one of the leading figures of the Muʿtazilah and the father of the Naẓẓāmiyyah sect. He had heretic views that were condemned by fellow Muʿtazilah.

211 Fakhr al-Dīn al-Rāzī believed that no body can be singular, but that every spatially extended entity must be composed of multiple conceptually indivisible (point-sized) atoms. For this reason, he argued that God must be

that they are singular, it is conceivable that they undergo divisions that are **infinite**."

وَأَعْجَبُ مِنْ هَذا أَنَّهُمْ يَجْعَلُونَ إِثْباتَ الجَوْهَرِ الفَرْدِ دِينَ المُسْلِمِينَ حَتَّىٰ يُعَدُّ مُنْكِرُهُ خارِجًا عَنِ الدِينِ، كَما قالَ أَبُو المَعالِي وذَوُوهُ: «اتَّفَقَ المُسْلِمونَ عَلَىٰ أَنَّ الأَجْسامَ تَتَناهَىٰ فِي تَجَزُّئِها وانْقِسامِها حَتَّىٰ تَصِيرَ أَفْرادًا، وكُلُّ جُزْءٍ لايَتَجَزَّأُ ولا يَنْقَسِمُ، ولَيْسَ لَهُ طَرَفٌ وحَدٌّ وجُزْءٌ شائِعٌ ولا يَتَمَيَّزُ. وإلىٰ هَذا صارَ المُتَعَمِّقونَ فِي الهَنْدَسَةِ وعَبَّرُوا عَنِ الجُزْءِ بالنُّقْطَةِ، فَقالوا: النُّقْطَةُ شَيْءٌ لا يَنْقَسِمُ.

Even more astonishing is that they have made [the belief in] the [conceptually] indivisible atom into a part of the religion of the Muslims, to the extent that they have excommunicated those who rejected the existence of the indivisible atom, as Abu al-Maʿālī claims: "Muslims

---

incorporeal if He is to be truly One, for He would otherwise be composite and consisting of multiple indivisible atoms. Ibn Taymiyyah rejected this view of al-Rāzī and maintained that God has a tremendous measure and a spatial location above the world while also stressing that He is One God who is not composed of atoms or substances that are located in distinct spaces.

By contrast, the Philosophers believed that spatially extended bodies are singular as long as they are divisible only potentially and are not actually divided into smaller parts. This potential divisibility continues indefinitely without an end in their view.

In disagreement with both the views of al-Rāzī and those of the Philosophers, Ibn Taymiyyah made the more nuanced distinction between conceptual divisibility on the one hand, and actual (or potential) divisibility on the other. He argued that all bodies are conceptually divisible ad infinitum, but that composite bodies are divisible to an end both actually and potentially.

unanimously agree that bodies are divisible to an end, such that they reduce to single atoms which are indivisible, inseparable [in themselves], and have no sides, spatial limits, or discernible extension. This is also the position of geometricians, for they refer to this atom as a [geometric] **point** and say that it is indivisible.

وصارَ الأَكْثَرونَ مِنَ الفَلاسِفَةِ إلىٰ أنَّ الأجْسامَ لا تَتَناهىٰ في تَجَزُّئِها وانْقِسامِها، وإلىٰ هَذا صارَ النَظّامُ مِنْ أهْلِ المِلَّةِ. ثُمَّ اعْتَرَفوا بِأنَّهُ تَنْتَهي قِسْمَتُها بالفِعْلِ ولا تَنْتَهي قِسْمَتُها بالقُوَّةِ، ويَعْنُونَ بالقُوَّةِ صَلاحِيَّةَ الجُزْءِ للانْقِسامِ. والعَجَبُ أنَّهُمْ اتَّفَقوا عَلىٰ أنَّ الأجْرامَ مُتَناهِيَةُ الحُدودِ والأقْطارِ، مُنْقَطِعَةُ الأطْرافِ والأكْثافِ، وكَذَلِكَ عَلىٰ كُلِّ جُمْلَةٍ ذاتِ مَساحَةٍ فَإنَّ لَها غاياتٍ ومُنْقَطَعاتٍ بالجِهاتِ، ثُمَّ قَضَوْا بِأنَّها تَنْقَسِمُ أجْزاءً بِلا نِهايَةٍ. والجُمْلَةُ المَحْدودَةُ كَيْفَ تَنْقَسِمُ أجْزاءً لا تَتَناهىٰ ولا يُحاطُ بِها؟!»

However, most Philosophers take the [other] position [and claim] that bodies may be divided indefinitely. This is also the position taken by al-Naẓẓām [who is] counted among the followers of the religion. The [Philosophers] admitted that physical bodies are divided actually to an end, but [claimed that they] are divisible potentially without an end. By 'potential' [divisibility], they mean to say that the part accepts division. And it is strange how they agree that physical bodies have finite limits, diameters, spatial extensions, and densities, and also that every sum of a given surface has a spatial limit and a boundary to its dimensions, but then claim that the physical bodies divide indefinitely into smaller parts. [For] how can a limited sum be divided into a countless and infinite number of parts?!"

قُلْتُ: والكَلامُ فِي ذَلِكَ مِنْ وَجْهَيْنِ:

I say: This claim [by Abu al-Maʿālī] can be criticized from two aspects:

The First Response

أَحَدُهُما: أنّا نَعْلَمُ بالاضْطِرارِ مِنْ دِينِ الإسْلامِ أنَّ الرَسولَ والصَحابَةَ والتابِعينَ وأئِمَّةَ المُسْلِمينَ لَمْ يَبْنُوا شَيْئًا مِنْ أَمْرِ الدِينِ عَلىٰ ثُبوتِ الجَوْهَرِ الفَرْدِ ولا انْتِفائِهِ. ولَيْسَ المُرادُ بِذَلِكَ أَنَّهُمْ لَمْ يَنْطِقوا بِهَذا اللَفْظِ، فَإنَّهُ قَدْ تَجَدَّدَ بَعْدَهُمْ أَلْفاظٌ اصْطِلاحِيَّةٌ يُعَبَّرُ بِها عَمَّا دَلَّ عَلَيْهِ كَلامُهُمْ في الجُمْلَةِ، وذَلِكَ بِمَنْزِلَةِ تَنَوُّعِ اللُغاتِ وتَرْكيبِ الأَلْفاظِ المُفْرَداتِ. وإنَّما المَقْصودُ أنَّ المَعْنىٰ الّذي يَقْصِدُهُ المُثْبِتَةُ والنُفاةُ بِلَفْظِ «الجَوْهَرِ الفَرْدِ» لَمْ يَبْنِ عَلَيْها أَحَدٌ مِنْ سَلَفِ الأُمَّةِ وأَئِمَّتِها مَسْأَلَةً واحِدَةً مِنْ مَسائِلِ الدِينِ ولا رَبَطوا بِذَلِكَ حُكْمًا عِلْمِيًّا ولا عَمَلِيًّا.

The first aspect is to say that we know by necessity from the religion of Islam that the Prophet (may God elevate his mention), his Companions, their righteous followers, and the leading scholars of Islam did not predicate anything of the matters of the religion on the existence or the nonexistence of the indivisible atoms. And we are not merely saying that they did not mention the term ['indivisible atom']. Indeed, new terms which generally indicate what they meant were introduced later; this is like the variety in languages and in expression. Rather, we are saying that the **very meaning** denoted by the 'indivisible atom' was not considered by the early Muslims and their leading scholars to be a foundation for a single matter in the religion, nor have they associated it with any matter of belief or practice.

فَدَعْوَىٰ المُدَّعِي انْبِناءَ أَصْلِ الإيمانِ باللهِ واليَوْمِ الآخِرِ عَلىٰ ذَلِكَ يُضاهي دَعْوَىٰ المُدَّعِي أَنَّ ما بَيَّنوهُ مِنَ الإيمانِ باللهِ واليَوْمِ الآخِرِ لَيْسَ هُوَ عَلىٰ ما بَيَّنوهُ، بَلْ إمّا أَنَّهُمْ ما كانُوا يَعْلَمونَ الحَقَّ، أو يَجُوزُ الكَذِبُ في هَذا البابِ لِمَصْلَحَةِ الجُمْهورِ، كَما يَقولُ نَحْوَ ذَلِكَ مَنْ يَقولُهُ مِنَ المُنافِقِينَ مِنَ المُتَفَلْسِفَةِ والقَرامِطَةِ ونَحْوِهِمْ مِنَ الباطِنِيَّةِ. فَإِنَّهُمْ إذا أَثْبَتوا مِنْ أُصولِ الدينِ ما يُعْلَمُ بالاضْطِرارِ أَنَّهُ لَيْسَ مِنْ أُصولِ الدينِ لَزِمَ قَطْعًا تَغْييرُ الدينِ وتَبْدِيلُهُ. ولِهَذا زادَ أَهْلُ هَذا الفَنِّ في الدِينِ ونَقَصُوا مِنْهُ عِلْمًا وعَمَلًا،

[Indeed,] for one to claim that the belief in God and the Last Day is predicated on the existence of indivisible atoms is **comparable** to claiming that these matters of the Faith which they [the Pious Predecessors] have mentioned are not in actual fact as they have described, but that they were either ignorant of the truth, or [that they believed that it is] permissible to lie in such matters for the benefit of the masses, just as it is claimed by the hypocritical Philosophers, the Qarāmiṭah, and other such esotericists.[212] For if the [Kalām theologians] hold as a religious foundation that which is known by necessity to be otherwise, it necessarily implies that they are changing and replacing the religion. In this way have the proponents of the science [of Kalām] added beliefs and practices to the religion while

212 These are extremely heretical groups that distinguish between an outer (exoteric) and an inner (esoteric) meaning in the revealed texts. Arabic: *Bāṭiniyyah*.

subtracting others.

وإذا كانَ كَذَلِكَ لَمْ يَكُنِ الخَوْضُ في هَذِهِ المَسْألَةِ مِمّا يُبْنَىٰ عَلَيْهِ الدِينُ، بَلْ مَسْألَةً مِنْ مَسائِلِ الأُمورِ الطَبيعِيَّةِ، كالقَوْلِ في غَيْرِها مِنْ أحْكامِ الأجْسامِ الكُلِّيَّةِ.

If that is the case, the engagement in the topic of [conceptually] indivisible atoms will instead be a subject of **natural science**, not a matter of religion, just like the other universal descriptions of natural bodies [i.e. the laws of physics] are also a topic of natural science.

وأيْضًا: فَإنَّهُ أَطْبَقَ أئِمَّةُ الإسْلامِ عَلىٰ ذَمِّ مَنْ بَنىٰ دِينَهُ عَلىٰ الكَلامِ في الجَواهِرِ والأعْراضِ.

Moreover, the leading scholars of Islam have unanimously considered it blameworthy for people to predicate their religious convictions on discussions in substances and accidents [as the Kalām theologians do].

ثُمَّ هَؤُلاءِ الّذين ادَّعَوْا تَوَقُّفَ الإيمانِ باللهِ واليَوْم الآخِرِ عَلىٰ ثُبوتِهِ قَدْ شَكُّوا فيهِ وقَدْ تَوَقَّفُوا في آخِرِ عُمُرِهِمْ، كَإمام المُتَأخِّرينَ مِنَ المُعْتَزِلَةِ أبي الحُسَيْنِ البَصْرِيِّ، وإمامِ المُتَأخِّرينَ مِنَ الأشْعَرِيَّةِ أبي المَعالي الجُوَيْنِيِّ، وإمامِ المُتَأخِّرينَ مِنَ الفَلاسِفَةِ والمُتَكَلِّمينَ أبي عَبْدِ اللهِ الرازِيِّ.

And those [theologians] who have predicated the belief in God and the Last Day on the existence of [conceptually indivisible atoms] themselves became undecided about the [existence of these atoms] in the end, as was the case of the *imām* of the later day Muʿtazilah: Abu al-Ḥusayn al-Baṣrī, the *imām* of the later day Ashʿarīyyah: Abu al-Maʿālī al-Juwaynī, and the *imām* of the later day Philosophers and Kalām theologians: Abū ʿAbdullāh al-Rāzī.

فَإِنَّهُ في كِتابِهِ بَعْدَ أنْ بَيَّنَ تَوَقُّفَ المَعادِ عَلىٰ ثُبوتِهِ – وذَكَرَ ذَلِكَ غيرَ مَرَّةٍ في أثْناءِ مُناظَرَتِهِ للفَلاسِفَةِ – قالَ في المَسْألَةِ بِعَيْنِها، لَمّا أَوْرَدَ حُجَجَ نُفاةِ الجَوْهَرِ الفَرْدِ، فَقالَ: «وأمّا المُعارَضاتُ الّتي ذَكَروها فاعْلَمْ أنَّ مِنَ العُلَماءِ مَنْ مالَ إلىٰ التَوَقُّفِ في هَذِهِ المَسْألَةِ بِسَبَبِ تَعارُضِ الأدِلَّةِ، فَإنَّ إمامَ الحَرَمَيْنِ صَرَّحَ في كِتابِ «التَلْخيصِ في أُصولِ الفِقْهِ» أنَّ هَذِهِ المَسْألَةَ مِنْ مَحاراتِ العُقولِ، وأبو الحُسَيْنِ البَصْرِيُّ – هُوَ أحْذَقُ المُعْتَزِلَةِ – تَوَقَّفَ فيها. ونَحْنُ أيْضًا نَخْتارُ هَذا التَوَقُّفَ».

Indeed, in his [same] book, after explaining that the [knowledge of] Resurrection is predicated on [first knowing] the existence of [the indivisible atom], [al-Rāzī] later states in the course of his debate with the Philosophers and his mentioning of their counter-arguments: "In regards to the counter arguments presented [by the Philosophers against the indivisible atom], do know that some scholars have indeed inclined towards suspending judgement on this matter due to conflicting arguments. The Imām of the Two Mosques [Abu al-Maʿālī al-Juwaynī] explicitly mentions in his *'Talkhīṣ fī Uṣūl al-Fiqh'* that this matter is puzzling. Abu al-Ḥusayn al-Baṣrī, one of the most erudite Muʿtazilah, also became undecided about it in the end. Similarly, we choose to suspend judgement on this issue."

فَأَيُّ ضَلالٍ فِي الدِينِ وخُذْلانٍ لَهُ أَعْظَمُ مِنْ هَذا؟

So can there be a greater misguidance and fall from (divine) grace than this?

The Second Response

الوَجْهُ الثاني: دَعْواهُمْ أنَّ هَذا قَوْلَ المُسْلِمِينَ أو قَوْلَ جُمْهورِ مُتَكَلِّمِي المُسْلِمِينَ. ومِنَ المَعْلوم أنَّ هَذا إنَّما قالَهُ أبو الهُذَيْلِ العَلَّافُ ومَنِ اتَّبَعَهُ مِنْ مُتَكَلِّمِي المُعْتَزِلَةِ والَّذين أَخَذُوا ذَلِكَ عَنْهُمْ.

The second aspect [of the criticism] is the [false] claim of a unanimity on this issue, or even an agreement of the majority. For it is known that those who affirmed [the existence of the indivisible atoms] were only Abu al-Huḏhayl al-ʿAllāf[213] and his followers among the Muʿtazilah as well as the [later theologians] who took the idea from them.

وقَدْ نَفَىٰ الجَوْهَرَ الفَرْدَ مِنْ أئِمَّةِ المُتَكَلِّمِينَ مَنْ لَيْسُوا دُونَ مَنْ أَثْبَتَهُ، بَلِ الأئِمَّةُ فيهِمْ أَكْثَرُ مِنَ الأئِمَّةِ في أولَئِكَ. فَنَفاهُ حُسَيْنٌ النَّجّارُ وأصْحابُهُ كأبِي عيسىٰ بَرْغُوثَ ونَحْوِهِ، وضِرارُ بنُ عَمْرٍو وأصْحابُهُ كَحَفْصٍ الفَرْدِ ونَحْوِهِ، ونَفاه أيْضًا هِشَامُ بنُ الحَكَمِ وأتْباعُهُ، وهُوَ المُقابِلُ لأبِي الهُذَيْلِ، فإنَّهُما مُتَقابِلانِ في النَّفْيِ والإثْباتِ. ونَفَتْهُ الكُلّابِيَّةُ أبو مُحَمَّدٍ عَبْدُ اللهِ بنُ سَعيدِ بنِ كُلّابٍ وذَوُوهُ، ونَفاهُ أيْضًا طائِفَةٌ مِنَ الكَرّامِيَّةِ كَمُحَمَّدِ بنِ

213 Abū Huḏhayl al-ʿAllāf (d. 235H) was one of the leading figures of the Muʿtazilah and the father of the Huḏhayliyyah sect.

صابِرٍ، ونَفاهُ ابْنُ الراوَنْدِيِّ.

Leading Kalām theologians who have rejected [the existence of] the indivisible atom are no lesser than the theologians who affirmed its existence. In fact, the leading theologians in the former camp are more than in the latter. For it was rejected by Ḥusayn al-Najjar[214] and his followers like Abū ‘Isa al-Bargūth[215] and others, Ḍirār bin ‘Amr[216] and his followers like Ḥafṣ al-Fard[217], and Hishām bin Ḥakam[218] and his followers – [this Hishām] is the inverse of Abu al-Huḏhayl [al-‘Allāf], for the two [men] are [exact] opposites [of each other] in

214 Ḥusayn al-Najjar (d. 220H) is the father of the Najjariyyah sect. They agreed with the Mu‘tazilah on the negation of God’s attributes and falsely claimed that God will not be seen in the hereafter.

215 Muḥammad bin ‘Īsā al-Bargūth was the father of the Bargūthiyyah sect and one of the leading Kalām theologians of the Jahmiyyah. In his debate with Aḥmad ibn Hanbal during the Inquisition, he tried to accuse Aḥmad of holding the position that God is a body, and so Aḥmad expressed his refusal to both affirm or negate that God is a body, as the term ‘body’ is ambiguous and was neither attributed to God nor negated from Him in Scripture.

216 Ḍirār bin ‘Amr (d. 190H) was the father of the Ḍirāriyyah sect. Some have counted him among the Jabriyyah, while others counted him among the Mu‘tazilah.

217 Ḥafṣ al-Fard was a Mu‘tazilī who later adopted the views of the Jabriyyah (i.e. the fatalists). In his debate with Imām al-Shafi‘ī, the latter excommunicated him for claiming that the Qur’ān is a creation of God and not His divine attribute.

218 Hisham ibn al-Ḥakam was one of the two founders of the Rāfiḍī sect known as the Hishāmiyyah, the other being Hishām ibn Sālim al-Jawālīqī. The two went to foolish extremes in their affirmation of God’s attributes, to the extent that they speculated about hair color and claimed that God shines like pearls. They were excommunicated by some Muslim scholars for this impiety.

their affirmations and negations. So was [the indivisible atom] rejected by the Kullābiyyah (the followers of Abū Muḥammad ʿAbdullāh bin Saʿīd bin Kullāb) and a group of the Karrāmiyyah like Muḥammad bin Ṣābir. Ibn al-Rāwandī[219] also rejected it.

وَلَيْسَ نَفْيُ هَؤُلاءِ مُوافَقَةً مِنْهُمْ لا لِلفَلاسِفَةِ ولا لِلنَظّامِ، بَلْ قَوْلُ النَظّامِ ظاهِرُ الفَسادِ، وكَذَلِكَ قَوْلُ الفَلاسِفَةِ أَيْضًا. وأَكْثَرُ هَؤُلاءِ الّذينَ ذَكَرْناهُمْ مِنَ النَجّارِيَّةِ والضِرارِيَّةِ والكُلّابِيَّةِ والكَرّامِيَّةِ وغَيْرِهِمْ لايَقولونَ في ذَلِكَ بِقَوْلِ النَظّامِ ولا الفَلاسِفَةِ، ولايَقولونَ بإِثْباتِهِ.

And those here who negate the existence of point-sized atoms do not do so in agreement with [Aristotelian] Philosophers or al-Naẓẓām. Rather, the position chosen by al-Naẓẓām is clearly false, as is the position of the Philosophers. Most of those we mentioned here among the Najjāriyyah, the Ḍirāriyyah, the Kullābiyyah, the Karrāmiyyah and others accept neither the position of al-Naẓẓām nor [the position of] the Philosophers, but [nevertheless] they do not affirm existence for the [conceptually] indivisible atom.

219 An atheist who was famous for his hypocrisy (d. 298H). He was once a follower of the Muʿtazili school.

The Rational Position

وذَلِكَ أنَّ دَعْوَىٰ الفَلاسِفَةِ قَبولَ الأجْسامِ والحَرَكاتِ والأزْمِنَةِ الانْقِسامَ إلىٰ غَيْرِ نِهايَةٍ باطِلٌ كَما ذَكَرَهُ المُثْبِتونَ، وكَذَلِكَ قَوْلُ مُثْبِتِيْهِ باطِلٌ بِما ذَكَرَهُ نُفاتُهُ مِنْ أَنَّهُ لا بُدَّ مِنِ انْقِسامِهِ، حَتّىٰ إنَّ أبا المَعالي وغَيْرَهُ اعْتَرَفوا بِأَنَّهُ غَيْرُ مَحْسوسٍ.

For the Philosophers' assertion that physical bodies, their motions, and their time[220] divide [potentially] to no end is false, as it is known from the arguments of [the Kalām theologians] who affirm [the existence of the indivisible atom]. Equally, the claims of those [Kalām theologians] who affirm its existence are known to be false by the argument of those [Philosophers] who negate its existence, [which is] that an atom must be [conceptually] divisible. Even Abu al-Maʿālī himself and others have admitted that the indivisible atom is unknowable through sense perception[221].

220 Ibn Taymiyyah is speaking here of *zaman*, a positive attribute that is defined as the measure of motion of a given physical body or system.

221 Ibn Taymiyyah was an empiricist: he believed that all ontological existents are knowable through sense perception, including the smallest constituents of matter. For Ibn Taymiyyah, if a substance cannot be observed in principle, then it does not exist. This rule extends to all matters of the Unseen, including the souls, angels, and even God Himself. The believers will be able to see God on the Day of Resurrection and when they enter Paradise, although they will never see Him in this life and before they die.

وَمَنْ تَدَبَّرَ أَدِلَّةَ الفَلاسِفَةِ القائِلِينَ بِما لا يَتَناهىٰ مِنَ الانْقِسامِ، والقائِلِينَ
بِوُجودِ الجُزْءِ الّذِي لا يَقْبَلُ الانْقِسامَ= وَجَدَ أَدِلَّةَ كُلِّ واحِدَةٍ مِنَ الطّائِفَتَيْنِ
تُبْطِلُ الأُخْرىٰ. والتَحْقِيقُ أَنَّ كِلا المَذْهَبَيْنِ باطِلٌ. والصَوابُ ما قالَهُ مَنْ
قالَهُ مِنَ الطّائِفَةِ الثّالِثَةِ المُخالِفَةِ للطّائِفَتَيْنِ: إِنَّ الأَجْسامَ إذا تَصَغَّرَتْ
أَجْزاؤُها فَإِنَّها تَسْتَحِيلُ، كَما هُوَ مَوْجودٌ في أَجْزاءِ الماءِ إذا تَصَغَّرَ فَإِنَّهُ
يَسْتَحِيلُ هَواءً أو تُرابًا.

And whoever ponders on the arguments of the Philosophers who claim infinite divisibility and the arguments of [the Kalām theologians] who claim the existence of indivisible atoms will find that the arguments of each party invalidate the arguments of the other. And the fact of the matter is that both opinions are false and that the truth lies in a third opinion. That opinion is **that the smallest parts in [the natural] bodies totally change**[222] [upon division][223], just like the smallest constituents of water totally change into air[224] or dust.

---

222 Meaning that substances are brought into existence in place of others, such that one thing perishes and another is created.

223 The reverse of this process is referred to as *ittiḥād*, or union. Ibn Taymiyyah mentions elsewhere that the union of two created things into a single entity is impossible without the two things changing substantially into a new creation. He writes in *Kitāb al-'Ubūdiyyah*: "It is not possible for the Creator to merge with something else. In fact, it is not possible for any two things to merge with each other unless they both change substantially and are annihilated, such that their union gives rise to a third thing that is not identical to the two." [*Majmū' al-Fatāwā*, Vol 10 p. 220]

224 Today, it is understood that water changes into oxygen and hydrogen in a chemical reaction known as water splitting. The equation that describes this endothermic process is: $2\,H_2O \rightarrow 2\,H_2 + O_2$

فَلا يَبْقَىٰ مَوْجودٌ مُمْتَنِعٌ عَنِ القِسْمَةِ كَما يَقولُهُ المُثْبِتونَ لَهُ، فَإِنَّ هَذا باطِلٌ بِما ذَكَرَهُ النُفاةُ مِنْ أَنَّهُ لا بُدَّ أَنْ يَتَمَيَّزَ جانِبٌ لَهُ عَنْ جانِبٍ. ولا يَكونُ قابِلًا لِلقِسْمَةِ إِلىٰ غَيْرِ نِهايَةٍ، فَإِنَّ هَذا أَبْطَلُ مِنَ الأَوَّلِ. بَلْ يَقْبَلُ القِسْمَةَ إِلىٰ حَدٍّ ثُمَّ يَسْتَحِيلُ إِذا كانَ صَغيرًا.

Thus, there can never exist a [conceptually] indivisible existent as the affirmers of the [point-sized] atom believe. This [claim] is false, for all objects must have discernable sides as those who negate [the existence of these atoms] correctly point out. [Conversely,] an existent cannot be divided indefinitely [as the Philosophers believe], for this position is even more flawed than the first. Rather, an existent accepts [actual and potential] division to a point and then totally changes when it becomes very small.

ولَيْسَ اسْتِحالَةُ الأَجْسامِ في صِغَرِها مَحْدودًا بِحَدٍّ واحِدٍ. بَلْ قَدْ يَسْتَحِيلُ الصَغيرُ ولَهُ قَدْرٌ يَقْبَلُ نَوْعًا مِنَ القِسْمَةِ، وغَيْرُهُ لا يَسْتَحِيلُ حَتّىٰ يَكونَ أَصْغَرَ مِنْهُ. وبِالجُمْلَةِ فَلَيْسَ في شَيْءٍ مِنْها قَبولُ القِسْمَةِ إِلىٰ غَيْرِ نِهايَةٍ، بَلْ هَذا إِنَّما يَكونُ في المُقَدَّراتِ الذِهْنِيَّةِ،

And bodies do not change at the same extent [of division] as they are divided. Rather, one body may totally change at a size which accepts some kind of [further] division[225] while another changes only at a

225 Although Ibn Taymiyyah believed that large-scale composite structures do not change substantially upon division but simply rearrange into new configurations, he also believed that the composition of a divisible substance at the smaller scales can be necessary to its existence, such that the disassembly of its components would be impossible. In these latter cases, dividing the

smaller size [and a more fundamental level].[226] But overall, none of those bodies are [actually or potentially] divisible to no end. Such [infinite division] can occur only in conceptual estimations [and not in the real world].

فَأمّا وُجودُ ما لا يَتَناهَىٰ بَيْنَ حَدَّيْنِ مُتَناهِيَيْنِ فَمُكابَرَةٌ، وسَواءٌ كانَ بالفِعْلِ أو بالقُوَّةِ، ووُجودُ مَوْجودٍ لا يَتَمَيَّزُ جانِبٌ لَهُ عَنْ جانِبٍ مُكابَرَةٌ، بَلِ الأجْسامُ تَسْتَحِيلُ مَعَ قَبولِ الانْقِسامِ، فَلا يَقْبَلُ شَيْءٌ مِنْها انْقِسامًا لا يَتَناهَىٰ، كَما أنَّها إذا كَثُرَتْ وعَظُمَتْ تَنْتَهي إلىٰ حَدٍّ تَقِفُ عِنْدَهُ ولا تَذْهَبُ

composite substance would necessitate a change in its identity, such that the constituents of the substance must cease to exist and change totally into something else. This is because the constituents of such a substance cannot exist in isolation, but must attach to other constituents if they are to continue existing. Otherwise, if the constituent does not attach to others, it necessarily must change into something else, as it cannot endure on its own after that final point of division. [*Al-Ṣafadiyyah*, Vol 1 p. 118]

226 Ibn Taymiyyah's *argument for the creation of matter* demonstrates that fundamental matter particles cannot exist eternally. When these fundamental particles are overpowered and subjected through appropriate means, they must undergo complete and total change, whereby the original particles will cease to exist, giving rise to new forms of existence. In line with this view, it is now confirmed experimentally that subatomic matter particles, when subjected to collision with their antiparticle counterparts, annihilate into radiation and then change into other forms of energy in the surroundings such as heat and potential energy. Such a process of change cannot be described as mere rearrangement of already existing matter since the kinetic and potential energy that begin to exist are not identical to the original matter particles that have ceased to exist. Rather, this process is more accurately described as a complete and total change, which explains its scientific name 'Matter creation' and 'Annihilation'.

إلىٰ أبْعادٍ لا تَتَناهَىٰ.

[For] the claim that an infinite number [of things] can exist within a finite [spatial] limit is absurd, whether that [existence] is said to be actual or potential. And it is [equally] absurd to claim that an object can exist without discernible sides. Instead, [natural] bodies change totally while undergoing division [at that minuscule level]. They may not be divided indefinitely, just as they do not amount to an infinite length when they are plentiful and vast, but rather must stop at a definite limit.

ولَكِنْ بَنَىٰ هَذِهِ الطائِفَةُ المَشْهورَةُ مِنَ المُتَكَلِّمِينَ عَلىٰ مُسَمَّىٰ هَذا الاسْمِ الهائِلِ - الّذي هُوَ «الجَوْهَرُ الفَرْدُ» عِنْدَهُمْ - إثْبَاتَ الخالِقِ والمَعادِ. وَهُوَ عِنْدَ التَحْقيقِ ما لا يُمْكِنُ أَحَداً أنْ يَحْصُرَهُ بِحِسِّهِ باتِّفاقِهِمْ، وعِنْدَ المُحَقِّقِينَ لامَسَّ لَهُ.

Nonetheless, this famous group of Kalām theologians [i.e. the Ashʿarīyyah] has predicated its belief in the Creator and in the Resurrection on this grand label: 'the indivisible atom' – although, as a matter of fact, this atom is undetectable by anyone according to their consensus and is unknowable according to the *Muḥaqqiqīn* (the most astute and inquisitive scholars).

وما أَشْبَهَهُ بـ«المَعْصوم المَعْلومِ» الّذي بَدَعَتْهُ القَرامِطَةُ، و«المُنْتَظَرِ المَعْصومِ» الّذي بَدَعَتْهُ الرافِضَةُ، و«الغَوْثِ» الّذي بَدَعَتْهُ جُهّالُ الصُوفِيَّةِ.

And just how similar is [this invention of theirs] to the [concept of the] 'known infallible one' invented by the Qarāmiṭah, the 'awaited infallible [*imām*]' invented by the Rāfiḍah, and the *'ghawth'* invented by ignorant Ṣūfis!

وهُوَ[٢٢٧] نَظيرُ ما يُعَظِّمُهُ مُقابِلَ هَؤُلاءِ الفَلاسِفَةُ المَشَّاؤونَ[٢٢٨] وأتْباعُهُمْ مِنَ الجَوْهَرِ المُجَرَّدِ، وهُوَ ما يَدَّعُونَهُ في النُفوسِ[٢٢٩] والعُقولِ مِنْ أنَّها شَيْءٌ لا داخِلَ العالَمِ ولا خارِجَهُ ولا مُتَحَرِّكٌ ولا ساكِنٌ ولا مُتَّصِلٌ بِغَيْرِهِ ولا مُنْفَصِلٌ عَنْهُ وأمْثالِ هَذِهِ التُرَّهاتِ. فَقَوْلُ هَؤُلاءِ في إثْباتِ هَذا الجَوْهَرِ المُجَرَّدِ كَقَوْلِ أولَئِكَ في الجَوْهَرِ الفَرْدِ.

And [their indivisible atom] is paralleled by the 'abstract substance' which their opposing camp, the Peripatetic Philosophers, hold in high regard: [the substance] which they claim is found in the form of **souls** and the **intellects**, [and which they claim to be something] neither inside the world nor outside the world, neither moving nor still, and neither connected to other things nor disconnected from them, and [which they describe with] similar nonsense. Indeed, the claim of those [Philosophers] in affirmation of this abstract substance is analogous to the claim of those [Kalām theologians] in affirmation of the indivisible atom.

ثُمَّ إنَّ هَؤُلاءِ وهَؤُلاءِ يَدَّعُونَ أنَّ هَذا حَقيقَةُ الإنْسانِ. هَؤُلاءِ يَدَّعُونَ أنَّهُ هَذا الجَوْهَرُ المُجَرَّدُ. وهَؤُلاءِ يَقولونَ إنَّهُ جَوْهَرٌ واحِدٌ مُنْفَرِدٌ، أو جَواهِرُ كُلٌّ مِنْها يَقومُ بِهِ حَياةٌ وعِلْمٌ وقُدْرَةٌ، أو تَقومُ الأعْراضُ المَشْروطَةُ بالحَياةِ

٢٢٧ في الأصل الخطي والمطبوع: «هو» من غير واو عطف.

٢٢٨ في الأصل الخطي والمطبوع: «المشائين»، خطأ.

٢٢٩ في الأصل الخطي والمطبوع: «النفس»، والمثبت أشبه.

بِبَعْضِها ويَثْبُتُ ٢٣٠ الحُكْمُ للجُمْلَةِ. وعَلىٰ هَذِهِ المَقالاتِ يَبْنُونَ المَعادَ.

Moreover, both parties [the Philosophers and the Kalām theologians] claim that [their theorized substance] is the [very] reality of the human being[231]. The [Philosophers] claim that [the reality of the human being] is an 'abstract substance' [i.e. the soul], whereas the [Kalām theologians] claim that [the reality of the human being] is one 'indivisible atom', or numerous 'indivisible atoms' each of which is a substrate of life, knowledge and power – or, [alternatively, only] some of which are substrates for the accidents that are conditional on life, with the attribution [nevertheless] being predicated to the [human being in his] entirety. Moreover, both [parties] establish [the belief in] Resurrection[232] on these claims.

---

٢٣٠ في الأصل الخطي والمطبوع: «وثبت»، ولعل المثبت أشبه.

231 Ibn Taymiyyah believed that the human being ought to be defined as the entirety of two distinct entities, both of which are substances: the human body and the human soul. At death, the soul leaves the body and lives on, and the body then perishes into the earth. The body will then be re-created out of the earth on the Day of Resurrection, and the soul will be reunited with it in preparation for God's judgement. Ibn Taymiyyah's position here contrasts with the view of many Kalām theologians who falsely assume that souls are accidents.

232 Philosophers believe that only souls are gathered in the Resurrection, and they deny that the material bodies will be re-created. By contrast, all Muslims believe that the Resurrection will be both of body and soul, and that the denial of this is an outright rejection of Scripture.

مسألة حدوث العالم

اشتراط المادة لحدوث المخلوق
On Material Conditions

The Ambiguity of "Originated from Nothing"

وَالمَقْصُودُ هُنا: أَنَّ القُرْآنَ يَنْفِي أَنْ يَكُونَ الإِنْسانُ خُلِقَ مِنْ غَيْرِ شَيْءٍ، وَأَخْبَرَ أَنَّهُ خَلَقَهُ وَلَمْ يَكُنْ شَيْئًا؛ فَلا نَحْتاجُ أَنْ نَقُولَ: إِنَّهُ خُلِقَ مِنْ عَدَمٍ. فَإِنَّ العَدَمَ لَيْسَ بِشَيْءٍ.

[But] the purpose here is to say that the Qur'ān negates [the claim] that man was created from nothing[233], and it [also] mentions that [God] created him when he was nothing[234]. Thus, we do not need to [further] say that he was created "from nothing", for nonexistence is not a thing.

فَإِذا قُلْنا «خُلِقَ مِن عَدَمٍ»، يَظُنُّ الظانُّ أَنَّهُ خُلِقَ مِنْ غَيْرِ شَيْءٍ خَلَقَهُ. بَلْ خُلِقَ مِنْ خالِقٍ خَلَقَهُ، وَهُوَ حَيٌّ قَيُّومٌ عَلِيمٌ سَمِيعٌ بَصِيرٌ قَدِيرٌ؛ فَلَمْ يَكُنْ مَوْجُودٌ إِلّا مِنْ مَوْجُودٍ، وَلَمْ يَكُنْ وُجُودٌ عَنْ عَدَمٍ مَحْضٍ.

If we say [that man was] originated "from nothing", one may [falsely] assume that [we are saying that] he was originated without any-

---

233 Meaning that the Qur'ān negates that man was originated without a Creator. This is mentioned in 52:35.

234 Qur'ān 19:9

thing that originated him. Rather, man was originated by a Creator, [one who is] Living, Self-sufficient, Knowing, Hearing, Seeing and Powerful. There was never an [originated] existent except from an existent, and there was never an [originated] existent from absolute nothingness.

وبَطَلَ بِهَذا ما يُورِدُهُ المُتَفَلْسِفَةُ علىٰ المُتكَلِّمِينَ في هَذا المَقَامِ؛ فَإِنَّ أَهْلَ الكَلامِ لَمّا قَالوا أنَّهُ «وُجِدَ مِنْ عَدَمٍ» أو «عَنْ عَدَمٍ»، فَإِنَّما أرادوا بِذَلِكَ أَنَّهُ وُجِدَ بَعْدَ العَدَمِ، لَمْ يُرِيدوا بِذَلِكَ أَنَّ نَفْسَ العَدَمِ خَرَجَ مِنْهُ شَيْءٌ؛ فَإِنَّ العَدَمَ لا شَيْءٌ. لَيْسَ العَدَمُ فِيما يُمْكِنُ أَنْ يُقَدَّرَ خُروجُ شَيْءٍ مِنْهُ، ولا دُخولُ شَيْءٍ فيهِ. وإِنَّما الذِهْنُ القَاصِرُ يُقَدِّرُ العَدَمَ كَأَنَّهُ مَوضِعٌ مُظْلِمٌ، أو خَلاءٌ وَراءَ العالَمِ، أو نَحْوُ ذَلِكَ مِنَ الخَيالاتِ؛ فَيَتَوَهَّمُ دُخولَ شَيْءٍ فِيهِ أو خُروجَ شَيْءٍ مِنْهُ.

And this invalidates the objections raised by the Philosophers against the Kalām theologians on this point. Indeed, by saying that [man] was "originated from nothing", the Kalām theologians intended that he was originated after being non-existent. They did not intend to say that the very nonexistence gave rise to something. For nonexistence is not a thing; it is not anything from which existents may be assumed to come out or into which existents may [be assumed to] enter. It is only that the limited mind envisions nonexistence as a dark location or a [substantial] space beyond the world, or a picture of the like, and thus mistakenly thinks that something [may] enter into nonexistence or come out of it.

ولِهَذا أَعْرِفُ أَنَّ بَحْثًا جَرَىٰ مَعَ طَائِفَةٍ مِنَ الفُضَلاءِ الّذِينَ كُنَّا نُجَالِسُهُمْ في قَولِهِ ﴿لَآ إِلَٰهَ إِلَّا ٱللَّهُ﴾ وما ذَكَرَهُ النُحاةُ مِنْ أنَّ «خبَرَ لا» مَنْفِيٌّ[٢٣٥] لِكَوْنِهِ مَعْلومًا، كَما حُذِفَ «عَامِلُ الظَرْفِ» في «خَبَرِ المُبْتَدَإِ» و نَواسِخِهِ مِثْل «بابِ إنَّ» و «بابِ كانَ» و «بابِ ظَنَنْتُ» ، وأنَّ التَقْديرَ عِندَ النُحاةِ: «لا إلَهَ في الوُجودِ» أو «لا إلَهَ كائِنٌ»؛ فَأَوْرَدَ بَعْضُهُمْ عَلىٰ ذَلِكَ: أنَّا إذا قَدَّرْنا «لا إلَهَ في الوُجُودِ» ، يَقْتَضي[٢٣٦] مَفْهومُ الكَلامِ أنَّ في العَدَمِ إلـٰهًا. فَقُلْتُ لَهُمْ: العَدَمُ لَيْسَ شَيْئًا حَتّىٰ يُقالَ: فيهِ إلَهٌ، أو لَيْسَ فيهِ. وهَذا ظاهِرٌ عَلىٰ قَوْلِ أَهْلِ السُنَّةِ أنَّ المَعْدومَ لَيْسَ بِشَيْءٍ.

For this reason, [when] I was [once] with a group of distinguished colleagues examining the [following] verse: **{[There is] no [true] deity but Allah}** and what the grammarians had mentioned [about its grammatical structure] – [namely] that the predicate of [the genus-negating] 'No' is elided because it is obvious, just as is the case of the adverbs of time and place which qualify the [elided] predicate of the *mubtadā* (subject) and its *nawāsikh* such as *inna* (verily), *kāna* (was), and *ẓanantu* (I thought); and thus the estimation, according to the grammarians, is: "**No true deity <u>is in existence</u>** [but Allah]" or "**No true god <u>exists</u>** [but Allah]" – some of the [attendees] suggested that if we were to assume [the verse to mean] "No [true] deity is **in existence** [but Allah]", the statement would be implying that there is another [true] deity within [the realm of] nonexistence. So, I replied that nonexistence is not a thing such that it may be [meaningfully] said to include a deity or not include [a deity]. This is ap-

---

٢٣٥ كذا في الأصل والمطبوع، والمراد أنه محذوف.

٢٣٦ في الأصل والمطبوع: «ينفي»، والظاهر أنه تصحيف عن المثبت.

parent from the position of Ahl al-Sunnah, who say that non-existents are not things [in external reality].

وَمَنْ قَالَ: إِنَّ المَعْدومَ شَيْءٌ، فَقَدْ يُورَدُ هٰذَا السُّؤَالُ عَلىٰ أَصْلِهِ. وقَدْ يُجِيبُ عَنْهُ بِأَنَّ النِّزَاعَ إِنَّما هُوَ فِي المَعْدومِ المُمْكِنِ. وأَمَّا المُمْتَنِعُ فَلَيْسَ بِشَيْءٍ بِالاتِّفَاقِ. والشَّريكُ مِنَ المَعْدومِ المُمْتَنِعِ، لَيْسَ مِنَ المُمْكِنِ. فَيَمْتَنِعُ أَنَ يَكُونَ فِي العَدَمِ. لَكِنْ يُقَالُ لَهُ: فَيَبْقىٰ المَفْهومُ أَنَّهُ فِي المَعْدومِ المُمْكِنِ.

As for someone who believes that non-existents are things [in external reality], this question can [indeed] be raised against his principle. And he may answer it by [pointing out] that the dispute [over whether non-existents are things or not] concerns only non-existents that are possible. As for impossibilities, they are not things by consensus. A partner [of God] is among the **impossible** non-existents, not among the possible non-existents. Thus, there cannot be [any] partner [with God] that dwells in nonexistence. However, it could be retorted that the statement [of the verse] would [still] be implying that there could be [another true god] within [the realm of] possible non-existence.

ولا رَيْبَ أَنَّ قَوْلَ مَنْ قَالَ: إِنَّ المَعْدومَ شَيْءٌ فِي الخَارِجِ قَوْلٌ باطِلٌ، وإِنَّما أَصْلُهُ اشْتِباهُ ما فِي الأَذْهانِ بِما فِي الأَعْيانِ، واشْتِباهُ الوُجودِ العَيْنِيِّ بِالعِلْمِيِّ. وذَلِكَ أَنَّهُ رَأَىٰ أَنَّ المَعْدومَ يَتَمَيَّزُ مِنْهُ المَقْدورُ مِنْ غَيْرِ المَقْدورِ، والمُرادُ مِنْ غَيْرِ المُرادِ. والامْتِيازُ لا يُعْقَلُ فِي النَّفْيِ المَحْضِ، فَقَالَ: لا

بُدَّ أنْ يَكُونَ المَعْدومُ ثَابِتًا لِيَحْصُلَ فِيهِ الامْتِيازُ. ثُمَّ عَلِمَ بِعَقْلِهِ أَنَّهُ لَيْسَ بِمَوْجودٍ، فَفَرَّقَ بَيْنَ الوُجودِ والثُّبوتِ، فَقالَ: هُوَ ثَابِتٌ وَلَيْسَ بِمَوْجودٍ.

[Anyhow,] the claim of one who says that non-existents are things in the external world is undoubtedly a false claim. The root of this [misconception] is [his] conflation of that which is in the mind with that which is in [extra-mental] reality, and [his conflation of] particular [ontological] existence with mental [epistemic] existence. That is because he had perceived that non-existents are [distinct from one another in regards to their possibility and impossibility, and therefore] distinct in regards to their inclusion in the power [of the omnipotent God] and their exclusion therefrom; and [that they are also distinct] in regards to their being intended [from the act] and their not being intended [from it]. However, distinctions are inconceivable in absolute negations. Thus, he claimed that the non-existent must be established [in reality] in order for this distinction to take place. But then he realized that non-existents do not exist. Therefore, he [found it necessary to] make a distinction between the existence [of something] and [its] establishment, and thus he said that the non-existent is established [in reality] but is not existing [in reality].

وكَثيرٌ مِمَّنْ رَدَّ عَلىٰ هَؤُلاءِ أَطْلَقَ القَوْلَ بِأَنَّ المَعْدومَ لَيْسَ بِشَيْءٍ. ورُبَّما كانَ في كَلامِهِ ما يَقْتَضِي أَنَّهُ لَيْسَ بِشَيْءٍ لا في العِلْمِ ولا العَيْنِ، لا في الذِهْنِ ولا الخارِجِ عَنِ الذِهْنِ، وهَذا غَلَطٌ؛ بَلِ الصَوابُ أَنَّهُ ثَابِتٌ مَوْجودٌ في العِلْمِ، بِمَعْنىٰ: أَنَّهُ يُعْلَمُ.

And many of the people who respond to those [theological groups] claim that "non-existents are not things" **unequivocally**. At times, their responses imply that non-existents are neither a thing in knowledge nor a thing in [particular] concretes, and [that they are] neither a thing in the mind nor a thing outside the mind. But this is [an] incorrect [response]. Instead, the truth is that non-existents are [both] established [in knowledge] and existing **in knowledge**, meaning that they **can be known** – [even though they are neither established nor existing in concrete reality.]

وَالتَّمْيِيزُ يَتْبَعُ العِلْمَ. فَإِذَا كَانَ مَعْلُومًا بِالعِلْمِ، مُيِّزَ بِالعِلْمِ بَيْنَ المُمْتَنِعِ وَالوَاجِبِ وَالجَائِزِ، وَالمُرَادِ وَغَيْرِ المُرَادِ. وَذَلِكَ لَا يُوجِبُ كَوْنَهُ ثَابِتًا فِي الخَارِجِ، فَإِنَّا نَعْلَمُ بِالاضْطِرَارِ أَنَّا نَتَصَوَّرُ فِي أَنْفُسِنَا مَا لَا حَقِيقَةَ لَهُ فِي الخَارِجِ.

And the distinction [between non-existents] follows from the **knowledge** [of them]. If a non-existent is known, it will be differentiated by knowledge into [the categories of] the impossible, possible, and necessary, and the intended and unintended. However, this [epistemic] distinction does not necessitate that the non-existent is established in the external reality. Rather, we know by necessity that we [are able to] conceptualize within ourselves [many] things which have no reality in the external world.

يُبَيِّنُ ذَلِكَ: أَنَّا نَتَصَوَّرُ الوُجُودَ المُطْلَقَ فِي أَنْفُسِنا، وَالوُجُودُ المُطْلَقُ لَا يَكُونُ ثَابِتًا فِي العَدَمِ وَلَا فِي الخَارِجِ. وَكَذَلِكَ سَائِرُ الكُلِّيَّاتِ المُطْلَقَةِ؛ فَإِنَّا نَتَصَوَّرُهَا مُطْلَقَةً، وَهِيَ لَا تَكُونُ فِي الخَارِجِ كُلِّيَّاتٍ مُطْلَقَةً. وَإِنَّا نَتَصَوَّرُ

المُمْتَنِعَ كَما نَتَصَوَّرُ المُمْكِنَ، والمُمْتَنِعُ لَيْسَ بِثابِتٍ في الخارِجِ بالاتِّفاقِ.

This is made clear by [the fact] that we [are able to] conceptualize **absolute existence** within ourselves, even though absolute existence is established neither in nonexistence nor in the external reality, [but is only established in knowledge and conception]. Likewise, all [other] absolute **universals** [are not established in external reality]; we indeed conceive of these universals as being absolute even though they do not exist as absolutes in external reality. Moreover, we [are able to] conceptualize the **impossible** just as we [are able to] conceptualize the possible, even though impossibilities are by consensus not established in external reality.

وقَدْ نَفىٰ اللهُ عَنِ الإنْسانِ أنْ يَكونَ شَيْئًا قَبْلَ خَلْقِهِ بِقَوْلِهِ: ﴿وَقَدْ خَلَقْتُكَ مِن قَبْلُ وَلَمْ تَكُ شَيْـًٔا﴾ [مريم: ٩]، وبِقَولِهِ: ﴿أَوَلَا يَذْكُرُ ٱلْإِنسَٰنُ أَنَّا خَلَقْنَٰهُ مِن قَبْلُ وَلَمْ يَكُ شَيْـًٔا﴾ [مريم: ٦٧].

[Furthermore,] God has negated [the claim] that man was something before his creation, such as when He says: **{I created you before, when you were nothing}**, and says: **{Does man not remember that We created him before, when he was nothing?}**.

وأمّا قَوْلُهُ: ﴿إِنَّمَآ أَمْرُهُۥٓ إِذَآ أَرَادَ شَيْـًٔا أَن يَقُولَ لَهُۥ كُن فَيَكُونُ﴾ [يس: ٨٢]، وقَوْلُهُ: ﴿إِنَّ زَلْزَلَةَ ٱلسَّاعَةِ شَىْءٌ عَظِيمٌ﴾ [الحج: ١] وقَوْلُهُ: ﴿وَلَا تَقُولَنَّ لِشَاْىْءٍ إِنِّى فَاعِلٌ ذَٰلِكَ غَدًا ۝٢٣ إِلَّآ أَن يَشَآءَ ٱللَّهُ﴾ [الكهف: ٢٣-٢٤]، فَفيهِ جَوابانِ:

As for [the argument that the non-existent is referred to as a thing in the following verses] where God says: **{His command, when He intends a thing, is only that He says unto it, "Be!" and it is}**, and says: **{O mankind! Fear your Lord. Indeed, the earthquake of the Hour is a tremendous thing}**, and says: **{And never say of anything, "Indeed, I shall do that tomorrow," except [when adding], "If Allah wills"}**, it can be answered in two ways:

أَحَدُهُما: أنَّهُ شَيْءٌ في العِلْمِ والقَوْلِ، وإنْ لَمْ يَكُنْ بَعْدُ صارَ في الخارِجِ لَهُ ثُبوتٌ ولا وُجودٌ. الثاني: أنَّهُ عِنْدَ وُجودِهِ يَصيرُ شَيْئًا، وهَذا في الزَّلْزَلَةِ أَظْهَرُ مِنْهُ في الآيَتَينِ.

The first [answer] is that non-existents are a **{thing}** in knowledge and speech, even though they are not yet a thing that is established or existing in the external world. The second [answer] is that they become a **{thing}** at [the moment of] their existence. This [second answer] is more evident in [the verse of] the earthquake than it is in the [other] two verses.

وقَوْلُهُ: ﴿إِذَآ أَرَادَ شَيْـًٔا﴾ بِمَنْزِلَةِ قَوْلِهِ: «أرادَ مَوْجودًا». ولا يَسْتَلزِمُ ذَلِكَ أنْ يَكونَ مَوْجودًا في الخارِجِ قَبْلَ وُجودِهِ. يُبَيِّنُ ذَلِكَ أنَّهُ عَلَّقَ الإرادَةَ بِنَفْسِ الشَّيْءِ، لا بِإِثْباتِ صِفَةِ الوُجودِ لَهُ، فَعُلِمَ أنَّهُ يُريدُ الشَّيْءَ وأنَّهُ يُكَوِّنُ الشَّيْءَ، لا أنَّهُ يَجْعَلُ لِلشَّيْءِ الثابِتِ الغَنِيِّ عَنْهُ صِفَةً لَمْ تَكُنْ.

And His saying that **{He intends a thing}** is like saying: "He willed an existent"; it does not necessitate that the existents are existing in the external world prior to their [coming into] existence. This is [further] clarified by [the fact] that [God] has attached His will to the very {**thing**}, not to the endowment of [that thing] with the attribute of existence. Thus, it becomes known that He is willing and originating the [very] {**thing**}, and that He is not [merely] making a new attribute [of existence] for a thing which is independent of Him and [already] established [in the external world].

وَإِذَا تَبَيَّنَ أَنَّ مَقْصُودَ أَهْلِ الْكَلَامِ مِنَ الْمُسْلِمِينَ فِي قَوْلِهِمْ «إِنَّ الْمُحْدَثَاتِ وُجِدَتْ عَنْ²³⁷ عَدَمٍ» أَيْ: وُجِدَتْ بَعْدَ عَدَمِهَا، وَأَنَّهَا وُجِدَتْ مِنْ غَيْرِ وُجُودٍ مَخْلُوقٍ؛ لَا يَعْنُونَ بِذَلِكَ أَنَّهَا وُجِدَتْ مِنْ غَيْرِ مُوجِدٍ خَالِقٍ؛ عُلِمَ أَنَّهُ لَيْسَ عَلَيْهِمْ فِي الْمَعْنَى الَّذِي قَصَدُوهُ دَرَكٌ، وَإِنْ كَانَ فِي الْعِبَارَةِ لَبْسٌ، وَعِبَارَةُ الْقُرْآنِ أَحْسَنُ وَأَبْيَنُ.

Once it becomes clear that the intention of the Muslim *Kalām* theologians who say that originated things exist "from nothing" is that they [begin to] exist "after their nonexistence" and "without [prior] created existents", [and that] they do not intend to say that they [begin to] exist "without a Creator who causes them into existence", it will be understood that the meaning which they have intended is above reproach. Nevertheless, their statement is ambiguous, whereas the statement of the Qur'ān is better and clearer.

---

٢٣٧ كذا في الأصل هنا، وقد سبق بلفظ «من» مرارًا.

The Philosophical Arguments for the Eternality of the World

لَكِنِ اعْتَرَضَ عَلَيْهِمُ المُتَفَلْسِفَةُ فَقالوا: لا يُعْقَلُ مَوْجودٌ عَنْ عَدَمٍ؛ لأَنّا ما رَأَيْنا شَيْئًا يَحْدُثُ إلّا مِنْ مادَّةٍ؛ كَحُدوثِ الحَيَوانِ والنَباتِ والمَعادِنِ مِنَ المَوادِّ المَشْهودَةِ؛ كَما تَحْدُثُ الثِمارُ مِنَ الأَشْجارِ، وكَما يَحْدُثُ الإنْسانُ مِنَ المَنِيِّ النازِلِ مِنْ أَبَوَيْهِ، وأَمْثالِ ذَلِكَ؛ فَإبْداعُ شَيْءٍ لا مِنْ شَيْءٍ لَمْ نَعْهَدْهُ.

But the Philosophers [further] objected to the Kalām theologians [with an argument from induction] and said: "It is inconceivable that something would [begin to] exist from nothing, for we have never seen anything originating except from [prior] matter – such as the animals, plants, and minerals that originate from the observed materials, the fruits that originate from the trees, and the human beings that originate from the seed emitted by their parents. [Indeed,] we have never witnessed anything originating from nothing."

ومَقْصودُهُمْ بِذَلِكَ أَنْ يُبْطِلوا القَوْلَ بِحُدوثِ الحَوادِثِ مِنْ غَيْرِ مادَّةٍ مُتَقَدِّمَةٍ، فَيَلْزَمُ مِنْ ذَلِكَ قِدَمُ المادَّةِ.

And their intention from this [statement] was to disprove the claim that created things [may] originate **without prior materials**, [an invalidation] which [in turn] would imply that matter is eternal.

كَما قَصَدوا أيْضًا إبْطالَ حُدوثِ الحَوادِثِ مِنْ رَبٍّ قَديمٍ؛ فَقالوا: إنْ كانَتِ العِلَّةُ الأزَلِيَّةُ لِوُجودِ العالَمِ تامَّةً، وَجَبَ قِدَمُ مَعْلولِها؛ فَيَلْزَمُ قِدَمُ العالَمِ. وإنْ كانَتْ غَيْرَ تامَّةٍ، فَلا بُدَّ لِتَمامِها مِنْ سَبَبٍ. والقَوْلُ فيهِ كالقَوْلِ في حُدوثِ العالَمِ؛ فَيَبْطُلُ الحُدوثُ. فَيَتَعَيَّنُ الأوَّلُ: وهُوَ أنْ تَكونَ العِلَّةُ القَديمَةُ تامَّةً، فَيَجِبُ قِدَمُ العالَمِ. وهَذا أعْظَمُ شُبَهِ المُتَفَلْسِفَةِ المَشّائينَ أتْباعِ أَرِسْطو، كابْنِ سينا وابْنِ الهَيْثَمِ وأمْثالِهِما.

Also, they intended to disprove [the notion that] the created [world] was **originated** by [the agency of] an eternal Lord. They argued [for this in the following way]: "If the eternal Cause of the world was complete [in eternity], then its effect must [also] be existing [with it] in eternity, which would mean that the world is eternal. But if the Cause [of the world] was not complete [in eternity], then there must have been a cause for why it [later] became complete, [i.e. there must be a cause for its creating after not creating]. [But] what we say of this [cause] is similar to what was said of the origination of the world: [If its Cause was complete in eternity, it must be eternal; otherwise there must be a cause for that completion]. [The infinite regress in the completion of the Cause ensues], and thus origination is invalidated. Only the first option remains, which is that the eternal Cause was [always] complete. The world must therefore be eternal." This is the greatest argument of the Peripatetic Philosophers, followers of Aristotle, such [figures] as Avicenna, Alhazen[238], and their ilk.

238 Ibn al-Haytham (d. 430H) is an Arab philosopher famous for his work on optics.

وَالشُّبْهَةُ الأُولَىٰ، وَهُوَ أَنَّ الحادِثَ لا بُدَّ لَهُ مِنْ مادَّةٍ، ذَكَرُوا عَنْ مُعَلِّمِهِمْ أَرِسْطو أَنَّهُ اسْتَدَلَّ عَلَىٰ ذَلِكَ أَيْضًا بِأَنَّ المُحْدَثَ قَبْلَ حُدوثِهِ لا بُدَّ أَنْ يَكونَ مُمْكِنًا. وَالإِمْكانُ وَصْفٌ ثُبوتِيٌّ، فَلا بُدَّ لَهُ مِنْ مَحَلٍّ، فَيَجِبُ أَنْ يَتَقَدَّمَ المُحْدَثَ مَحَلٌّ يَقومُ بِهِ الإِمْكانُ، وَذَلِكَ يُوجِبُ قِدَمَ المادَّةِ.

And regarding the first misconception, which is [their claim] that all originated things must have [come from] materials, [the Philosophers] have reported that their pedagogue, Aristotle, had additionally concluded this from [the following argument]: (1) All originated things must be possible prior to their origination. (2) [This] possibility is an ontologically positive attribute and must therefore have a substrate. (3) Therefore, a substrate for the possibility must precede [the existence of] the originated thing. And this necessitates that the matter is eternal.

فَهَذا وَنَحْوُهُ هُوَ كَلامُ هَؤُلاءِ الفَلاسِفَةِ الدَّهْرِيَّةِ في مِثْلِ هَذا، وَهُمُ الَّذِينَ يَقولونَ: لا يُعْقَلُ مَوْجودٌ عَنْ عَدَمٍ.

This [argument] and the like is the statement of the *Dahriyyah*[239]. And it is they who claim that it is inconceivable for something to [begin to] exist from nothing [i.e. without prior matter].

---

239 Dahriyyah are the philosophers who claim that the world is eternal.

Responses to the Argument from Induction

وما قالوهُ خَيالاتٌ عِنْدَ أُولِي الأَلْبابِ النُبَلاءِ، وإنْ كانَ كَثيرٌ مِنَ الناسِ يَظُنّونَ أنَّها مِنْ أعْظَمِ الحُجَجِ عِنْدَ فُضَلاءِ العُقَلاءِ.

[Now,] according to noble men of reason, these claims [by the Philosophers] are mere figments of imagination, even though many people [falsely] assume that they are among the greatest of arguments [conceded] by the best of rational minds.

وبَيانُ ذَلِكَ أنْ يُقالَ: قَوْلُكُمْ «لا يُعْقَلُ مَوْجودٌ عَنْ عَدَمٍ» لَفْظٌ مُجْمَلٌ كَما تَقَدَّمَ. أتُريدونَ بِهِ: لا يُعْقَلُ مَوْجودٌ مِنْ غَيْرِ مُبْدِعٍ أبْدَعَهُ وصانِعٍ صَنَعَهُ؟ أمْ تُريدونَ: لا يُعْقَلُ مَوْجودٌ مِنْ غَيْرِ مادَّةٍ خَلَقَهُ مِنْها الصانِعُ المُبْدِعُ؟

This is resolved by saying [to these Philosophers]: Your statement that "it is inconceivable for something to [begin to] exist from nothing" is **ambiguous**, just as [we have] stated [previously]. Do you intend [to claim] that it is inconceivable for something to [begin to] exist without an Originator or Maker that originated it and made it? Or do you [instead] intend [to claim] that it is inconceivable for something to [begin to] exist without a [prior] material out of which the Originator [or] Maker caused [the thing] into existence?

فَإنْ أرَدْتُمُ الأَوَّلَ، فَهَذا لا يَقولهُ مُسْلِمٌ و لا مِلِّيٌّ، بَلِ المُسْلِمونَ وسائِرُ

أَهْلِ المِلَلِ مُتَّفِقونَ علىٰ أنَّهُ لا يَكونُ مَوْجودٌ مُمْكِنٌ إلا مِنْ مَوْجودٍ واجِبٍ، وأَنَّ كُلَّ مَوْجودٍ غيْرَ اللهِ فاللهُ خالِقُهُ.

If you intend the first, then this is not the belief of any Muslim nor an adherent of [any other] faith. Rather, Muslims and the followers of all [other] faiths agree that there cannot be a contingent existent except from a Necessary existent, and that every existent other than God is created by God.[240]

وقَدْ ذَكَرْنا أنَّ القُرْآنَ جاءَ بِلَفْظِ «مِنْ» في مِثْلِ ذَلِكَ، كَما في قَوْلِهِ: ﴿أَمْ خُلِقُواْ مِنْ غَيْرِ شَيْءٍ أَمْ هُمُ ٱلْخَٰلِقُونَ﴾ [الطور: ٣٥]، وقَوْلِهِ: ﴿وَمَا بِكُم مِّن نِّعْمَةٍ فَمِنَ ٱللَّهِ﴾ [النحل: ٥٣]، وقَوْلِهِ: ﴿وَسَخَّرَ لَكُم مَّا فِى ٱلسَّمَٰوَٰتِ وَمَا فِى ٱلْأَرْضِ جَمِيعًا مِّنْهُ﴾ [الجاثية: ١٣]. والمَعْنىٰ مُتَّفَقٌ عَلَيْهِ بَيْنَ المُسْلِمينَ.

And we have [already] mentioned that the Qurʾān came with the term 'from' in such [affirmations of God's causal agency], such as when [God] says: **{Or were they created *from* nothing, or were they the creators?}**, and says: **{Whatever you have of favor, it is *from* Allah}**, and says: **{He has made of service unto you whatsoever is in the heavens and whatsoever is in the earth; it is all *from* Him}**. This meaning is agreed upon by the Muslims.

240 Elsewhere, Ibn Taymiyyah states: "The intuition that every originated thing must have an originator is stronger than the intuition that every originated thing must have a prior material from which it is created and a final cause for which it is created. Indeed, many of the rational minds dispute with the latter, but never with the former." [*Majmūʿ al-Fatāwā*, Vol 13 p. 151].

وإنْ قُلْتُمْ: لا يَكونُ مَوْجودٌ إلا مِنْ مادَّةٍ خَلَقَهُ مِنْها الصَانِعُ، فَيُقالُ لَكُمْ: فَتِلْكَ المادَّةُ هِيَ مَوْجودةٌ لا مِنْ مادَّةٍ.

[But] if you [instead intend to] say that it is inconceivable for something to [begin to] exist without a [prior] material out of which the Maker caused [the thing] into existence, then it will be said to you [in response]: That matter [substrate] does not exist from [prior] materials, [for it is according to you an eternal effect of the Maker and accompanies Him in eternity.]

وهُمْ مُعْتَرِفونَ بِما لا بُدَّ لَهُمْ مِنْهُ مِنْ أنَّ المَوْجوداتِ القَديمَةِ هِيَ مَوْجودَةٌ مِنْ غَيْرِ مادَّةٍ تَقَدَّمَتْ عَلَيْها كانَتْ مِنْها، بَلْ أَبْدَعَها الرَبُّ إبْداعًا مِنْ غَيْرِ مادَّةٍ. هَذا قَوْلُ الإلَهِيِّينَ مِنْهُمُ المُقِرُّونَ بِواجِبِ الوُجودِ المُبْدِعِ.

And the [Philosophers] do admit this conclusion which they cannot avoid, [namely] that the [alleged] eternal existents [of this world, such as the celestial spheres,] are made to exist [by their Maker in eternity] without the antecedence of any material from which they came into existence. Indeed, [they believe that] the Lord caused these [eternal existents] without [prior] materials. This is the position of the **theistic Philosophers** who accept the existence of the Necessary Maker.

وإنْ قُدِّرَ الكَلامُ مَعَ مَنْ يُنْكِرُ مِنَ الطَبيعِيِّينَ[٢٤١] أنْ يَكونَ لِلعالَمِ مُبْدِعٌ، كانَ جَوابُهُ أَظْهَرَ. فَإنَّهُ يُقالُ لَهُ: يا أَحْمَقُ! إذا جَوَّزْتَ أنْ يَكونَ مَجْموعُ العالَمِ مِنْ غَيْرِ مُبْدِعٍ ولا مادَّةٍ، كَيْفَ يَمْتَنِعُ أنْ يَكونَ بَعْضُهُ مِن غَيْرِ مادَّةٍ مَعَ كَوْنِهِ

٢٤١ في المطبوع: «الطبعيين»، والتصحيح من المخطوط.

مِنْ صانِعٍ؟!

But if the conversation is assumed to be with a [philosophical] **Naturalist** who denies that the world has a Maker, then the response [to his claim] will be more evident. For it will be said to him: "O fool! If you claim that it is possible for the entirety of this [contingent] world to exist without a Maker and from no [prior] material, then how can it be impossible for [only] part of it to exist without [prior] material if it is [effected] by a Maker?!"

وَمَعْلُومٌ أَنَّ الأَوَّلَ هُوَ أَبْعَدُ فِي العَقْلِ، بَلْ هُوَ مُمْتَنِعٌ فِي العَقْلِ، بِخِلافِ الثاني. فَإِنَّ هَذِهِ الحَوادِثَ المَشْهودَةَ، إِنْ قالَ: إِنَّ المَوادَّ أَحْدَثَتْها، فَقَدْ أَثْبَتَ فاعِلًا مُبْدِعًا مُحْدِثًا بِلا مادَّةٍ. وَإِنْ قالَ: لَها مُحْدِثٌ فاعِلٌ غَيْرُ المادَّةِ، فَقَدْ أَثْبَتَ فاعِلًا مُحْدِثًا لَها مِنْ مادَّةٍ، وَهَذا إِقْرارٌ بِالصانِعِ، فَيَلْزَمُهُ إِثْباتُهُ، وَصارَ مِنَ القِسْمِ الأَوَّلِ. فَما فَرَّ إِلَيْهِ شَرٌّ مِمّا فَرَّ مِنْهُ عَلىٰ كُلِّ تَقْدِيرٍ. وَهَذا حالُ أَهْلِ الباطِلِ دائِمًا؛ لا يُكَذِّبونَ بِحَقٍّ لِشُبْهَةٍ إِلا لَزِمَهُمْ ما هُوَ أَشَدُّ مِنْها.

And it is known that the first [proposition] is farther away in reason; rather it is impossible in reason, unlike the second [option]. For if he claims that these originated [things] which are witnessed [to come into existence] are originated by the [very] materials, then he has affirmed [the existence of] a maker that brought [them] into existence without [prior] matter. [But] if he says that they are originated by some agent other than the materials, then he has affirmed [the existence] of an agent who brought them into existence out of [prior] matter. And this is a recognition of the Maker. Thus, he must affirm His existence, and will revert back to the first group [i.e. the theistic Philosophers]. [Indeed,] that to which he fled is worse than that from which he fled in every respect. Such is the condition of the people of falsehood: they cannot reject a truthful [proposition] due to some misconception without falling into an [even] worse [proposition as a] consequence.

وإذا قالوا: نَحْنُ نُسَلِّمُ وُجودَ المَوْجوداتِ القَديمَةِ مِنْ غَيْرِ مادَّةٍ، وإنّما الكَلامُ في المَوْجودَاتِ المُحْدَثَةِ عَنْ عدَمٍ - وهَذا حَقيقَةُ قَوْلِهِم - ظَهَرَ فَسادُ مَذْهَبِهِمْ أيْضًا.

And if the [Philosophers] reply: "We do acknowledge that the eternal existents [of this world] are not from [prior] materials," and that "[our] statement [that materials are necessary] is only true for existents that [are said to] **originate** anew from nothing" – which is [indeed] the reality of their claim – then the fallacy of their position will also become evident.

فَإنَّهُ إذا ثَبَتَ أنَّ إبْداعَهُ لِلأشْياءِ لا يَفْتَقِرُ إلىٰ مادَّةٍ، بَلْ نَفْسُهُ كافِيَةٌ في إبْداعِها مَعَ القِدَمِ، فَلأَنْ تَكونَ نَفْسُهُ كافِيَةً في إبْدَاعِها مَعَ الحُدوثِ أَوْلَىٰ. فإنَّهُ مِنَ المَعْلومِ أنَّ المُحْدَثَ أضْعَفُ مِنَ القَديمِ وأَقَلُّ في الوُجودِ، وأنَّ ذاكَ أكْمَلُ وأقْوَىٰ؛ فإذا كانَ مُكْتَفِيًا بِنَفْسِهِ في إبْدَاعِ الأكْمَلِ الأقْوَىٰ، فَكَيْفَ لا يَكْتَفِي بِنَفْسِهِ في إبْدَاعِ الأنْقَصِ الأضْعَفِ؟!

For if it is established that His causing of things is not dependent on materials, but that His [very] Self is sufficient for causing them as **eternal** [existents], then His [very] Self is all the more sufficient for causing them as **originated** [existents]. For it is known that an originated [thing] is inferior and weaker in existence than an eternal [thing], and that [an eternal thing] is stronger and more perfect. Thus, if God is in and of Himself sufficient for making the stronger and more perfect [existent], how can He not be in and of Himself sufficient for making the weaker and inferior [existent]?![242]

ومِن المَعْلوم بِبَدائِه[٢٤٣] العُقولِ أنَّ الفاعِلَ لِلأكْمَلِ الأقْوىٰ بِنَفْسِهِ لا يَكونُ مُحْتاجًا في الأنْقَصِ الأضْعَفِ إلىٰ غَيْرِهِ، لا مادَّةٍ ولا غَيْرِ مادَّةٍ.

And it is known intuitively that the one who is by Himself a doer of something stronger and more perfect cannot be in need of anything else in doing what is weaker and lesser; neither [in need of] matter nor [of] something besides matter.

وهَذا بَيِّنٌ واضِحٌ ولَيْسَ عَليهِ سُؤالٌ، لَكِنْ غايَتُهُمْ أنْ يَقولوا: يَمْتَنِعُ أنْ يَحْدُثَ عَنْهُ شَيْءٌ بَعْدَ أنْ لَمْ يَكُنْ حَادِثًا، لأنَّ ذَلِكَ يقْتَضِي سَبَبًا حادِثًا. وهَذِهِ حُجَّتُهُمُ الأُخْرَىٰ - وهِيَ الكَبيرَةُ - وسَنُبَيِّنُ إنْ شاءَ اللهُ فَسادَها.

---

242 This *a fortiori* argument is binding on Philosophers who claim that this world is an eternal effect of God. Indeed, if it is possible to cause an eternal world without materials, then it is with greater reason possible to cause originated effects such as animals and trees without materials. However, such an argument is not binding on Ibn Taymiyyah as he believed that all contingent effects are necessarily originated after their nonexistence. For Ibn Taymiyyah, it is impossible for a contingent world to be eternal, and so he cannot conclude from this argument alone that creation without materials is a possibility.

٢٤٣ في المطبوع: «ببداية».

And this is clear and evident, and the [Philosophers] cannot object to it. But the most they may say is that it is impossible for something to originate from God after it was not originating [from Him], because that [itself] would require an originating cause, [and so on and so forth, which would result in an infinite regress in the completion of the Cause]. This is their other argument, and it is the bigger one. We will clarify the fallacy of this [argument later], God willing.

وَإِنَّما المَقْصودُ هُنا: بَيانُ فَسادِ حُجَّتِهِمْ مِنْ جِهَةِ إِثْباتِ المادَّةِ، وأَنَّ الحادِثَ لا بُدَّ لَهُ مِنْ مادَّةٍ قَديمَةٍ، لِأَنَّ الوُجودَ عَنِ العَدَمِ المَحْضِ لا يُمْكِنُ؛ فإِنَّ هَذِهِ الحُجَّةَ فيها إِجْمالٌ يُوهِمُ المُسْتَمِعَ أَنَّهُ يُوجَدُ بِلا مُوجِدٍ. ومَعْلومٌ أَنَّ هَذا باطِلٌ، ومَقْصودُهُمْ أَنَّهُ يُوجَدُ مِنْ غَيْرِ مادَّةٍ.

For the purpose now is to demonstrate the fallacy of their argument concerning the affirmation of the matter [substrate] and that originated [things] must have [come from] eternal materials, [namely] because of [the claim that] it is impossible [for things to begin] to exist from absolute nothingness. Indeed, there is an ambiguity in this argument which misleads the listener into assuming that [the Kalām theologians' position is tantamount to saying that] originated things exist without a Cause – which is obviously false. [Rather,] the intention of the [Kalām theologians] is [to say] that [originated] things [are caused to] exist without [prior] matter.

ومَعْلومٌ أَنَّهُ لا يَجِبُ فيما يُبْدِعُهُ الباري أَنْ يَكونَ لَهُ مادَّةٌ، فإِنَّهُ يُبْدِعُ القَديمَ عِنْدَهُمْ بِلا مادَّةٍ. فَعُلِمَ أَنَّهُ وَحْدَهُ مُسْتَغْنٍ في إِبْداعِ ما يُبْدِعُهُ عَنْ مادَّةٍ، وأَنَّهُ وَحْدَهُ يُبْدِعُ الأَكْمَلَ الأَعْلَىٰ، فَكَيْفَ لا يُبْدِعُ وَحْدَهُ الأَنْقَصَ الأَدْنَىٰ؟

And it is known that it is unnecessary for [the things] which God originates to have [come from prior] matter. For God makes the eternal [existents] without [prior] matter according to their opinion. Thus, it is known that God alone is independent of materials in His causing of whatever He makes. He independently makes the higher, more perfect [existent], and so how can He not independently make the lower, less perfect [existent]?!

فتبيَّنَ أنَّ كَوْنَ المَوْجودِ وُجِدَ عَنْ عَدَمٍ سِوَىٰ الخَالِقِ لَيْسَ بِمُمْتَنِعٍ، وأنَّ وُجودَ الخَالِقِ لا بُدَّ مِنْهُ، وأنَّهُ وَحْدَهُ غَنِيٌّ عَنْ كُلِّ ما سِواهُ في كُلِّ ما يَخْلُقُهُ. ولِهَذا قالَ سُبْحانَهُ: ﴿وَقُلِ ٱلْحَمْدُ لِلَّهِ ٱلَّذِى لَمْ يَتَّخِذْ وَلَدًا وَلَمْ يَكُن لَّهُۥ شَرِيكٌ فِى ٱلْمُلْكِ وَلَمْ يَكُن لَّهُۥ وَلِىٌّ مِّنَ ٱلذُّلِّ ۖ وَكَبِّرْهُ تَكْبِيرًۢا﴾ [الإسراء: ١١١]، فَهُوَ سُبْحانَهُ لَيْسَ لَهُ شَريكٌ في مُلْكِهِ عَاوَنَهُ علىٰ خَلْقِ شَيْءٍ، لا مادَّةٌ ولا غَيْرُها، ولا لَهُ وَلِيٌّ مِنَ الذُّلِّ كَما يَتَوَلَّىٰ المَخْلوقُ مَنْ يَتَعَزَّزُ بِهِ. بَلْ يَتَوَلَّىٰ عِبادَهُ رَحْمَةً وإحْسانًا إلَيْهِمْ، لا احْتِياجًا ولا اسْتِعَانَةً بِهِمْ.

It therefore becomes clear that it is not impossible for a thing to [begin to] exist from nothing [else] beside [its] Creator, and that the existence of the Creator is necessary [for the thing to begin to exist]. And [it also becomes clear] that God alone is independent of all others in everything He creates. This is why the exalted God says: **{And say: Praise be to Allah, who has not taken unto Himself a son, and who has no partner in the Sovereignty, nor does He have protector on account of any weakness. And proclaim His greatness}**. For He, glorified is He, does not have a partner in His Sovereignty – neither matter nor anything besides matter – that assisted Him in creating anything. And He [also] does not have a [protecting] friend on account of any weakness, as do created beings ally [themselves] with [others] that provide reinforcement. Rather, He takes His servants as friends out of [His] mercy and kindness, not out of need or in pursuit of assistance.

ولِذَلِكَ قالَ سُبْحانَهُ: ﴿قُلِ ٱدْعُواْ ٱلَّذِينَ زَعَمْتُم مِّن دُونِ ٱللَّهِ لَا يَمْلِكُونَ مِثْقَالَ ذَرَّةٍ فِى ٱلسَّمَٰوَٰتِ وَلَا فِى ٱلْأَرْضِ وَمَا لَهُمْ فِيهِمَا مِن شِرْكٍ وَمَا لَهُۥ مِنْهُم مِّن ظَهِيرٍ﴾ [سبأ: ٢٢]، فَبَيَّنَ أَنَّهُ سُبْحانَهُ لَيْسَ لَهُ ظَهِيرٌ يُظاهِرُهُ ويُعاوِنُهُ عَلىٰ شَيْءٍ مِنَ الأشْياءِ، بَلْ هُوَ الغَنِيُّ عَنْ كُلِّ شَيْءٍ في كُلِّ شَيْءٍ، وأنَّ ما خَلَقَهُ مِنَ الأسْبابِ لَمْ يَخلُقْهُ لِحاجَتِهِ في خَلْقِ المُسَبَّبِ إلَيْهِ، بَلْ لِأنَّ لَهُ في خَلْقِهِ مِنَ الحِكْمَةِ ما لَهُ في خَلْقِ المُسَبَّباتِ أيْضًا، كَما قالَ تَعالىٰ لَمَّا أَمَرَ المُؤْمِنينَ بِجِهادِ الكُفّارِ: ﴿ذَٰلِكَ وَلَوْ يَشَآءُ ٱللَّهُ لَٱنتَصَرَ مِنْهُمْ وَلَٰكِن لِّيَبْلُوَاْ بَعْضَكُم بِبَعْضٍ﴾ [محمد: ٤].

For this reason, the exalted [God] says: **{Say (O Muḥammad): "Call upon those whom you set up [as gods] beside Allah!" They possess not an ant's weight in the heavens or in the earth, nor have they any share in either, nor has He an auxiliary among them.}** [In this verse,] God has clarified that He has no helper that assists Him in [causing] anything. Rather, He is independent *of* all things *in* all things. [Also, He has clarified] that the [natural] causes which He has created do not assist Him in [His act of] creating their effects. Rather, He creates [these natural causes] because He has a wise purpose in creating them, just as He also has [a wise purpose] in creating [their] effects. As God says when He commands the believers to strive against the unbelievers: **{And if Allah willed He could have punished them (without you), but (thus it is ordained) that He may test some of you by means of others.}**

وإنْ قالوا: لَمْ نَشْهَدْ حادِثًا إلا مِنْ مادَّةٍ، قِيلَ لَهُمْ: ولَمْ نَشْهَدْ مَوْجودًا مِنْ غَيْرِهِ بِلا مادَّةٍ، وأنْتُمْ تَقولونَ أنَّ الأفْلاكَ حَدَثَتْ عَنْهُ بِلا مادَّةٍ مُتَقَدِّمَةٍ عَلَيْها. فَكَيْفَ أَثْبَتُّمْ اسْتِغْناهُ في إبْداعِ المَوْجودِ الأكْمَلِ عَنِ المادَّةِ – ولَمْ تَشْهَدوا ذَلِكَ – وجَعَلْتُموهُ مُحْتاجًا في إبْداعِ المَوْجودِ الأنْقَصِ إلى المادَّةِ لِكَوْنِكُمْ لَمْ تَشْهَدوا حادِثًا إلا مِنْ مادَّةٍ؟!

And if the [Philosophers] reply: "We have never witnessed anything **originating** [anew] without [prior] matter", then it will be said to them [in response]: We have [also] never witnessed any [contingent] thing **existing** from a [cause] besides it [to exist] without [prior] matter. But you [Philosophers] claim that the celestial spheres [of this world] were caused by God [in eternity] without preceding materials. So how did you affirm His independence of the materials in His causing of the more perfect, [eternal] existents – even though you have never witnessed it – but then claimed that He is in need of the materials in His causing of the less perfect, [temporary] existents, [merely] because you have never witnessed anything originating without [prior] matter?!

بَلْ كانَ طَرْدُ قَوْلِكُمْ أنْ تُنْكِروا وُجودَ مَوْجودٍ مِنْ غَيْرِهِ إلا مُحْدَثًا، فَإنَّكُمْ لَمْ تَشْهَدوا مَوْجودًا بِغَيْرِهِ إلا مُحْدَثًا عَنْ عَدَمٍ. إذْ[٢٤٤] كُلُّ ما شَهِدْتُموهُ

٢٤٤ في المطبوع: «أو»، والتصحيح من المخطوط.

مَوْجودًا مِنْ غَيْرِهِ - مِثْلَ الحَيَوانِ والنَباتِ والمَعادِنِ - لَمْ تَشْهَدوهُ إلا حادِثًا.

Rather, the implication of your position would be to reject the existence of anything [that exists] from a [cause] except what is originated [and not eternal]. Indeed, all of the existents which you have witnessed to exist by a [cause] are **originated** after [their] nonexistence, for everything you observe to be existing from [a cause] besides it – such as animals, plants, and minerals – you have only found it to be originated [anew and not eternal].

فَإذا تَبَيَّنَ أنَّ السَماواتِ والأرْضَ مُمْكِناتٌ مُفْتَقِراتٌ إلىٰ مُبْدِعٍ أَبْدَعَها، وَجَبَ أنْ تَجْعَلوها حادِثةً، لِأَنَّكُمْ لَمْ تَشْهَدوا مَفْعولًا إلا مُحْدَثًا.

So, if it is evident that the heavens and the earth are contingent things that depend on a Cause which made them, then you must [also] deem them originated. For you have only witnessed **originated** effects, [not eternal ones].

وهَذِهِ طَريقَةٌ سَلَكَها كَثيرٌ مِنْ أهْلِ الكَلامِ، وهِيَ خَيْرٌ مِنْ كَلامِ الفَلاسِفَةِ. فَإنَّهُ إذا حَصَلَ الاتِّفاقُ وعُلِمَ بالدَليلِ أنَّ السَماواتِ مُبْدَعَةٌ مُفْتَقِرَةٌ إلىٰ مُبْدِعٍ فَعَلَها، ولَمْ نَشْهَدْ مُبدَعًا مَفْعولًا إلا مُحْدَثًا، وَجَبَ القَوْلُ بِحُدوثِها. فَإنَّ تَقَدُّمَ الفاعِلِ المُبْدِعِ - الّذي هُوَ خالِقُ كُلِّ شَيْءٍ - عَلىٰ فِعْلِهِ هُوَ أقْرَبُ في العَقْلِ مِنْ كَوْنِ الفاعِلِ المُبْدِعِ يَفْتَقِرُ إلىٰ مادَّةٍ.

And this argument was used by many of the Kalām theologians, and it is better than the statement of the Philosophers. For if it is agreed upon and known with evidence that the heavens are [contingent] effects [that are] dependent on a Maker which made them, and [since, additionally,] we have only witnessed effects that are originated, then we must [likewise] say that the heavens are originated [after their nonexistence]. Indeed, [the claim] that the Maker and Creator of all things must precede His effect [in time] is more rational than [the claim] that the Maker depends on materials [for His act of creation].

يُبَيِّنُ ذَلِكَ: أَنَّ كَوْنَ الفاعِلِ مُتَقَدِّمًا عَلىٰ المَفْعولِ أَمْرٌ مُسْتَقِرٌّ في العَقْلِ والحِسِّ، مَعَ أَنَّهُ لا يَحْتاجُ إِلىٰ شَهادَةِ الحِسِّ، ولَوْ قِيلَ: مُتَقَدِّمٌ بالذاتِ. بِخِلافِ كَوْنِ المَفْعولِ أَوِ المُحْدَثِ يفْتَقِرُ إِلىٰ مادَّةٍ، فَهَذا لَيْسَ مَعْلومًا بالعَقْلِ، وإِنَّما شُبْهَةُ قائِلِهِ كَوْنُهُ لَمْ يُحِسَّ مُحْدَثًا إِلا كَذَلِكَ. وأَيْنَ قَضِيَّةٌ تُعْلَمُ بالعَقْلِ والحِسِّ مِنْ قَضِيَّةٍ لا تُعْلَمُ بِواحِدٍ مِنْهُما، ولَكِنْ لَمْ يَشْهَدْها الحِسُّ؟!

This is clarified by the fact that the [temporal] precedence of the agent with regards to its effect is well-established in [both] reason and sense perception, even though it does not require the testimony of sense perception [to be accepted]; [this is] even when the agent is assumed to be ontologically prior [to its effect]. [However,] this is unlike [the belief] that the effects or originated things must have [come from] matter. For this [latter statement] is not known by reason. The misconception of the one who claims [this position] only [arises] because his observation was limited to things which originate in this way [i.e. out of matter]. [So] how can a statement known by [both] reason and sense perception [ever] be equated with a statement that is known by neither [reason nor sense perception,] but is [at the most] something [contrary to that which was] not perceived by sense perception?!

ومَعْلومٌ أنَّ عَدَمَ شَهادَةِ الحِسِّ لا تَنْفِي ثُبوتَ ما لَمْ يَشْهَدْهُ. ولَوْ كانَ كُلُّ ما لَمْ يَشْهَدْهُ الإنْسانُ بِحِسِّهِ يَنْفِيْهِ، لَبَطَلَتِ المَعْقولاتُ والمَسْموعاتُ. وقَدْ قالَ تَعالىٰ: ﴿بَلْ كَذَّبُواْ بِمَا لَمْ يُحِيطُواْ بِعِلْمِهِۦ وَلَمَّا يَأْتِهِمْ تَأْوِيلُهُۥ﴾ [يونس: ٣٩]، فإذا كانَ المُكَذِّبُ بِما لم يَعْلَمْهُ بِوَجْهٍ مِنَ الوُجوهِ مَذْمومًا في الشَرْعِ كَما هُوَ مُخَالِفٌ لِلعَقْلِ، فَكَيْفَ المُكَذِّبُ بِما لَمْ يَعْلَمْهُ بِحِسِّهِ فَقَطْ؟ وإذا كانَ عَدَمُ العِلْمِ لَيْسَ عِلْمًا بالعَدَمِ، فَكَيْفَ يَكونُ عَدَمُ الإحْساسِ عِلْمًا بالعَدَمِ؟!

And it is known that the absence of the perception of the senses does not negate the existence of that which was not perceived. If man were to negate the existence of everything which he has not perceived by his own senses, then all rational inferences and testimonies would be invalidated. [This is as] God says [concerning the unbelievers]: **{Rather, they have denied that which they encompass not in knowledge and whose manifestation (in events) has not yet come to them}**. So, if a person who denies [the statements] which he does not know through any one of the routes [of knowledge] is [both] blameworthy in the Divine Law and in opposition to [sound] reason, how then is [the state of] a person who denies what he does not know through mere sense perception?! And if the absence of knowledge is not knowledge of absence, how can the absence of sense perception be knowledge of absence?!

The Objection to Aristotle's Argument

وَأَمَّا الشُّبْهَةُ الثَّانِيَةُ وَقَوْلُهُمْ: إنَّ المُحْدَثَ يَتَقَدَّمُهُ الإمْكَانُ فَلَا بُدَّ لَهُ مِنْ مَحَلٍّ ثُبوتِيٍّ، فَيُقَالُ لَهُمْ:

As for their second misconception [regarding the necessity of the materials], [which is] their [Aristotelean] argument that "originated things are preceded by [their] possibility, and [this possibility] must therefore have an [ontologically] positive [material] substrate", it is answered by saying:

الإمْكَانُ لَيْسَ وَصْفًا مَوْجُودًا لِلمُمْكِنِ زَائِدًا عَلَىٰ نَفْسِهِ؛ بَلْ هُوَ بِمَنْزِلَةِ الوُجوبِ والحُدوثِ والوُجودِ والعَدَمِ ونَحْوِ ذَلِكَ مِنَ القَضَايَا الَّتِي تُعْلَمُ بِالعَقْلِ. ولَيْسَ العَدَمُ زَائِدًا عَلَىٰ المَعْدومِ في الخَارِجِ، ولَا وُجودُ الشَّيْءِ زَائِداً عَلَىٰ مَاهِيَّتِهِ في الخَارِجِ، ولَا الحُدوثُ زَائِدًا عَلَىٰ ذاتِ المُحْدَثِ في الخَارِجِ، ولَا الإمْكَانُ زَائِدًا عَلَىٰ ذاتِ المُمْكِنِ في الخَارِجِ، ولَا الوُجوبُ زَائِدًا عَلَىٰ ذاتِ الواجِبِ في الخَارِجِ.

Possibility is not an attribute of possible existents that exists in addition to their [very] being. Rather, it is analogous to [meanings such as] necessity, origination, existence, nonexistence, and similar statements that are appreciated by reason. [Indeed,] nonexistence is not [a thing that is] added to the non-existent in external reality, nor is the existence of something [a thing] added to its quiddity in external reality, nor is origination [a thing] added to the essence of the originated existent in external reality, nor is possibility [a thing] added to the essence of the possible existent in external reality, nor is necessity[245] [a thing] added to the essence of the necessary existent in external reality.

والمَقْصودُ هُنا: الإمْكانُ. فالمُمْكِنُ إمّا أنْ يَكونَ مَعْدومًا أو مَوْجودًا. فَإذا كانَ مَعْدومًا فَلَيْسَ لَهُ صِفَةٌ ثُبوتِيَّةٌ أصْلًا، إذِ المَعْدومُ لا يَتَّصِفُ بِصِفَةٍ ثُبوتِيَّةٍ.

And the interest here lies in **possibility**. So [we say in response to the Aristotelean argument]: It is either the case that a possible thing is nonexistent or existing. If it is **nonexistent**, then it does not have an [ontologically] positive attribute at all. For non-existents cannot be described with positive attributes, [i.e. the possible non-existent does not have an ontologically positive attribute of 'possibility', and so no material substrate is needed.]

وإنْ كانَ مَوْجودًا، فَقَدْ صارَ واجِبًا بِغَيْرِهِ؛ فإنَّهُ ما شاءَ اللهُ كانَ وما لَمْ يَشَأْ لَمْ يَكُنْ؛ فَما شاءَهُ وَجَبَ وُجودُهُ، وما لَمْ يَشَأْهُ امْتَنَعَ وُجودُهُ، لَكِنْ وَجَبَ بِغَيْرِهِ وامْتَنَعَ لِغَيْرِهِ، وهُوَ في نَفْسِهِ يَقْبَلُ الوُجودَ والعَدَمَ. وقَوْلُنا في المَوْجودِ: «مُمْكِنٌ» مَعْناهُ: أنَّهُ مَوْجودٌ بِغَيْرِهِ.

245 Elsewhere, in what is probably a later development, Ibn Taymiyyah stresses that the necessity of God is a meaning that has positive ontology. [*Dar' Ta'ārud al-'Aql wa al-Naql*, Vol 5 p. 111]

[But] if the [possible thing] is **existing**, then [it also cannot have an ontologically positive 'possibility', because] the possible thing [in this option] will have become **necessary** through another; [it is no longer merely *possible* given the existence of its necessitating cause.] For everything God wills **must** happen, and everything He wills not must not. Whatever thing He wills exists **necessarily**, and whatever thing He wills not cannot possibly exist, although [the thing] is necessary or impossible *due to another*, while it *in itself* accepts [both] existence and nonexistence. [Indeed,] when we say that an existing thing is "possible", the meaning is [simply] that it **exists by another** [i.e. by an external agent].

وَمِمَّا يُبَيِّنُ ذَلِكَ: أَنَّ الإِمْكَانَ لَوْ كَانَ صِفَةً زَائِدَةً عَلَىٰ المُمْكِنِ لاَمْتَنَعَ قِيَامُهُ بِغَيْرِهِ، إِذْ صِفَةُ الشَّيْءِ لا تَقُومُ بِغَيْرِهِ. وَقَبْلَ وُجُودِ المُمْكِنِ لَيْسَ لَهُ صِفَةٌ. فَيَمْتَنِعُ وُجُودُ إِمْكَانٍ هُوَ صِفَةٌ لَهُ قَبْلَ وُجُودِهِ. فَتَبَيَّنَ أَنَّ مَا يَدَّعُونَهُ فِي إِثْبَاتِ إِمْكَانٍ وُجُودِيٍّ مِنْ مَحَلٍّ قَبْلَ وُجُودِ المُمْكِنِ خَيَالٌ مَحْضٌ.

The [fallacy of the Aristotelean argument] can [also] be explained [in the following way]: If possibility were an attribute that exists [ontologically] in addition to the possible existent, then this attribute [must be subsisting in the very existent and] must not be subsisting in other [existents]. For the [very] attribute of one thing cannot subsist in another thing. [Now,] before the possible thing was in existence, it could not have had any attributes. Therefore, the possibility [of that possible existent] could not have been an attribute of it that existed prior to it. Thus, it becomes clear that the [Philosophers'] claim that there exists an [ontologically] positive 'possibility' in a [material] substrate that precedes the possible existent is pure fantasy.[246]

ثُمَّ يُقَالُ: نَحْنُ نَشْهَدُ بِالحِسِّ حُدوثَ الصُّوَرِ مِنَ الحَيَواناتِ والنَّباتِ والمَعْدَنِ، ونَشْهَدُ أَنَّ هَذِهِ الصُّوَرَ الحادِثَةَ كانَتْ بَعْدَ أَنْ لَمْ تَكُنْ. وإِنْ كانَتْ خُلِقَتْ مِنْ غَيْرِها، فَلَيْسَتْ هِيَ ذَلِكَ الغَيْرَ ولا بَعْضَهُ، ولَكِنْ ذاكَ اسْتَحالَ وعُدِمَتْ صُورَتُهُ الأُوْلىٰ، وأَحْدَثَ اللهُ صُورَةً غَيْرَ تِلْكَ. فَهَذِهِ الصُّورَةُ مَوْجودَةٌ بَعْدَ العَدَمِ حادِثَةٌ بَعْدَ أَنْ لَمْ تَكُنْ، وهَذا مَشْهودٌ.

Moreover, it should be said [to these Philosophers who believe in the eternality of the matter substrate]: We witness with our senses the origination of the [very] forms of the animals, plants, and minerals, and we witness that these forms are originated after they did not exist. Despite their being created from other things, these [originated] forms are neither the other things [from which they were created], nor are they part of them. Rather, that [preceding thing] has changed totally [and substantially], and its initial form was annihilated, whereupon God originated an entirely different form. As such, this [new] form is existing after its nonexistence [and is] originated after it [once] did not exist. This is [a fact] witnessed [with our very eyes].

---

246 Later in *Nubuwwāt*, Ibn Taymiyyah accepted the position that the possibility of the *origination* of a creation is a positive attribute and must therefore subsist in a prior material. This later position implies that there must be one material or another in existence as long as the origination of created things is possible. More clearly, it implies the necessity of the infinite regress in the material conditions and in the created effects of God, such that every creation is originated by God only out of a preceding creation. Nevertheless, this later position does not imply the eternality of any one of the individual materials.

فإنَّ هَذا اللَحْمَ وهَذِهِ الثَمَرَةَ لَمْ يَكُنْ مَوْجوداً أصْلاً بِوَجْهٍ مِنَ الوُجُوهِ، فَوُجِدَ بَعْدَ عَدَمِهِ. وتِلْكَ الصُوَرُ المَوْجودَةُ - كالنَباتِ الّذي رَعَتْهُ الشاةُ والمَنِيِّ الّذي اسْتَحالَ وَلَداً - عُدِمَتْ بَعْدَ وُجودِها. فَهَذا وُجودٌ بَعْدَ عَدَمٍ وعَدَمٌ بَعْدَ وُجودٍ مَشْهودٌ.

Indeed, this [very] **flesh** and that [very] **fruit** was [previously] not existing at all in any way. It then existed after it was non-existent. Also, these [very] forms which exist, such as the **grass** on which the sheep grazes and the **semen** which changes into a child, go out of existence after they are existing.[247] Hence, these are witnessed [examples of things] existing after [their] nonexistence and not existing after [their] existence, [which is clear evidence against the claim that the matter substrate is eternal.]

247 The philosophical position which denies the existence of substantial origination in processes of biological development and chemical change prevents many people from appreciating the full range of color and diversity in God's creation. Instead of viewing a homogeneous world that is constituted of merely a few kinds of elementary particles that are in constant rearrangement, early Muslims understood that this world is constituted of an endless variety of different substances that come into existence and go out of existence. For example, it is famously reported that when Imām al-Shāfiʿī was asked to provide evidence for God's existence and oneness, he replied: "Consider the leaf of a berry tree; it has a single taste. Yet it changes to silk when consumed by a silkworm, honey when consumed by a bee, manure when consumed by sheep and cattle, and musk when consumed by deer".

Responses to the Avicennian Argument

وأمّا الحُجَّةُ الكُبْرَىٰ لَهُمْ عَلىٰ القِدَمِ، وهُوَ أنَّ العِلَّةَ التامَّةَ تَسْتَلْزِمُ مَعْلولَها، فَلا يَجوزُ تَأَخُّرُ العالَمِ عَنْ عِلَّتِهِ التامَّةِ= فَيُقالُ لَهُمْ:

As for their greatest argument for the eternality [of the world, which is the Avicennian argument] that "[God is] a complete Cause [who] necessitates [His] effect, and therefore the world cannot be delayed [in time] after its complete Cause [but must accompany God from eternity]", it is answered by saying:

نَحْنُ نَشْهَدُ هَذِهِ الحَوادِثَ الّتِي تَحْدُثُ مِنَ الحَيَوانِ والنَباتِ والمَعْدَنِ. فالمُوجِبُ لِحُدوثِها إنْ كانَ عِلَّةً تامَّةً قَديمَةً، بَطَلَ قَوْلُكُمْ: إنَّ قِدَمَ العِلَّةِ يُوجِبُ قِدَمَ المَعْلولِ.

We [indeed] witness these creations that **originate** [in the world], such as the animals, the plants and the minerals. If the necessitating cause of their origination is an eternal complete Cause, then this invalidates your claim that the eternality of the Cause implies the eternality of its effect.

وإنْ كانَ المُوجِبُ لَها مَعَ العِلَّةِ القَديمَةِ حُدوثَ أَمْرٍ مِنَ الأُمورِ، إمّا حَرَكَةَ الفَلَكِ أو غَيْرَها، فَذَلِكَ الحادِثُ إنْ حَدَثَ عَنِ العِلَّةِ التامَّةِ القَديمَةِ، بَطَلَ

قَوْلُكُم. وإنْ تَوَقَّفَ عَلىٰ حُدوثٍ آخَرَ، فالقَوْلُ فيهِ كالقَوْلِ في الأَوَّلِ.

[But] if the necessitating cause [of their origination] is some originating occurrence in addition to the eternal Cause –whether this [occurrence] is [assumed to be] the motion of the celestial sphere or anything else – then: (i) If that occurrence is originated by the eternal Cause, your claim [that the eternality of the Cause implies the eternality of its effect] will be invalidated. But (ii) if that [occurrence] is conditional on [yet] another occurrence, then what we say of this [second occurrence] will be similar to what we said of the first [occurrence].

وهَذِهِ الحَوادِثُ - سَواءٌ كانَتْ مُتَناهِيَةً أو غَيرَ مُتَناهِيَةٍ - تَسْتَلْزِمُ إمّا صُدورَها عَنْ عِلَّةٍ تامَّةٍ قَديمَةٍ، وإمّا صُدورَها عَنْ غَيْرِ فاعِلٍ بالكُلِّيَّةِ. والثاني أَظْهَرُ بُطْلانًا مِنَ الأوَّلِ، وهُوَ باطِلٌ بالعَقْلِ الصَريحِ وبالاتِّفاقِ. والأَوَّلُ يَسْتَلْزِمُ صُدورَ الحَوادِثِ عَنْ عِلَّةٍ تامَّةٍ قَديمَةٍ، وذَلِكَ يُبْطِلُ أصْلَ حُجَّتِهِمْ.

[Now,] these [originating] occurrences – whether they are finite or infinite – are necessarily either: (a) proceeding from the eternal complete Cause, or (b) proceeding from no agent whatsoever. The second option is more clearly erroneous than the first, and is [known to be] false by sound reason and consensus. The first option entails that **originating events proceed from an eternal complete Cause**, which invalidates the basis of their argument [for the eternality of the world and its celestial spheres, as the origination of the world can equally be said to proceed from the eternal complete Cause in this option].

وَمَعْلُومٌ أَنَّ حَقِيقَةَ قَوْلِهِمْ أَنَّ الحَوادِثَ المُتَعاقِبَةَ الَّتِي لا تَتَناهىٰ صادِرَةٌ

عَنْ عِلَّةٍ تامَّةٍ قَدِيمَةٍ. ثُمَّ يَجْعَلونَ ذَلِكَ هُوَ حَرَكَةَ الفَلَكِ التاسِع. وقَوْلُهُمْ

فِي غايَةِ التَناقُضِ؛ فَإِنَّ حَرَكَةَ التاسِع لَيْسَتْ هِيَ السَبَبَ، بَلْ لِكُلِّ فَلَكٍ

حَرَكَةٌ تَخُصُّهُ لَيْسَ سَبَبَها حَرَكَةُ هَذا الفَلَكِ، وإِنْ كانَ مُتَحَرِّكًا بالعَرَضِ

حَرَكَةً تابِعَةً لِحَرَكَتِهِ.

And it is known that the reality of their [cosmological] assumptions is that an infinite regress of successive events is proceeding from an eternal complete cause. They then claim that the complete cause [for these successive events] is the motion of the ninth celestial sphere [that is above the rest of the world][248]. [But] their claim is most self-contradicting. For the ninth [sphere] is not the [complete] cause [for the motions below it]. Rather, each [one of the lower] spheres has a distinct motion that is not determined by the motion

---

248 In opposition to Abrahamic monotheism, the Philosophers described God as a simple and eternally complete Cause that has no will. When attempting to explain how originated things can proceed from such a God, they promoted ideas from Neoplatonic cosmology that posit an intermediary celestial hierarchy between God and His creation. This celestial hierarchy includes ten intellects and nine celestial spheres, each sphere with its own soul. In this view, God cannot originate anything of the creation through will, but rather emanates the world in eternity through this celestial hierarchy of eternal intellects and spheres. The higher intellect gives existence to a celestial sphere and a lower intellect, which in turn gives existence to a lower celestial sphere and a lower intellect. The hierarchy ends at the tenth intellect and the sphere of the moon, by which this intellect causes everything that occurs below on the earth. In this way, these Philosophers believed that the creations are fully originated by the rotations of the celestial spheres, and ultimately by the motion of the outermost ninth sphere.

of this [ninth] sphere, although [each sphere] does move accidentally in accordance with its rotation.[249]

وَالفَلَكُ الثَّامِنُ فِيهِ كَوَاكِبُ عَظِيمَةٌ تَقْتَضِي أَسْبَابًا بِعَدَدِهَا. وَالأَطْلَسُ فَوْقَهُ بَسِيطٌ لَا يَصْدُرُ عَنْهُ كَثْرَةٌ، فَلَا بُدَّ لِتِلْكَ الكَثْرَةِ مِنْ أَسْبَابٍ. وَهَذَا مِنْ مَحَارَاتِهِمُ المُفْسِدَةِ لِقَوْلِهِمْ؛ فَقَدْ صَدَرَتْ حَرَكَاتٌ مُخْتَلِفَةٌ عَنْ عِلَلٍ تَامَّةٍ قَدِيمَةٍ مَعْلُولَةٍ لِعِلَّةٍ تَامَّةٍ قَدِيمَةٍ.

And the eighth celestial sphere [is a starry sphere that] has an enormous number of stars, requiring explanations as many [as their number]. But the starless, [ninth] sphere [that rotates] above it is **simple**, and multiplicity cannot proceed from it [at all]. [Indeed,] there must be [many] reasons for the multiplicity [of existents in the contingent world below the ninth sphere, which this sphere cannot account for]. And this is one of the conundrums that spoils their claim, for [the reality of their claim is that] **diverse** motions have proceeded from **eternal complete causes**, [in turn] proceeding from an **eternal complete Cause**.

وَغَايَتُهُمْ أَنْ يَقُولُوا: لَا يُمْكِنُ إِلَّا هَذَا. وَلَكِنْ بِكُلِّ حَالٍ فَقَدْ بَطَلَ اسْتِدْلَالُهُم عَلَىٰ أَنَّ الفَلَكَ قَدِيمٌ وَحَرَكَاتِهِ أَزَلِيَّةٌ أَبَدِيَّةٌ.

---

249 In Ibn Taymiyyah's time, the earth was believed to be a stationary sphere that is surrounded by a rotating system of celestial spheres that carry the sun, the moon, and the stars in their orbits around the earth. The first seven spheres carry the moon, Mercury, Venus, the sun, Mars, Jupiter and Saturn. The eighth sphere carries the fixed stars. The outermost ninth sphere explains a certain eastward motion of the other eight spheres.

And the most they may respond is that this is the only plausible option. But in any case, we have invalidated their argument for [the claim] that the celestial spheres are eternal and that their motions are without beginning or end.

وَذَلِكَ أَنَّ أَصْلَ حُجَّتِهِمْ أَنَّ كَوْنَهُ أَحْدَثَ الفَلَكَ بَعْدَ أَنْ لَمْ يَكُنْ مُحَالٌ؛ لِأَنَّ المُمْكِنَ إِنْ لَمْ يَكُنْ قَدْ تَمَّتْ أَسْبَابُ إِيْجَادِهِ افْتَقَرَ إِلَىٰ أَسْبَابٍ أُخْرَىٰ. والقَوْلُ فِيها كالقَوْلِ فِي الحادِثِ الأَوَّلِ؛ لِأَنَّهُ لا بُدَّ لَهُ مِنْ أَسْبَابٍ حادِثَةٍ، إِذِ الحُدوثُ بِدُوْنِ سَبَبٍ مُحَالٌ. وإِنْ تَمَّتْ، وَجَبَ القِدَمُ.

For indeed, the basis of their argument [for the eternality of the world] is that it is impossible for God to have originated the celestial sphere after He had not [done so, arguing that]: (i) If the [divine] causes for the existence of the contingent [sphere] were not complete [in eternity], then [the sphere must] depend on additional causes [for its origination]. The case with these [additional causes] is similar to that of the first origination: [If their divine causes were not complete in eternity, they must depend on yet other causes for their origination.] For the [completion that occurs in time] must have originating causes, as origination without a cause is impossible. [But] (ii) if the [divine] causes [of the celestial sphere] were complete [in eternity], then [the sphere] must [also] be existing in eternity.

ثُمَّ عَيَّنُوا القِسْمَ الثانِيَ تَحَكُّماً وتَناقَضُوا فيهِ، فَصارَتْ حُجَّتُهُم باطِلَةً مِنْ وُجوهٍ:

The Philosophers then selected the second option, [namely that the causes were complete in eternity and that therefore the celestial sphere is eternal, doing so] arbitrarily and falling into contradiction. Thus, their argument became flawed from numerous aspects:

مِنْها أنْ يُقالَ: ولِمَ لا يَجوزُ أنْ يَكونَ حُدوثُهُ مَوْقوفًا علىٰ حادِثٍ بَعْدَ حادِثٍ؟ وهَذا لَيْسَ بِمُمْتَنِعٍ عِنْدَكُم، فَإنَّ الحَوادِثَ هِيَ كَذَلِكَ عِنْدَكُمْ.

One [aspect] is to say [to them]: Why is it not possible for [the world to have been originated by God after its nonexistence along with] its origination [being] **conditional** on a [prior] origination, [and that origination] on [another] origination, [in an infinite regress of events and conditions]? For this [regress of conditions][250] is not im-

250 The regress of events and conditions is not impossible according to Ibn Taymiyyah and the Philosophers, unlike (i) the regress of dependencies and efficient causes and (ii) the regress in the basis of efficient causation, which are impossible by the consensus of rational minds, and (iii) the regress in the completion of the very efficacy of the Cause, which is impossible by the agreement of the majority of rational minds. [*Dar' Ta'āruḍ al-'Aql wa al-Naql*, Vol 2 pp. 282-288].

In agreement with the Philosophers, Ibn Taymiyyah accepted that the Kalām theologians' doctrine of Creation – namely that God became an efficient cause after He was not – is impossible because it leads to a regress in the completion of the very efficacy of the Cause, as is suggested in the Avicennian argument. However, Ibn Taymiyyah also rejected the Philosophers' doctrine of emanation which they proposed as a solution – namely that God is an eternally complete Cause for the world – because this doctrine necessitates that nothing may occur in the world, which contradicts observation, and likewise entails that this world is eternal, which contradicts its contingency. Instead, Ibn Taymiyyah promoted a third intuitive position that is in line with the belief of the Pious Predecessors of the Muslim nation, namely that God was perpetually acting from eternity by His will, such that it is of His very nature to become a complete efficient cause for a specific originating effect after He becomes a

possible according to you, as [natural] occurrences likewise [regress into the past] in your view.[251]

ومِنْها أنْ يُقالَ: إنْ كانَ تَوَقُّفُ الحادِثِ عَلىٰ حَوادِثَ لا تَتَناهىٰ مُمْتَنِعًا – كَما تَقولُهُ طَوائِفُ كَثيرَةٌ مِنْ أَهْلِ الكَلامِ والفَلْسَفَةِ كالمُعْتَزِلَةِ ومَنِ اتَّبَعَهُمْ – لَزِمَ إمَّا بُطْلانُ الحُدوثِ، وهُوَ خِلافُ المُشاهَدَةِ، وإمّا بُطْلانُ قَوْلِكُمْ بِأَنَّ هَذِهِ الحَوادِثَ المَشْهودَةَ مُتَوَقِّفَةٌ عَلىٰ حَوادِثَ لا تَتَناهىٰ.

Another [second aspect] is to say [to them]: If the infinite regress of events and conditions is [assumed to be] **impossible** – as it is claimed by many of the groups of Kalām theology and philosophy, such as the Muʿtazilah and their followers – then [one of two things] is necessary: Either (a) origination is impossible, which would contradict observation, or (b) your claim that "the observed [natural] occurrences are conditioned on [others] in an infinite regress" is false, [which would mean that the world cannot be eternal].

وإنْ كانَ جائِزًا – كَما تَقولُهُ طَوائِفُ مِنْ أَهْلِ الفَلْسَفَةِ والكَلامِ والحَديثِ

---

complete efficient cause for a preceding originating effect. This third position does not imply an impossible regress in the completion of the very efficacy of the Cause; rather, it implies a regress in completions of *individual* causations of successive originating effects, one after the other, which is a permissible regress of conditions.

251 The Philosophers claimed that the celestial spheres are eternal, ever-rotating existents, and that the creations may only exist in the terrestrial sphere that lies below the moon. Ibn Taymiyyah points out that the Philosophers cannot provide evidence for such a distinction. Rather, God creates both the celestial and terrestrial bodies out of matter.

وغَيرِهِمْ - أَمْكَنَ تَوَقُّفُ العالَمِ أوِ الفَلَكِ علىٰ حَوادِثَ لا تَتَناهىٰ، سَواءٌ قِيلَ: حَدَثَتْ في ذاتِ القَديمِ أو غَيْرِهِ.

[But] if the regress [of events and conditions] is [said to be] **permissible** – as it is claimed by [some of] the groups of philosophy and Kalām, Ḥadīth, and others – then it will be possible for [the entire origination of] this world and its celestial spheres to be conditional on [other] events in an infinite regress, [and so the origination of this world after its nonexistence cannot be ruled out as an option]. This is equally the case whether these [conditions] are said to [be divine actions that] subsist in the eternal [God], or [are said to include occurrences that exist] in [His] creation [and that regress into the past].

فَإنَّ حُدوثَ الحَوادِثِ في القَديمِ لَيْسَ مُمْتَنِعًا عِنْدَكُم ولا عِنْدَ طَوائِفَ مِن أَهْلِ المِلَلِ، بَل أَكْثَرِ أَهْلِ المِلَلِ. فَإنَّكُمْ وهَؤُلاءِ تُبْطِلون قَوْلَ مَنْ يَسْتَدِلُّ بالحَرَكَةِ عَلىٰ حُدُوثِ مَحَلِّها.

Indeed, [the theological position] that ***ḥawādith* (events and acts) originate in the eternal [being]** is not false according to you, nor according to [many of the] adherents of the faiths. Actually, [it is not false according to] most adherents of the faiths. Indeed, [both] you and those [people] refute the assertions of [theological groups] who argue for the originated-ness of entities based on [their being substrates of] motion [or *ḥawādith*][252], [i.e. both of you have no objection against the belief that God is an eternal Creator being who is

252 This is the Argument from the Origination of Bodies that was discussed earlier.

perpetually acting and originating things after their nonexistence by His will, including this world and its celestial spheres.]

وما تَذْكُرونَهُ في واجِبِ الوُجودِ مِنْ نَفْيِ الصِفاتِ الّذي تُسَمّونَهُ نَفْيَ التَرْكيبِ في غايَةِ الفَسادِ، كَما قَدْ أُوْضِحَ في غَيْرِ هَذا المَوْضِعِ.

As for [your additional objection that God, unlike the celestial spheres, cannot be a substrate of motion and activity, which you predicate on] your **negation** of the [divine] **attributes** from the Necessary existent, [or] what you [otherwise] refer to as a negation of composition [and an affirmation of God's simplicity][253], it is an entirely **false** [argument], as this has been clarified elsewhere.

ومِنْها: أنَّ هَذا بِعَيْنِهِ يُقالُ في الحَوادِثِ المَشْهودَةِ: إنْ تَمَّتْ أَسْبابُها في القِدَمِ وَجَبَ قِدَمُها، وإنْ لَمْ تَتِمَّ افْتَقَرَتْ إلىٰ أَسْبابٍ أُخْرىٰ!

Another [third aspect] is to say [to the Philosophers]: This very thing [which you say about the celestial spheres] can [also] be said about the originated things we witness [in the natural world, such as the animals, the plants, and the minerals. You might as well ridiculously argue that]: "If the causes of these [creations] were complete in eternity, these [creations] must [also] be eternal. But if their causes were not complete [in eternity], then they must be dependent on additional causes, [and their origination would be invalidated!"]

والثَلاثَةُ عائِدَةٌ إلىٰ أَصْلٍ واحِدٍ. فَقَدْ ظَهَرَ فَسادُ عُمْدَتِهِمُ العُظْمَىٰ في

253 This is the Argument from the Contingency of Bodies that was mentioned earlier, also known as the Argument from Composition. The argument is not to be confused with the contingency argument.

إثْباتِ قِدَمِهِ.

These three [responses] go back to the same root. Thus, the fallacy of their greatest argument for the eternality of the world is now evident...

And the last of our prayers is

"All praise is due to God, the Lord of Creation"

Appendix

The following pages comprise of flowcharts summarising the arguments found in the main text.

Figure 1: Demonstrating the impossibility of creation without prior matter (*pp. 193-197*)

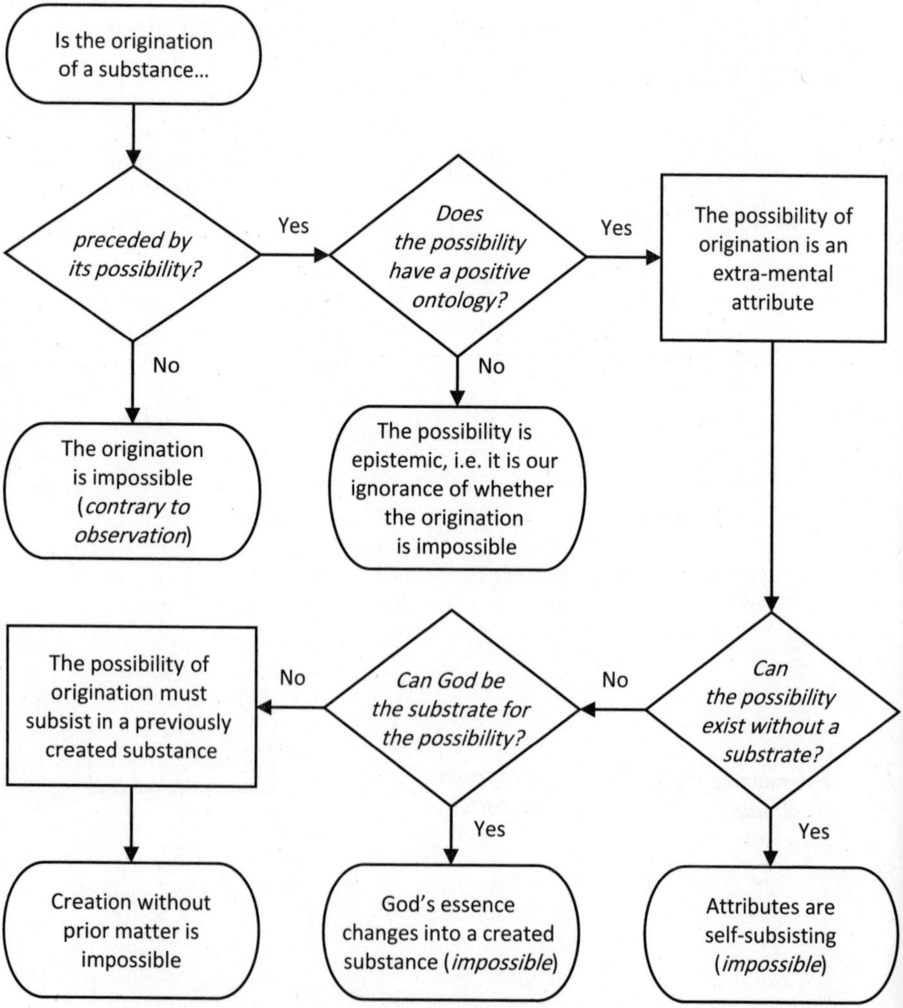

Figure 2: Demonstrating that matter is created and annihilated (*pp. 223-227*)

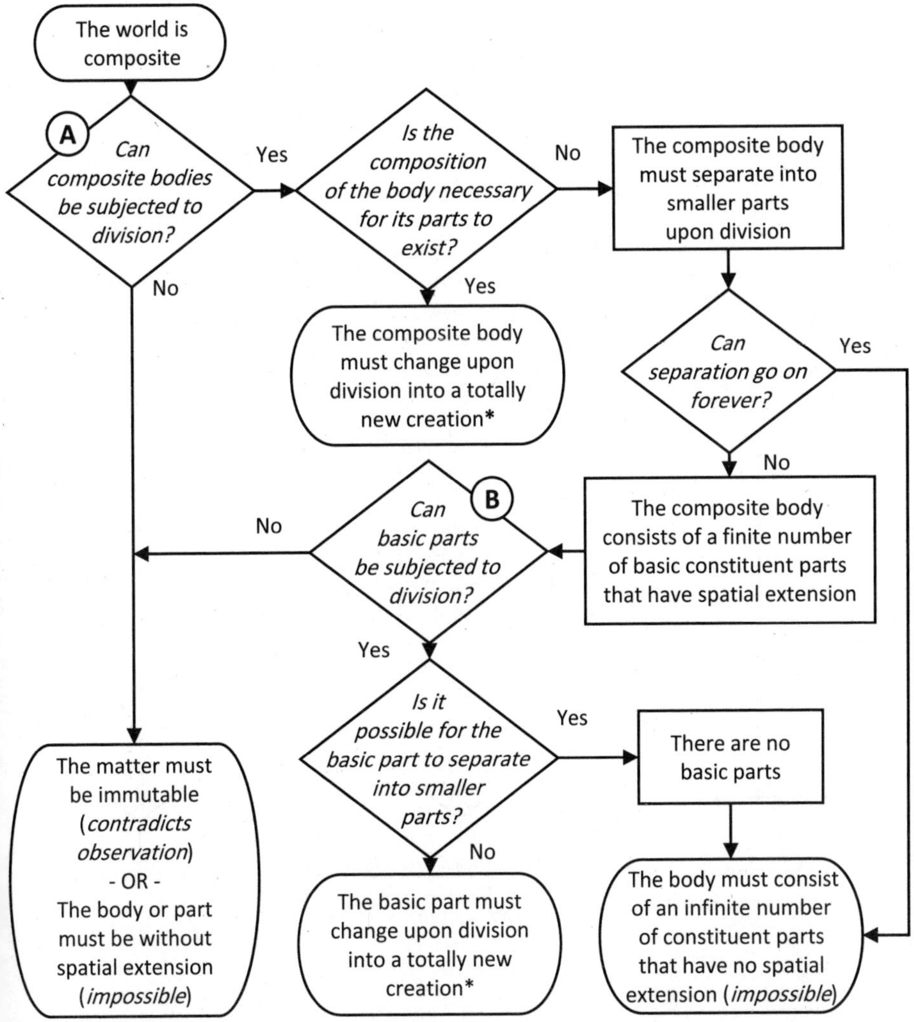

** If the newly created substance is a composite, then repeat route A. If it is basic, then repeat route B. If the new creation is a form of energy that is predicated of the surrounding substances, then the division does not apply to the energy on its own, but rather to the material body which serves as its substrate.*

Figure 3: Ibn Taymiyya's early refutation of the impossibility of creation without prior matter (*pp. 261-264*)

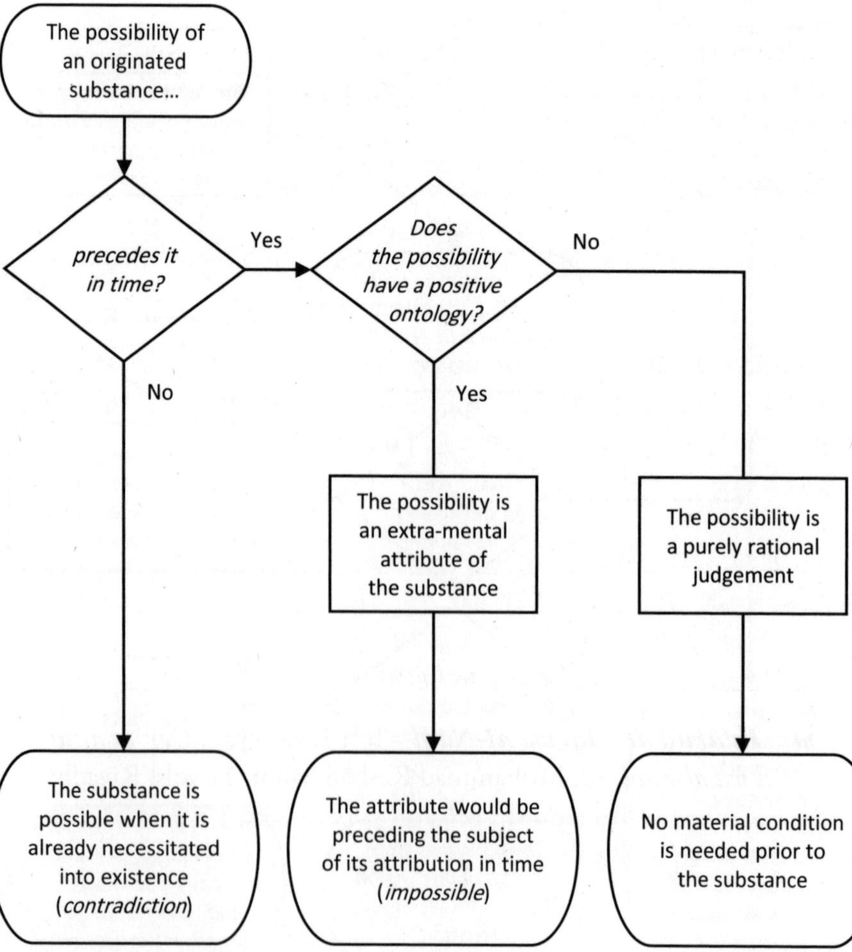
The possibility of an originated substance...
precedes it in time?
Yes
Does the possibility have a positive ontology?
No
No
Yes
The possibility is an extra-mental attribute of the substance
The possibility is a purely rational judgement
The substance is possible when it is already necessitated into existence (contradiction)
The attribute would be preceding the subject of its attribution in time (impossible)
No material condition is needed prior to the substance

Bibliography

The Arabic text was translated from the following works:

Nubuwwāt = Ibn Taymiyyah, *Kitāb al-nubuwwāt*, ed. 'Abd al-'Azīz b. Ṣāliḥ al-Ṭuwayyān. 2 vols. in 1. Riyadh: Maktabat aḍwā' al-salaf, 1420/2000.

Bayān Talbīs al-Jahmiyyah = Ibn Taymiyyah, *Bayān talbīs al-Jahmiyyah fī tǎsīs bida'ihim al-kalāmiyyah*, ed. Yaḥyā b. Muḥammad al-Hunaydī, 10 vols. Medina: Majma' al-Malik Fahd li-tibā'at al-muṣḥaf al-sharīf, 1426, second printing.

Ḥudūth al-'Ālam = Ibn Taymiyyah, *Mas'alat ḥudūth al-'ālam*, ed. Yūsuf b. Muḥammad Marwān b. Sulaymān al-Uzbakī al-Maqdisī. Beirut: Dār al-bashā'ir al-Islāmiyya, 1433/2012.

The following works were cited in the footnotes:

Majmū' al-Fatāwā = *Majmū' fatāwā* Shaykh al-Islām Aḥmad ibn Taymiyyah, ed. 'Abd al-Raḥmān ibn Muḥammad ibn Qāsim and Muḥammad ibn 'Abd al-Raḥmān ibn Muḥammad, 37 vols. Medina: Mujammā' al-Malik Fahd, 1425/2004.

Dar' Ta'āruḍ al-'Aql wa al-Naql = Ibn Taymiyyah, *Dar' ta'āruḍ al-'aql wa al-naql*, ed. Muḥammad Rashād Sālim, 11 vols. Riyadh: Jāmi'at al-Imām Muḥammad b. Sa'ūd al-Islāmiyya, 1979-1983, second printing 1411/1991.

Minhāj al-Sunnah al-Nabawiyyah = Ibn Taymiyyah, *Minhāj al-sunnah al-nabawiyyah fī naqḍ kalām al-Shīʿah al-Qadariyyah*, ed. Muḥammad Rashād Sālim, 9 vols. Riyadh: Jāmiʿat al-Imām Muḥammad b. Saʿūd al-Islāmiyya, 1406/1986.

Ṣafadiyyah = Ibn Taymiyyah, *Kitāb al-Ṣafadiyyah*, ed. Muḥammad Rashād Sālim, 2 vols. 1406, second printing.

Sharḥ al-Aṣfahāniyyah = Ibn Taymiyyah, *Sharḥ al-Aṣbahāniyyah*, ed. Muḥammad b. ʿOuda al-Saʿawī. Riyadh: Maktabat dār al-minhāj, 1430/2009.

Al-Kāfiyah al-Shāfiyah = Ibn al-Qayyim, *Al-kāfiyah al-shāfiyah fī al-ʾintiṣār li al-firqat al-nājiyah*, ed. Muḥammad b. ʿAbd al-Raḥmān al-ʿArīfī, Nāṣir b. Yaḥyā al-Ḥunaynī, ʿAbdullāh b. ʿAbd al-Raḥmān al-Hudhail, and Fahd b. ʿAlī al-Musāʿid, 3 vols. Riyadh: Dār ʿaṭāʾāt al-ʿilm, Beirut: Dār Ibn Ḥazm, 1440/2019, fourth printing.

Further reading:

Sāmī b. Ṣāliḥ al-Samīrī, *Mafātīḥ al-ḥikmah wa al-kalām*. Beirut: Muʾassasat al-ʿulūm li al-dirāsāt wa al-nashr, 1443/2022, second printing.